SECOND EDITION

Focus:
Writing Paragraphs
and Essays

MARTHA E. CAMPBELL
St. Petersburg Junior College

PRENTICE HALL, UPPER SADDLE RIVER, NEW JERSEY 07458

Library of Congress Cataloging-in-Publication Data

Campbell, Martha E.
  Focus : writing paragraphs and essays / Martha E. Campbell. — 2nd
ed.
    p.   cm.
  Includes index.
  ISBN 0-13-896465-3 (pbk.)
    1. English language — Rhetoric.   2. English language — Paragraphs.
3. English language — Grammar.   4. Report writing.   I. Title.
  PE1408.C2835   1999
  808′.042 — DC21   98-24400
                                                          CIP

Editor-in-Chief: Charlyce Jones Owen
Senior Acquisitions Editor: Maggie Barbieri
Director of Production and Manufacturing: Barbara Kittle
Senior Managing Editor: Bonnie Biller
Senior Project Manager: Shelly Kupperman
Manufacturing Manager: Nick Sklitsis
Prepress and Manufacturing Buyer: Mary Ann Gloriande
Director of Marketing: Gina Sluss
Creative Design Director: Leslie Osher
Interior and Cover Designer: Carmela Pereira
Editorial Assistant: Joan Polk

This book was set in 11/14 Janson by Digitype and printed by Courier – Westford.
The cover was printed by Courier – Westford.

Acknowledgments
Martin Luther King, Jr. "I Have a Dream." Reprinted by permission of Intellectual
    Properties Management, Atlanta, GA.
Katherine Preble, "Chasing Suspects Costs Innocent Lives," editorial, June 7, 1994.
    Reprinted by permission of *Tampa Tribune*, Tampa, FL.

© 1999, 1996 by Prentice-Hall, Inc.
Upper Saddle River, New Jersey 07458

Printed in the United States of America
10 9 8 7 6 5 4 3 2

ISBN: 0-13-896465-3

Prentice-Hall International (UK) Limited, *London*
Prentice-Hall of Australia Pty. Limited, *Sydney*
Prentice-Hall Canada, Inc., *Toronto*
Prentice-Hall Hispanoamericana, S.A., *Mexico*
Prentice-Hall of India Private Limited, *New Delhi*
Prentice-Hall of Japan, Inc., *Tokyo*
Prentice-Hall Asia Pte. Ltd., *Singapore*
Editora Prentice-Hall do Brasil, Ltda., *Rio de Janeiro*

To my loving family
and in memory of two special teachers,
Kathy and Len

Contents

CHAPTER 2: FOCUS ON THE PARAGRAPH   24

x *Contents*

CHAPTER 5:   FOCUS ON OBSERVATION   106

CHAPTER 6:   FOCUS ON COMPARISON/CONTRAST   136

CHAPTER 7: FOCUS ON THE ESSAY 160

CHAPTER 9:   FOCUS ON THE PERSUASION ESSAY   226

CHAPTER 10:   REVISING AND EDITING STRATEGIES   256

Preface

To the Instructor

PURPOSE/OVERVIEW

This second edition of *Focus: Writing Paragraphs and Essays* offers a readable, practical, and engaging text for students who have returned to school and need to brush up their composition skills as well as for students who have graduated from high school but have not mastered the fundamentals of writing needed for the classroom and the workplace.

What differentiates this writing text from many others is its integration of rhetoric and grammar. Grammar and punctuation rules are presented within specific writing contexts—not isolated in a separate section. The purpose of this integrated approach is to help your students to improve their writing and prepare themselves for the challenges of writing in their college courses and in their careers.

SPECIAL FEATURES OF THE SECOND EDITION

This second edition offers three new features not found in many developmental writing textbooks:

- A "Writers as Spiders" section in each chapter, containing links to World Wide Web sites to reinforce grammatical/rhetorical concepts
- An ESL Appendix addressing the concerns of students for whom English is not the native language
- Answers to selected odd-numbered exercises

Another feature of this edition is many additional exercises, particularly in Chapters 3 through 5.

Furthermore, the second edition continues to offer features that have contributed to the success of this textbook:

- Focus on the writing process
- Extensive use of student writing samples
- Emphasis on peer review, including guide questions for each assignment
- Many choices of writing topics
- Specific organizational, revising, and editing strategies for each rhetorical purpose
- Focus on transition in each rhetorical context

- Abundant exercises to reinforce grammar, punctuation, and diction skills.
- Paragraph-level editing exercises
- Revising and editing strategies for the computer
- Appendices on outlining and manuscript form
- Glossary of key grammatical terms

ORGANIZATION OF CHAPTERS

Chapter 1 introduces students to the stages of the writing process and includes a student work-in-progress.

Chapter 2 discusses the topic sentence paragraph while reviewing the basic grammatical structure of sentences.

Chapters 3 through 6 each focus on a particular purpose for writing paragraphs. Development by example, narration, observation, and comparison/contrast paragraphs are each introduced, along with related grammatical, punctuation, and diction skills.

Chapter 7 creates a bridge from the paragraph to the essay. Your students will build on their development by example and comparison/contrast paragraphs to compose essays.

Chapters 8 and 9 continue the discussion of the essay with the problem-solving and persuasive essays. This experience in essay writing should build your students' confidence as they prepare to enter their freshman composition courses.

Chapter 10 introduces students to general revising and editing strategies as well as techniques for revising and editing with a computer.

ACKNOWLEDGMENTS

The comments of the reviewers of this second edition have been invaluable. These reviewers included Janet Cutshall of Sussex County Community College; Suzanne G. Metzger of Indiana Wesleyan University; Mary A. Eastland of Hill College; and Elsa Luciano of the University of Puerto Rico–Arecibo.

I am especially indebted to Jan Ballantine, my great friend and fellow traveler, as well as the author of "Appendix A, Tips for ESL Students."

I am also grateful for my many students over the last twenty-five years—particularly those whose compositions appear within these pages. They have been a constant source of inspiration and surprise.

For listening to me and laughing with me, I thank my colleagues at St. Petersburg Junior College, Tarpon Springs Center.

As always, I appreciate the work of the Prentice Hall staff: sales representative Beth Rechsteiner, for first urging me to undertake this project; Phil Miller, President of Humanities and Social Sciences, for offering me a contract; Acquisitions Editor, Maggie Barbieri, for supporting and befriending me; and English Editorial Assistant, Joan Polk, for assisting me whenever I have asked.

Finally, I thank my mother and father, Evelyn and George Etheredge, for giving me a love for language; my husband, Dan, for loving me; and my daughters, Jenny and Leah, for teaching me.

Martha E. Campbell

To the Student

This textbook asks you to think about yourself as a writer. If you are like many other college students, you may be uncomfortable with the title. You think of yourself as a student, an adult, a friend, a son or daughter, a worker—but as a *writer*?

With the help of this textbook, you can become a confident writer. You will need time, energy, and patience. You must also believe that writing well is a necessary skill for your future success in the classroom and in the workplace.

You will probably need to review some basics—especially if you are not an active writer outside the classroom or if you have not recently been in school. So this book offers a thorough review of the writing process, paragraph and essay organization, and grammar and punctuation rules. All of these techniques are important for you to know.

But writing is more than grammatically correct, organized prose. Writing is a creative exchange between you and your reader. Unless your reader receives your intended message, your writing is not effective. Because your relationship with your reader is so important, this textbook also offers opportunities for you to read other students' writing and for other students to give you feedback about your work.

You are now part of a community of writers—your classroom. Your fellow students and your instructor will offer you support as you work to improve your writing. Keep practicing and learning. Remember that the more you learn about writing, the more you will want to know.

Martha E. Campbell

How to Use the Icons in This Book

In this textbook you will often find icons (visual images) in the margins. Each icon represents a grammatical concept or punctuation rule. Use these icons as your guide when you are searching for information. To improve your understanding, try to associate the icon with the related grammatical concept or punctuation rule.

Following is a list of the icons used in this text:

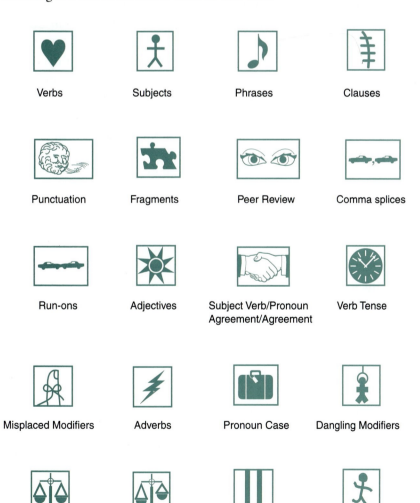

Verbs	Subjects	Phrases	Clauses
Punctuation	Fragments	Peer Review	Comma splices
Run-ons	Adjectives	Subject Verb/Pronoun Agreement/Agreement	Verb Tense
Misplaced Modifiers	Adverbs	Pronoun Case	Dangling Modifiers
Coordination	Subordination	Parallelism	Rhythm

CHAPTER 1

Focus on Writing

This book is designed to help you improve your writing skills by building upon your strengths as a thinker and communicator. Effective composition skills are vital to your success both in the classroom and in the workplace. In the classroom, teachers reward students who can express their understanding of an academic subject in a clear, organized composition. In the workplace, supervisors often evaluate an employee's ability to compose effective proposals and other forms of business communications before they consider the employee for a promotion.

Some students enter a writing classroom as experienced, self-assured writers. However, many beginning college students, for a variety of reasons, are not confident about their ability to write well. Yet these students know that improving their writing skills is an essential key to their future success.

As you begin the task of improving your writing, you are setting forth on a journey of discovery. You will be asked to think about yourself as a writer and a reader. You will also learn a variety of grammatical and composition skills that will enable you to write for different purposes. The path of discovery will not always be smooth. However, the goal of being an effective writer is worth the effort and commitment you will make. As you make this journey, remember that you are joining a community of students and teachers who, like their ancestors before them, use written language as a tool in the quest for knowledge and understanding.

WHY WRITE IN A HIGH-TECH WORLD?

Before the development of written language, humankind had to depend on visual representations to record thought. Today, thankfully, writers in the academic and career worlds have a written language to use to record their ideas and preserve our culture for generations to come.

Now, with the twenty-first century rapidly approaching, technological advances are occurring at a furious pace. There are more ways to send a message than ever before. You can pick up the phone and reach your neighbor next door or an acquaintance around the world. Soon the person on the other end of the phone will even be able to see you on a viewing screen as you converse. If you want to send a long message, you can record the message on an audiocassette or a videocassette, depending on your preference.

So, with all these communications tools readily available, why commit yourself to improving your writing skills?

Even with all the technological advances in the communications field, the task of writing has its own benefits for the writer:

- Writing is a means of self-discovery.
- Writing is a way to share these discoveries with a reader.
- The process of writing has its own rewards.

A Means of Self-Discovery

To write clearly, the writer, whether a beginning college student or a professional author, must turn inward, listen to his or her inner voice, and give that voice expression. The results are often surprising.

Many writers express themselves by keeping a diary or a journal. Diaries, which provide a day-to-day recording of events, not only teach writers much about themselves but preserve memories for future generations.

Mary Chestnut began a journal in 1861. As the wife of a former South Carolina senator who had resigned his office to serve the Confederacy, she used her pen to comment on the political and social changes that surrounded her. Today, students of Civil War history who read her journals are impressed by her courage and strength.

As she hid in an attic from the terror of the Nazis, Anne Frank wrote every day in her diary. She never expected that her diary would be read each year by thousands of students. She wrote in her diary because she needed a friend to talk to and share her secrets. Though she lived in an environment of terror, she discovered much about herself through her daily conversations with "Kitty."

Writing in a journal gives the writer a private place to record a conversation, a casual observation, a poem, or a memorable moment. The writer not only makes notes of events in the journal the same way a writer might in a diary, but also comments on those events in an attempt to understand them. These journal entries are then available as a resource for writing topics and/or a scrapbook for memories.

Diary or journal writing provides the writer a chance to think about common, everyday happenings that might otherwise just pass by. Keeping a diary or journal inevitably leads the writer to self-discovery.

A Way to Share Discoveries with the Outside World

Effective writers are intellectually curious and driven by a need to understand their environment and their places within it. Writers not only write *to express personal feelings*, but also to share their discoveries with others—by providing the reader with useful information, by persuading the reader to accept the writer's point of view, or by entertaining the reader through humor.

Much of the writing you read every day is written *to inform*. If you pick up the newspaper, you will find front-page articles designed to inform you of the events of the previous day. News journalists have prepared these articles so that you can learn the who, what, when, and where of each event. For example, a news article might present the latest crime statistics in a particular area. Informational writing is factual. Other examples of informational writing include textbooks, technical manuals, and encyclopedias.

Other writing is clearly meant *to persuade* you to adopt a particular viewpoint. If you turn to the editorial page of your newspaper, you can read editorials and columns designed to convince you to accept the writer's opinion. An editorial, for instance, might encourage the community to address a rise in criminal activity by passing a bond issue to build additional correctional facilities. Other examples of persuasive writing include print advertisements, sermons, letters of recommendation, and business proposals.

Some writers compose essays *to entertain*. In the newspaper, humorists write columns to amuse their readers by relating a story or by satirizing some aspect of their readers' daily lives. In the eighteenth century, Jonathan Swift published a satirical essay, "A Modest Proposal," which suggested that the Irish could solve the problem of famine by cannibalizing children. Today magazine and newspaper columnists still use satire to entertain their readers.

Effective writers—whether they are writing to express their personal feelings, to inform readers, to persuade others, or to entertain an audience— know that writing for a reader means that the focus of the communication is no longer on the writer but on the message. Because they are eager to send messages to the outside world, writers are always anxious to learn writing techniques that will help them attract readers.

Rewards from the Commitment to Writing Well

Any form of written communication involves risks on the part of the writer. "Will the reader enjoy what I have to say?" "Will the reader be bored?" Will the reader understand my message?" "Will the reader agree with my position?" All of these questions can lead initially to self-doubt. Yet for the writer who accepts these risks and communicates a message as best as he or she can, the most satisfying moment comes when the writing is finished and ready for a reader. Seeing the finished product, the writer can be proud of his or her accomplishment.

Accepting the challenge of communicating clearly to a reader also fosters intellectual growth. Writers are active learners for whom learning to write is a continual process of discovery. They are not passive observers of their environment but active participants ready to meet intellectual challenges.

Read each of the following topics. Depending on the topic's primary purpose, place the appropriate letter in the blank to the left: **X** (express personal feelings), **I** (inform), **P** (persuade), **E** (entertain).

_____ **1.** A lawyer's brief in support of a client's innocence

_____ **2.** An airline's list of airfare rates to China

_____ **3.** A scientific article on the effects of pollution on the ozone layer

_____ **4.** A political candidate's speech on the day before elections

_____ **5.** A teenager's diary

_____ **6.** A job application letter

_____ **7.** A charity's appeal for additional funds to feed the homeless

_____ **8.** A newspaper editorial in support of a new sports stadium

_____ **9.** A technical manual for installing an icemaker in a refrigerator

_____ **10.** A column about relatives who are really space aliens

SPEAKING VERSUS WRITING

All forms of communication feature three key elements:

- An audience or reader
- A speaker or writer
- A message or text

If you are like most people, you rely much more on oral communication than on written communication. Because you have more practice speaking than writing, you are probably more comfortable carrying on a conversation with another person than you are writing for a reader. Some writers try to make the transition from speaking to writing easier by thinking of writing as "speaking on paper." If you are writing for yourself, it may be helpful for you to think of writing in this way. However, if you are writing for a reader, it is essential that you think about some basic differences between speaking and writing.

When You Are Speaking, the Audience Is Present

The speaker can tell if the audience is listening attentively by looking for eye contact, head nods, and other gestures on the part of the audience.

If the audience fails to understand part of the message, they can ask questions. An alert speaker can also tell if the audience is not paying attention. For example, the audience may not be giving the speaker direct eye contact or may be paying attention to something other than the message the speaker is trying to communicate.

When You Are Writing, the Audience (Reader) Is Absent

The writer does not see the reader reading the message, so the writer has no way of knowing if the reader is concentrating on the written message. The reader could be distracted by any number of things, and the writer would not know it. Fortunately, readers are also generally writers, so they appreciate the work that has gone into sending the written message. However, what happens if the reader has a question about the paper or does not understand a sentence because some words are omitted? Generally the writer is not available to answer questions.

Most Everyday Speaking Is Associative

In other words, everyday conversations are not rehearsed. They move freely between the various speakers and are "off the cuff." Again, because the audience is present, the speaker plays off the audience and speaks the thoughts as soon as they occur.

Most Writing Must Be Organized

Unless the writing is self-expressive (such as diaries and journals), you are writing for an absent reader. That means you must plan what you want to write before you write it and present your message in such a way that the reader cannnot misunderstand your message. You cannot answer the reader's questions; your message must be clear, and to be clear, it must be organized.

Writers Have to Worry about Spelling and Punctuation

An audience cannot tell if words are misspelled on the speaker's note cards. However, readers may be confused by a large number of spelling errors in a written communication—particularly those errors that affect the clarity of the message. Similarly, an audience will never know if commas, semicolons, periods, and other punctuation marks are used correctly in the speaker's notes. However, the audience will notice dramatic pauses that the speaker uses for effect.

Writers Cannot Rely on Body Language to Help Communicate Their Messages

Speakers rely heavily on body language to help them communicate their messages. Some speakers wave their hands in the air while others seem to use their hands to cut the air like scissors. Furthermore, some speakers like to walk into the audience and maintain eye contact with their audience at all times. Writers cannot use body language to help them communicate. They must rely on other methods to attract the reader's attention.

INFORMAL VERSUS FORMAL WRITING

Writing for a reader means not only understanding the differences between speaking and writing, but also being able to distinguish between informal and formal writing styles. An effective writer knows that the reader's needs must be met. Sometimes the reader will expect an informal written message; other times the reader will require a message written at a formal level. It is the writer's responsibility to meet the reader's demands.

Informal Writing Style

An informal usage style is casual and generally used to communicate with yourself or with your friends and acquaintances. Some examples of informal academic writing include notes from class lectures, journals, narrative paragraphs, and personal experience essays. Informal writing in the workplace includes electronic mail (e-mail) correspondence, Internet chat room conversations and notes to coworkers.

One characteristic of informal writing is the writer's freedom to use slang. The words and expressions that are considered slang change from generation to generation, so the informal writing of today is quite different from that of the past. Such slang expressions as *groovy, out of sight,* and *neat* have been replaced by *bad, rad,* and *hip-hop.* Who knows what slang expressions the twenty-first century will bring?

Other characteristics of informal writing include the use of contractions (e.g., *don't, can't, won't*), and the use of first person (*I, me, my, mine, we, our, ours, us*) and second person (*you, your, yours*) pronouns. Also, shortened forms of expressions such as *thanks* for *thank you* are common.

Informal writing is appropriate when the writer knows the reader well because the writer can assume that the reader will understand the meaning of particular words. For example, if you were writing a letter to your best friend, you would naturally use an informal style. You would not worry about the organization of your letter, just write as if you were having a conversation with your friend. You probably would not worry about misspelled words, improper punctuation, or grammatical errors because your friend would undoubtedly understand your message despite these errors.

Formal Writing Style

Many writing situations—particularly in an academic or workplace setting—call for a formal style. Some examples of formal writing in an academic setting are problem-solving essays, persuasive essays, research papers, and responses to essay test questions. Formal writing in the workplace can be found in job proposals, letters of complaint, letters of thanks, and application letters.

A formal style, unlike an informal one, assumes a distance between the writer and the reader. In other words, the writer has often either never met the reader or does not know him or her well. Even if the writer does know the reader personally, the writing situation may require a formal written communication.

Because of the distance between the writer and the reader that is characteristic of a formal style, formal writing is generally highly organized. It also follows the rules of the Standard American English dialect (referred to throughout this textbook as SAE), one of many dialects spoken and written in America's multicultural society. The writer who uses a formal style is expected to be familiar with the standard punctuation, spelling, and grammar rules characteristic of this dialect. This book is designed to present the organizational skills and punctuation and grammar conventions associated with formal writing.

Unlike informal writing, formal writing is not characterized by the presence of slang. Readers of formal writing expect writers to use exact and specific vocabulary. What employer would consider seriously an application letter that begins: "I would like, you know, to apply for that rad job advertised in the mag I read yesterday"?

Other differences between informal and formal writing are evident. For example, many formal documents do not include the use of contractions. Also, the use of first and second person pronouns is less frequent in formal writing than in informal writing. While formal letters often require the use of first and second person pronouns, these pronouns are absent in many formal written communications.

EXERCISE 1.2

Write an informal letter to a friend whom you have not seen recently. Use contractions, first person pronouns, second person pronouns, and slang expressions. Then write a formal letter applying for a job advertised in the *Bay View Times* for a part-time sales clerk at Jane's Department Store. Be prepared to share your letters with a group in class. Be ready to answer the following questions: Which letter was easier to write? Why? What adjustments did you have to make as you shifted from writing an informal letter to writing a formal letter?

FOCUS ON THE READER

Every author needs a *reader* (referred to in some texts as the *audience*). The reader can be an individual or a group of readers. In some cases the writer knows the reader well, but many times the writer is writing for a reader with whom he or she has had little or no contact. All writers work hard to communicate to a reader, but how does the writer know what the reader expects?

Readers can be divided into two groups:

- General readers
- Specialized readers

When you are writing for a general reader, you do not expect the reader to have any specific knowledge about your topic, so you must be prepared to engage your reader's interest with the subject matter of your writing. You must also use vocabulary that you would expect the general public to know and define terms your reader will likely not understand. For example, if you were writing a restaurant review for a student newspaper, you would likely be writing for a general reader.

Specialized readers, on the other hand, already have knowledge of the subject matter. Therefore, you assume some interest on the part of the reader in what you are writing. You can also use vocabulary that you would expect this specialized audience to know. If you were writing a restaurant review in a magazine for gourmet cooks, you would be writing for a specialized reader.

One way to get a grasp on the reader's expectations is to ask yourself a series of questions about the reader. Keep in mind that you will not be able to answer every question if you do not know your reader well.

1. Who is likely to read this communication?

2. Is this person a general reader or a specialized reader?

3. In what age group is this reader?

4. What are this reader's interests?

5. What areas is this reader likely to be knowledgeable about?

6. How much knowledge about your topic does your reader have?

7. Has this reader read any of your writing before?

8. Based on your previous communication, what will this reader expect from this communication?

9. If your writing is designed to inform, is your reader likely to learn a great deal from your writing?

10. If your writing is designed to persuade, is your reader likely to agree or disagree with you? If your reader disagrees with you, is your writing likely to change his or her opinion?

If you want to become a successful writer, your writing must be "reader-friendly." Answering the above questions is a good start. Knowing something about your reader will help you decide what to write about and how to say what you want to communicate.

Consider each of the following types of writing. If the writing is aimed at a general reader, place a **G** in the blank. If the writing is aimed at a specialized reader, place the letter **S** in the blank.

EXERCISE 1.3

_____ **1.** A movie review in a daily newspaper

_____ **2.** A review of an art exhibit in a magazine for art historians

_____ **3.**   A cookbook for lovers of Louisiana Cajun cooking

_____ **4.**   An instruction manual for a portable television

_____ **5.**   A textbook for freshman composition students

_____ **6.**   A cookbook for beginning cooks

_____ **7.**   A technical manual for repairing videocassette recorders

_____ **8.**   A review of a new classical music CD for a magazine for classical music lovers

_____ **9.**   A review of a new CD for a local newspaper

_____ **10.** A guide to a foreign city for first-time visitors

Focus on the Writer

Not only must you consider your reader's needs and expectations, you must also understand the challenges of being a writer. What do you know about yourself as a writer?

EXERCISE 1.4

The following questions are designed to help you take inventory of your habits and challenges as a writer. Your responses to these questions will serve as a springboard for class discussion and will help form a framework for the remainder of this chapter. There are no right or wrong responses, and answers will vary greatly from student to student, so do not worry about your answers. As you respond to the questions, place a **0** in the blank for **Never,** a **1** in the blank for **Rarely,** a **2** in the blank for **Often,** or a **3** in the blank for **Always.**

_____ **1.**   I like to write for pleasure.

_____ **2.**   I enjoy taking classes that require writing assignments.

_____ **3.**   I allow enough time to complete any writing assignment.

_____ **4.**   My primary and secondary school teachers gave me plenty of opportunities to write.

_____ **5.**   The comments my teachers have made on my papers have been helpful in improving my writing.

_____ **6.**   My teachers have encouraged me to continue writing.

_____ **7.**   I like to plan what I am going to write before I begin a writing assignment.

_____ **8.**   I enjoy outlining my papers before I write them.

_____ **9.**   I like writing assignments that allow me to choose my own topic.

_____ **10.** I find it easy to write introductions and conclusions.

_____ **11.** I enjoy deciding how to support my main idea with details and examples.

_____ **12.** I find it easier to write the body of the writing assignment than introductions and conclusions.

_____ **13.** I read my papers aloud so I can check the flow of the sentences.

_____ **14.** I ask someone else to read my writing assignments aloud to me so I can check the flow of the sentences.

_____ **15.** I like to go back and rearrange my sentences to see if I can improve the flow of my writing.

_____ **16.** I make sure I allow some time after the writing assignment is finished and before I check my draft for mistakes.

_____ **17.** I read over my writing assignments many times looking for mistakes.

_____ **18.** I can work on a writing assignment for a long time without being distracted.

_____ **19.** I am satisfied with my writing assignments when I hand them in to my instructor.

_____ **20.** I reward myself when I complete a writing assignment to my satisfaction.

FOCUS ON THE WRITING PROCESS

Understanding your writing habits and your attitudes toward writing will help you think of yourself as a writer and a member of a writing community—your classroom. The more writing you do, the more you will be aware of the process that you use to complete your writing assignments.

Many students, for a variety of reasons, feel anxious when they are asked to complete writing assignments—a condition sometimes called *writer's anxiety*. If your answers to questions 1 through 6 above total between 0 and 7, you may be one of these students.

One of the characteristics of writing anxiety is *writer's block*, a frustrating situation for any writer. All writers at some time or another have faced a blank page and wondered whether they have anything worthwhile to say. Experienced writers know that this situation is temporary, but many student writers feel that they are the only ones who are nervous about the writing process. Some writers experience writing anxiety to such a degree that they procrastinate getting started on an assignment until the very last minute or never complete the assignment. Understanding the stages of the writing process can help students avoid the negative effects of writing anxiety. These stages are

- Planning
- Organizing
- Revising
- Editing
- Finishing

Stage 1. Planning

Once a writer has received a writing assignment or begun a writing project, the planning stage (often referred to as *prewriting*) begins. In this stage writers

- Plan how to approach the writing task
- Determine what they already know about various possible topics
- Consider what topic to write about
- Think about how they might focus the topic to meet the assignment's requirements
- Consider how much time will be needed to complete the project
- Collect ideas about a possible topic through freewriting, brainstorming, listing, or other prewriting activity

In the writer's inventory, if your responses to questions 7 through 10 totaled between 8 and 12, you enjoy the work of this stage. Perhaps you have already discovered that much of the pleasure of writing takes place before pen ever touches paper as the writer searches for ways to tackle a writing assignment.

One of the keys to being a successful writer is allowing enough time for this stage in the process. Writers learn from experience that some writing assignments take more planning time than others. For example, research papers and business proposals (as well as textbooks) are planning-intensive, and this first stage in the writing process may take more time than any other stage. Successful writers know that once they begin thinking about a writing assignment, ideas will flow, and the writing process will begin. On the other hand, procrastinators are generally poor planners, and putting off doing assignments until the last possible moment defeats the work of the planning stage. If you scored below 6 on questions 7 through 9, consider spending more time in the planning stage.

Chapter 2 of this textbook introduces techniques that you can use in the planning stage, including brainstorming, listing, freewriting, and clustering. Chapters 3 through 9 include guidelines for choosing a writing topic for a specific writing purpose—to develop by example, to narrate, to observe, to compare/contrast, to solve a problem and/or present a solution, and to persuade.

A teacher asked her students to write a paragraph on the following topic: "If I Won the Lottery, I Would . . ." During the planning stage the student completed the following freewriting:

Student Sample

If I won the lottery (hopefully about five million dollars), I would pay off my condo, which my grandparents are paying for, buy a new car, preferably a convertible, and remodel my condo. I would also pay off all my outstanding debts, put money away for my daughter to go to college, buy some real estate (some rental property), and purchase a new wardrobe. However, I should first join a health club to lose an extra forty pounds. I would then like to send my parents on a cruise and travel myself. My geography is terrible. I don't even know North from South half the time, so maybe traveling would help, I think I would retire for about ten years so I could really concentrate on school and get all sorts of degrees so that I could become a very knowledgeable and well-rounded person. I would like to spend more quality time with my daughter and understanding what parenting is all about. I would also like to have more kids, and I think having more money would bring this dream within reach. I could then spoil my children. I am sure I could do many more things than I have listed, but as the ideas come to me, I would pursue them.

Nicole Masko

Stage 2. Organizing

At this point writers have committed themselves to a topic and collected the ideas they plan to use. In this second stage writers should

- Decide how to narrow the topic
- Determine the main idea
- Consider which ideas they will use to support the main idea (and which they will omit)
- Decide in what order the ideas will appear
- Make a tentative formal or informal outline
- Write experimental draft(s)

The planning stage is writer-focused (that is, the writer makes the decisions, and any writing in this stage is for the writer's benefit). In the organizing stage, however, an important shift takes place. The writer arranges the ideas for a reader so that the writing becomes reader-focused. From this point on, the decisions are made so that the writer can communicate clearly with a reader.

Questions 10 through 12 in the writer's inventory relate to this stage. Some writers consistently find that it is easier to compose an introduction or conclusion of a piece of writing than to write the body. When these writers prepare the experimental draft in this second stage, they spend less time getting started and more time arranging the details in the body. Other writers find it easier to skip over the introduction and write the body of their experimental drafts first. Then these writers can back out and write the introduction and conclusion. If you frequently have difficulty beginning your first draft, think about your responses to questions 10 through 12 and try a different approach.

Chapter 2 discusses ways to narrow a topic and determine a main idea for a paragraph, and Chapter 7 presents strategies for choosing a topic and composing a main idea for an essay. Chapters 3 through 9 discuss methods of organizing details for specific purposes. In Appendix B, you will find informal and formal outlining guidelines designed to help you arrange your ideas effectively.

When the student submitted her freewriting to her teacher, the response was, "Good start! You have big plans for those lottery dollars. On the next draft, try narrowing your paragraph's focus to one of your plans and then developing that idea with specific details." The following is the experimental draft. Since the emphasis in the arranging stage is on shaping ideas rather than grammatical accuracy, this draft includes some spelling, punctuation, and grammatical errors.

Student Sample

I am happy with my condominium, and I love the neighborhood. My daughter and I have plenty of living space, a maintenance company to do all repairs and landscaping, a recreation center with pool, playground, tennis, and racquetball courts, and a nice pond surrounded by a picnic area and grill. If I won the lottery at this point in my life, I would choose to remodel my condominium. I would begin with my bedroom and bathroom. I have already spent a great deal of time and money in these rooms getting them the way I want; nevertheless, the rooms could still use a few final touches. I would add some pictures to my room as well as a builtin bookcase to hold all my little "clutter things." Aside from these minor things, this room would be complete. All the bathroom needs is a new sink and some pretty

→

ceramic tile for the shower and floor. My next job would be my daughters room. I would like to paint the bottom half pink and the top half white with a chair rail border to divide the two colors. Then, I would put in a cushioned window seat with two storage cupboards on each side. The window seat would store her endless supply of toys and stuffed animals while the cupboards would house her books and such. Finally, I would get new carpet, bedding, curtains and pictures. The room would then be the beautiful room I have pictured in my mind. The rest of the condo just needs a few minor (but expensive) details: tile for the guest bath, kitchen and front entryway floor. Paint and wallpaper for the dining and living room areas, pictures, coffee and end tables, a desk and new dining room set. Finally, I would add the finishing touches, getting the carpet cleaned, dishwasher and garbage disposal operating, and a screened door on the front door. You know—all those pesky little things that you bypass to do the fun things that really make changes noticeable. Of course, I may be the only one who likes to do the "fun" things first. More sensible people probably would fix the "foundation" before making it pretty. At any rate, I am sure that I would come up with many more ideas for my home, but I would have my whole life ahead of me to make additions or changes.

What differences do you note between Nicole's freewriting and her experimental draft? In her freewriting Nicole plans to pay off and remodel her condo, buy a car, pay off all her debts, start a college fund, buy a wardrobe, join a health club, travel, pursue a number of degrees, spend more time with her daughter, and have more kids. However, in her experimental draft Nicole limits her focus to her plans for her condo. Choosing a single focus allows her to add specific details that will interest the reader and support her main idea.

Nicole has also added a number of details to support her main idea—for example, her plans for a bookcase for her room, new fixtures for the bathroom, new furniture for the living and dining rooms, and others. These ideas help the reader to "see" Nichole's redecorating plans in a way that was not possible in her freewriting.

When Nicole submitted her experimental draft to her teacher, her teacher's response was, "The focus on remodeling your condominium is clear. You are ready to revise and edit your draft."

Stage Three. Revising

During this stage, writers should

- Rearrange sentences to improve the organization
- Rewrite sentences that may be unclear to the reader

- Omit ideas that are unrelated to the topic
- Add ideas that were omitted from the experimental draft(s)
- Insert transitional expressions to improve the flow of ideas
- Prepare revised draft(s)
- Rewrite outline to check for logical arrangement of ideas

Check your responses to questions 13 through 15 of the writer's inventory. If the total of your responses to these questions is below 6, then you may need to spend more time revising your papers. Revising requires discipline and concentration. Many writers find it difficult to revise ("to see again") their writing once the experimental draft is completed. Sometimes writers are so familiar with their message that they forget they are communicating to a reader. The key is to "see" your writing as readers will read it—a challenging task.

Chapter 10 is devoted to revision strategies. Although this chapter is the last of this textbook, it is not the least important. If you have difficulty revising your writing, try one or more of the strategies given in this chapter.

On Nicole's experimental draft, the teacher suggested that the student move the main idea to the first sentence and consider omitting sentences that were unnecessary and unrelated to the main idea. The following is her revised draft, which, like the previous draft, contains punctuation, spelling, and grammatical mistakes.

Student Sample

If I won the lottery, I would choose to remain in my condominium and do some remodeling. The room that I have the most plans for is my daughters room. First, I would paint the walls and woodwork. I want to paint the bottom half of the walls pink and the top half white with a chair rail border to divide the two colors. Then I would put in a cushioned window seat with a builtin bookcase on each side, going from ceiling to floor. The window seat would store her endless supply of toys and stuffed animals while the bookcases would house her books and such. Finally, I would get new carpet and matching bedding, curtains, and pictures. The room would then be the beautiful little girl's room that I have pictured in my mind. The rest of the condo just needs a few minor, but expensive, details: tile for the guest bath, kitchen, and foyer floors. Paint and wallpaper for the dining and living room areas, pictures, coffee and end tables, a desk, and a new dining room set. I am sure that if I won the lottery, I would come up with many more ideas for my home, but with all the money I would have, there would be plenty of time to do them all.

In her revised draft Nicole places the main idea of her paragraph—remodeling her condo—in the first sentence. She supports this idea by starting her plans for her daughter's room and then her plans for the rest of the condo. She has omitted those ideas in the experimental draft which do not support the main idea in her final draft and has added some ideas as well—for example, the floor-to-ceiling bookcase.

Stage 4. Editing

Once the composition has been revised, it is ready for editing. This stage includes

- Checking for effective word choice
- Correcting spelling errors
- Correcting punctuation errors
- Correcting grammatical errors
- Preparing edited draft(s)

If you scored between 6 and 9 on questions 16 through 18, you are probably an effective editor of your own work. However, for many writers this stage is the most challenging in the writing process. Many students confuse editing with revising and feel that if they have revised their drafts, they have also edited them and vice versa. The editing stage, however, is a distinct step in the process. Furthermore, many students underestimate the effect that a poorly edited (or, conversely, a well edited) draft will have on a reader. Most readers are accustomed to reading work that has been edited well and expect written work submitted to them to have been thoroughly edited. It is difficult for a reader—particularly an educated reader—to concentrate on the content of a text that has a large number of spelling, punctuation, and grammatical errors. Think about the reader's point of view. Would you consider seriously a business proposal that was full of spelling errors? Would you be more likely to consider a business proposal that was edited well and carefully laid out to attract the potential customer?

For many the work of this stage is time-consuming and sometimes tedious. Editing involves reading over the draft many times. This stage can also involve other readers. The section entitled "Focus on Peer Review" suggests ways for other students in the classroom to participate in this stage of the writing process.

Chapters 2 through 9 feature sections on punctuation, diction, grammar, and peer review designed to help you become an effective editor. Each section contains editing exercises to reinforce these skills. Chapter 10 discusses strategies for editing including using a computer.

When Nicole edited her revised draft, she discovered and corrected two misspellings as well as an incomplete sentence (see words in bold print). The following is her edited draft:

Student Sample

If I won the lottery, I would choose to remain in my condominium and do some remodeling. The room that I have the most plans for is my **daughter's** room. First, I would paint the walls and woodwork. I want to paint the bottom half of the walls pink and the top half white with a chair rail border to divide the two colors. Then I would put in a cushioned window seat with a **built-in** bookcase on each side, going from ceiling to floor. The window seat would store her endless supply of toys and stuffed animals while the bookcases would house her books and such. Finally, I would get new carpet and matching bedding, curtains, and pictures. The room would then be the beautiful little girl's room that I have pictured in my mind. The rest of the condo just needs a few minor, but expensive, details: tile for the guest bath, kitchen, and foyer floors, **paint and wallpaper for the dining and living room areas, pictures, coffee and end tables, a desk, and a new dining room set.** I'm sure that if I won the lottery, I would come up with many more ideas for my home, but with all the money I'd have, there would be plenty of time to do them all.

Stage 5. Finishing

This stage completes the work of the writer and includes

- Preparing the final draft according to the reader's (or teacher's) instructions
- Choosing a title
- Proofreading the final draft for last-minute corrections and legibility
- Presenting the text to the reader

This stage, like all the stages of the writing process, requires time and effort. The writer must meet the reader's expectations regarding manuscript form, including such details as whether the text must be typed, word processed, or handwritten; whether a cover page must be included; whether the assignment must be presented in a folder; and where and how the pages should be numbered. For additional information regarding manuscript form, see Appendix C. If you know your reader but are unsure of the expectations, be sure to ask. If you do not know your reader, then use your judgment to present your text in the best way possible.

During this stage the writer should select a title that is clearly related to the main idea of the paper and will interest the reader. Nicole gave her paper the title "If I Won the Lottery." She knew her reader would be curious about what would come next.

Some writers are reluctant to make any last-minute corrections to the final draft. Yet all writers have had the experience of finding a correction just before they turn in an assignment. Most readers do not mind corrections that are made neatly.

Because attention to these details can affect the reader's response to your text, this final stage of the writing process is critical to your assignment's success. When you complete the finishing stage, you are ready to hand in your assignment and reward yourself for a task well done.

Here is Nicole's finished draft:

Nicole Masko
Communications
Ms. Campbell

If I Won the Lottery

If I won the lottery, I would choose to remain in my condominium and do some remodeling. The room that I have the most plans for is my daughter's room. First, I would paint the walls and woodwork. I want to paint the bottom half of the walls pink and the top half white with a chair rail border to divide the two colors. Then I would put in a cushioned window seat with a built-in bookcase on each side, going from ceiling to floor. The window seat would store her endless supply of toys and stuffed animals while the bookcases would house her books and such. Finally, I would get new carpet and matching bedding, curtains, and pictures. The room would then be the beautiful little girl's room that I have pictured in my mind. The rest of the condo just needs a few minor, but expensive, details: tile for the guest bath, kitchen, and foyer floors, paint and wallpaper for the dining and living room areas, pictures, coffee and end tables, a desk, and a new dining room set. I'm sure that if I won the lottery, I would come up with many more ideas for my home, but with all the money I'd have, there would be plenty of time to do them all.

Although the stages of the writing process have been presented here in a step-by-step fashion, the writing experience is often circular—that is, writers often find themselves recycling through stages they thought they had finished. For example, a writer who is editing a misspelling may find a sentence that needs to be revised, or a writer may write an unsuccessful experimental draft and have to go back to the planning stage. Experienced writers know that this recycling through stages is a natural part of the process, but inexperienced writers sometimes think something is wrong because they cannot follow the stages in a lock-step manner. A key to success is to allow enough time for the writing process to take its natural course.

 ## FOCUS ON PEER REVIEW

As a student in a college classroom, you are a member of a community of writers consisting of your teacher and your fellow students. One of the advantages of being a member of a writing community is the chance to present your drafts to members of this community—not just your teacher but also your peers—for review. Whenever you show one of your drafts to another student or a group of students in your classroom, you are taking part in an activity known as *peer review*.

This activity offers you many advantages. You have a chance to submit your revised and/or edited draft to a reader for a trial run before you present your final draft to your teacher for evaluation. When your draft is accompanied by a list of guide questions for your peer editor to answer, you and your reader have the opportunity to think through your text together. After you receive the comments from your peer reviewers, you are then able to make revisions and editing corrections based on your reviewers' comments and prepare your final draft.

Many students feel uncomfortable at first about peer review. Some students feel that they themselves are too inexperienced with writing to make helpful comments about another student's written work. Other students are uneasy about making any comments that are critical of another student's composition. Remember, however, that students who participate in a peer review activity are a part of a writing community, so every peer reviewer should treat each composition with respect and try to be as helpful as possible. Peer reviewing is like any other writing activity—practice is the key.

Here are some common methods of peer review:

- Anonymous peer review
- Partner peer review
- Group peer review

Anonymous Peer Review

Using this method, you review a classmate's draft, but the draft is identified only by a number or some mark other than the student's name. Then you write down your comments about the draft, either on the draft itself or on a separate piece of paper. You identify your comments also with a number rather than with your name, or you can initial the draft. This method works best with a set of guide questions provided by your instructor or decided on by the classroom "community." This method also works well if you do not know the other students in your class well enough to feel comfortable about the peer review process. The disadvantage is that you cannot ask your peer reviewer questions face-to-face about any comments that may be unclear.

Partner Peer Review

This method involves working with another classmate and exchanging drafts. Some of the advantages of partner review include having someone to read your draft aloud to you or someone to listen to you read your draft. Reading the composition aloud allows you and your partner to hear your composition as well as see it. That way you can work together to check for clear as well as unclear sentences and for effective as well as poor word choice. Also, the writer is immediately available to answer questions about the draft. Again, this method works best with a set of guide questions. Your answers to the questions can be oral or written. However, if the responses are oral, you may want to take notes so that you will have a written record of your partner review when you begin to revise and/or edit your composition. A disadvantage is that working with a partner you do not know well can be uncomfortable, but most students realize that the advantages of partner review outweigh this disadvantage.

Group Peer Review

Small groups are particularly effective for peer review. You should provide enough copies of your draft so that each group member will have an opportunity to respond. In the group setting you will be able to read your draft aloud to the group or to hear your composition read aloud by a group member.

The advantages of this method depend on the willingness of the group members to participate in the peer review. Ideally, each member will make comments about each draft and build upon the comments of other members. This way the writer will have the opportunity to listen to the collective comments of a number of different writers. You may want to ask another member of the group to record the group members' comments so that you can concentrate on listening to the group's responses to your writing.

The goal of any peer review is to gather comments that will be helpful to you as you prepare your final draft to submit to your instructor. Working toward that common goal should be the concern of every member of the writing community. Sometimes, though, you may be puzzled by comments that do not seem relevant or are unclear. Do not feel obligated to revise and/or edit your composition to address every comment you receive. If you are unsure about whether a peer's comment will improve your composition, ask your instructor.

Chapters 3 through 9 feature guide questions for anonymous, partner, or group peer review. These guide questions are designed to reinforce the purpose for writing discussed in each chapter. Also included for your use are the following general guide questions for a paragraph-length writing assignment and an essay-length writing assignment. These guide questions will be applicable to the various types of writing assignment you will complete in the college setting.

GUIDE QUESTIONS FOR PARAGRAPHS

1. What is the main idea of the paragraph? Is this main idea stated? If so, where?

2. Does the writer include enough details in the rest of the paragraph to support the main idea? If not, what ideas could be added for support?

3. Are there any ideas that do not support the main idea and should be omitted? Where are they located?

4. Are any ideas unnecessarily repeated? Which ideas could be omitted?

5. Do the ideas in the paragraph flow well? Are the ideas logically arranged? What changes should the writer make to improve the paragraph's flow?

6. Does the closing sentence reinforce the main idea of the paragraph? If not, why?

7. Do any sentences need clearer wording? Why?

8. Are there any incomplete sentences? Where do they occur?

9. Are there any other grammatical errors? Where are they located?

10. Are there any punctuation errors? Where do they occur?

11. Are there any spelling errors? If so, where?

12. The strengths of this paragraph are _____
    _____ .

13. The weaknesses of this paragraph are _____
    _____ .

GUIDE QUESTIONS FOR ESSAYS

1. Does the introductory paragraph of the essay engage the reader's interest? If not, why?

2. What is the main idea of the essay? Where is it stated?

3. What is the main idea of each of the supporting paragraphs? How do these main ideas relate to the main idea of the essay?

4. Are there sufficient details in each of the supporting paragraphs to develop that paragraph's main idea? If not, what ideas could be added for support?

5. Are there any ideas in the supporting paragraphs that are unnecessarily repeated? If so, where?

6. Are there any ideas in the supporting paragraphs that do not relate to that paragraph's main idea or detract from the main idea of the essay? Which sentences could be omitted?

7. Do the ideas in the supporting paragraphs flow well? Are they logically arranged? If there is a break in the flow, where does it occur?

8. Does the closing paragraph reinforce the main idea of the essay? If not, why?

9. Are there any incomplete sentences? Where do they occur?

10. Are there other grammatical errors? Where are they located?

11. Are there punctuation errors? Where do they occur?

12. Are there spelling errors? If so, where?

13. This essay's strengths are _____

_____ .

14. This essay can be improved by _____

_____ .

The goal of peer reviewing your drafts is to help you see your writing from the viewpoint of a reader. In order to write well you must be able to stand back from your writing and evaluate its strengths and weaknesses. Peer reviewing will help you achieve what professional writers sometimes call *critical distance* from your own writing.

Writing is a continual process of discovery—a way for you to look at yourself and the world around you from new perspectives. Though the task of writing well may sometimes be tiresome and frustrating, the joys of communicating your ideas to a reader are worth your best efforts.

Writers as Spiders

The Internet is a network of computers around the world connected to each other by modems, phone lines, satellites, and fiber optics cable. The Internet was originally designed for research by educational and military organizations. Today the Internet has many users thanks to Internet service providers to which businesses and homes can subscribe for a fee.

One of the most popular components of the Internet is the World Wide Web (www). The "web" is a collection of "pages" which include both text and graphics. The user ("spider") is able to "see" the page (instead of the language used to create it) with a browser. The Internet service provider generally includes a browser with the user's subscription.

Each web page has an address. The address begins with **http://**followed by other letters and numbers. If users know the address of a web site, they can open its location using the browser. If they do not know the specific address, they can use a search engine. To use a search engine, the "spider" enters a keyword or a phrase. The search engine then compiles a list of www addresses related to the keyword entry.

Many students have access to the Internet, including the World Wide Web, at home, at work, or at school. If you have had little or no experience on the World Wide Web or if you just want to use the web more efficiently check out

http://www.spjc.cc.fl.us/0/research/home.html

This site gives an overview of using the World Wide Web as a tool for writing. The site also features instructions for conducting a search on the Internet, including links to various search engines, advantages and disadvantages of search engines, and information about keyword searches. You will further discover links to on-line writing labs to assist you when you check your papers for grammar and style.

A keywork search for *writing process* will suggest numerous sites for further exploration. Some of these sites include

http://leo.stcloud.msus.edu/acadwrite/writeproc.html

http://www.up.net/~wic/writing/wwwcom1.html

http://loge.umd.umich.edu/owc/writ/Tips/stage.html

http://cci.scbe.on.ca/departments/library/writproc.htm

Remember that changes to web sites occur frequently, so if you cannot access one site, try another. Also keep in mind that you must enter the address exactly. Any mistakes will result in failure to open that location. Watch out for similar symbols. What appears to be a zero (0), for instance, may be a capital O, or what seems to be the number one (1) may be the letter l.

Web Exercise

After you have read through one of the web sites above, answer the following questions:

1. What are the steps of the writing process as detailed in the web site you visited?

2. How are these steps similar to the ones presented in this chapter?

3. What are the differences between the writing process featured on the web site and the one in this chapter?

4. What new information did you learn from the web site?

Focus on the Paragraph

The paragraph, a group of sentences that combine to present a main idea to a reader, is the basic building block of all prose compositions. The word *paragraph* is derived from the Greek words *para* (meaning *beside*) and *graphein* (meaning *to write*). In medieval Latin the word *paragraphos* referred to a sign used to mark a new section of writing. The symbol for the paragraph (¶) can be found in many ancient documents.

Both readers and writers have long been dependent on the paragraph for making documents understandable. Think of what this textbook page would look like without the indentations marking the beginning of paragraphs. What you would see would be a solid block of type, and you as the reader would be expected to decide for yourself where one major idea ends and another begins. Writers, then, are responsible for dividing their compositions into paragraphs so that the reader can receive the message.

Paragraphs can generally be classified into three types:

- Topic sentence paragraphs
- Transition paragraphs
- Special paragraphs

Topic Sentence Paragraphs

The most common type of paragraph is the topic sentence paragraph. A topic sentence paragraph has a stated or implied main idea, a sufficient number of details to support that main idea, transitional expressions that help the reader understand the message, and a concluding sentence that reinforces the topic sentence. A single topic sentence paragraph is usually 100 to 300 words in length. A writer can develop a single topic sentence paragraph as a composition or compose a group of topic sentence paragraphs to form the body of an essay, research paper, textbook, or nonfiction book.

In this chapter, you will learn how to compose a topic sentence paragraph by narrowing the topic, forming a topic sentence, choosing relevant supporting details, linking ideas together using transition, and adding a concluding sentence. The remainder of the textbook will focus on writing topic sentence paragraphs for a variety of purposes—to develop by example, to narrate, to observe, to compare and/or contrast, to present a problem, to propose a solution, and to persuade. In Chapter 7, you will learn how to link several topic sentence paragraphs to form an essay.

Understanding the organization of topic sentence paragraphs for a variety of purposes is essential for success in the college classroom. Paragraph composition skills are critical for writing competency—and not just in English classes. Many instructors in other disciplines require their students to write paragraphs, essays, or research papers to demonstrate their understanding of the subject area. These instructors expect their students to be able to state a main idea in a topic sentence paragraph, support that main idea with a variety of details, and provide key words to communicate the message to the reader. These skills are not only important for writing competency but are also necessary for reading comprehension. In order to do well on tests, students must read the textbooks and understand the key concepts in each paragraph of each chapter. They must also comprehend the details that the author uses to support each key concept. Finally, they must be able to follow the author's progression from concept to concept.

The ability to write clear paragraphs is also essential in the workplace. Proposals, business letters, and abstracts are all based on the unit of the paragraph.

Transition Paragraphs

Transition paragraphs are used to help move the reader through a lengthy essay, research paper, or book. These paragraphs are generally short and lack topic sentences. The purpose of transition paragraphs is not to discuss a main idea but to create drama or link together sections of the composition. While transition paragraphs can add polish and style to a composition, they are not the essential building blocks that topic sentence paragraphs are. Thus, they are not the focus of this chapter.

Special Paragraphs

In an essay or lengthy composition, introductory paragraphs and concluding paragraphs are considered special paragraphs because they fulfill specific functions. Introductory and concluding paragraphs are necessary to form an essay, and both the introductory paragraph and the concluding paragraph have particular features. These special paragraphs are discussed in Chapter 7.

FOCUS ON GENERATING IDEAS

Each topic sentence paragraph begins with the choice of a topic. Sometimes your instructor will assign you a topic; sometimes you will choose your own topic. Often these topics are general, and you must narrow the topic before you can write your paragraph. Here are some examples of general topics that will be used in the first five exercises in this chapter:

- Challenges Facing College Students Who Work
- Characteristics of an Effective Leader
- Problems Facing Today's Adolescents
- Characteristics of a Good Parent
- Benefits of Regular Exercise

Each of the above topics could be the focus of a lengthy essay, a research paper, or even a book! One common error made by beginning college writers is trying to write on a topic that is too general or unfocused for a single paragraph. Your first step in limiting the topic should be to generate as many subtopics as you can and keep narrowing the topic until you find a focus for your paragraph. The following methods will help you discover your ideas on a particular subject and then choose a limited topic:

- Brainstorming
- Listing
- Freewriting
- Clustering

Brainstorming

Brainstorming can be done individually or in groups. When you brainstorm, you think about as many related topics as you can. The key is not to be self-critical and second-guess your responses but to generate numerous ideas. For example, if you were brainstorming the first topic above, you might ask yourself what challenges you face as a working college student. You might think about the difficulties involved with finding time to study, working too many hours, taking too many classes, eating on the run, not getting enough sleep, or not having time to spend with friends and family.

The fun of brainstorming, however, is sharing your ideas with someone else and then listening to that person's ideas about the subject. Another student, for instance, might bring up some benefits of being a working student such as having a support group at work or understanding the relationship between school and career.

Brainstorming in a small group works well, too, if everyone has a chance to speak and no one is critical of anyone else's ideas. If everyone in the group actively participates, the rewards of group brainstorming are great.

EXERCISE 2.1   In small groups of three or four, brainstorm one of the five topics above. Someone in your group should serve as a recorder who will report to the class your group's ideas about the subject. If more than one group brainstorms the same topic, what are the similarities and differences between the groups' responses?

Listing

Once you have brainstormed either individually, with a partner, or with a group, you are ready to list your ideas about the topic. It is not important that you list your ideas in any particular order; you will have the chance to organize them later. You can also list them in any way you choose—complete sentences, phrases, or individual words. What is essential is that your list is comprehensive enough so that you will be able to choose a narrowed topic as the focus of your paragraph.

Suppose you are making a list for the second topic above, "Characteristics of an Effective Leader." Here are some possibilities:

Courage

Risk-taking

Listening skills

Organizational skills

Clear communication of goals

Fairness

Charisma

Availability for meetings

Efforts to keep followers interested

Effective language use

Openness to criticism

Encouragement to work hard

Response to followers' needs

What characteristics would you add? Think about how many characteristics you could list if you were working with a group of three or four other students.

The value of list-making is that you will be able to generate ideas quickly and overcome "blank paper" anxiety.

EXERCISE 2.2

Create a list for any of the topics given at the beginning of this section. Be prepared to share your list in class. Compare and contrast the ideas on your list with the ideas of other students. Which method of generating ideas did you find easier—brainstorming or listing? Why?

Freewriting

When you freewrite, you write nonstop about a topic for a set length of time and see what comes to your mind. You can freewrite on a general topic, or you can wait until you have brainstormed and made a list and then freewrite on one of the ideas on your list. You should choose a specific amount of time before you begin. Once you start freewriting, do not stop moving the pen across the paper. If you cannot think of something, just write "I can't think of anything to say" until you can think of something to say! Do not stop to correct your spelling or punctuation. Keep going until the time is up.

Once you have finished, read over what you have written. Is there any sentence about which you could write more? If that is the case, you can freewrite again using that sentence as a focal point.

Following is a student's freewriting on "Benefits of Regular Exercise."

Student Sample

Exercise can be beneficial for things like keeping in shape and relieving stress. Exercise can also be strenuous. Some people go overboard with exercise. They do too much at one time, which can lead to muscle strain, overheating, or exhaustion. Exercise can lead to a longer life, a life which can be enjoyed without worry. Regular exercise normally consists of sit-ups, push-ups, walking, or running. Regular exercise to some people is weightlifting or aerobic exercise. A good diet also goes along with regular exercise. Eating three good meals a day along with an hour of daily exercise is beneficial to anyone's health. It's sad that so many people do not exercise. If more people exercised, health problems would be reduced. These are just a few common benefits of exercise.

Stephanie Clark

EXERCISE 2.3

Freewrite for five minutes on one of the five general topics. When you finish, read over your freewriting and circle a sentence about which you have more to say. Then freewrite for another five minutes. What advantages does freewriting offer you as a writer?

Clustering

Clustering is an effective way to generate ideas because it provides a visual representation of your ideas about a topic. To cluster, place one or two words representing the general topic in the center of a piece of paper (the larger the paper, the better). Draw a circle around the topic. Then extend lines out from the general topic and create subtopics—again represented by one or two words. Circle the subtopics. Then draw lines again as you generate words associated with the subtopics. Remember to make sure you draw lines between related words. Many students have found clustering helpful because the process reveals relationships between ideas which are essential to the writing process. Clustering is also helpful for students who have difficulties writing outlines (see Appendix A).

Here is one writer's cluster on the topic, "Characteristics of a Good Parent".

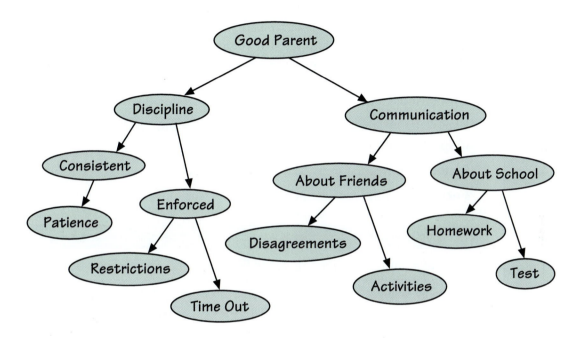

Create a cluster on one of the five general topics. Which of the ideas in your cluster might serve as a focal point for a paragraph?

EXERCISE 2.4

All of the above techniques will help you focus your topic. Not every technique, though, will work for every student or for every topic. Experiment until you find a method that helps you. After you have focused your topic, ask yourself if that topic can be discussed in a single paragraph. Even after you have chosen a narrowed topic, you may later discover that you have too much information and examples for one paragraph. If so, then brainstorm, freewrite, or cluster the topic again until you have a topic that is workable.

FOCUS ON THE TOPIC SENTENCE

Once you have chosen a limited topic, you are ready to write your topic sentence. Your topic sentence states your narrowed topic and expresses the single main idea you want to communicate in your paragraph. An effective topic sentence

- Announces the narrowed topic to the reader
- Focuses the reader's attention on your main idea
- Limits what you can discuss to those ideas related directly to the topic sentence

An effective topic sentence serves both you and your reader. The key words of the topic sentence direct the reader's attention to the main idea of your paragraph. The topic sentence will also keep your attention focused on your subject. Because the topic sentence controls the direction of your paragraph, you must be careful to write a topic sentence that can be discussed fully within the limits of a single paragraph. If you write an unfocused topic sentence, you will have so much to say that you must write a longer composition, such as an essay or a research paper, in order to be comprehensive.

Unfocused: College students who work face an uphill battle.

Focused: One challenge facing college students who work is finding time to spend with friends.

Unfocused: Regular exercise benefits everyone.

Focused: Regular exercise helps strengthen the lungs.

TABLE 2.1 Types of Topic Sentences		
Paragraph Purpose	*Topic Sentence Focus*	*Sample Topic Sentence*
To develop by example (Chapter 3)	To narrow the topic to a supportable main idea	One advantage of being a working college student is learning to manage study time effectively.
To relate a personal experience (Chapter 4)	To provide necessary information—who, what when, where	On a cold winter's day in November 1996, I visited an unforgettable place.
To describe a person, animal, or object (Chapter 5)	To communicate a dominant impression	My office desk is a wonderful example of organized chaos.
To compare or contrast (Chapter 6)	To explain similarities or differences	My two daughters differ greatly in their attitudes toward household chores.
To present a problem (Chapter 8)	Identify the problem	One problem I face at home is time management.
To propose a solution (Chapter 8)	Identify the solution	One way to increase personal savings is to prepare a weekly budget.
To persuade an audience (Chapter 9)	Give your position	Teenagers should not be subject to city-imposed curfews.

Each chapter of this book will provide guidelines to help you compose an effective topic sentence. The following table gives some examples of the types of topic sentences you will be writing in the following chapters. Each chapter focuses on a different purpose for writing, and the topic sentence for each paragraph you write will reflect that focus.

Read each of the sentences below. Place a check in the blank next to the sentences that you think would make good topic sentences. If the sentence is too general to be effective, place an **X** in the blank, cross through the sentence, and write a narrowed topic sentence in its place. (Each sentence is based on one of the topics presented in this chapter under the heading, "Focus on Generating Ideas.")

EXERCISE 2.5

_____ **1.** Students who attend college while employed face many challenges.

_____ **2.** Young people are often pressured to consume alcoholic beverages at an early age.

_____ **3.** There are many problems facing adolescents today.

_____ **4.** Working college students must budget study time carefully.

_____ **5.** A good parent maintains an active interest in his or her child's homework.

_____ **6.** An effective teacher uses class time wisely.

_____ **7.** Exercising regularly is beneficial in many ways.

_____ **8.** Good parents are hard to find.

_____ **9.** There are many characteristics of an effective teacher.

_____ **10.** One benefit of regular exercise is weight control.

For each of the general topics below, narrow the topic, and write a topic sentence. Use the first example as a model.

EXERCISE 2.6

1. Topic: Characteristics of an Ideal Job
Narrowed topic: <u>medical insurance coverage</u>
Topic sentence: <u>An ideal job offers employees excellent medical insurance coverage.</u>

2. Topic: What I Would Do if I Won a Lottery

Narrowed topic: _____

Topic sentence: _____

_____

3. Topic: A Great Place to Vacation

Narrowed topic: _____

Topic sentence: _____

_____

4. Topic: Qualities of a True Friend

Narrowed topic: _____

Topic sentence: _____

_____

5. Topic: Advantages of a College Education

Narrowed topic: _____

Topic sentence: _____

_____

A topic sentence can appear as the first or last sentence in the paragraph or can be implied. Most instructors encourage beginning college writers to place the topic sentence at the beginning of the paragraph to attract both the reader's and the writer's attention.

The following paragraph is an example in which the topic sentence is the first sentence:

An effective teacher shows respect for her students in the classroom. When a student asks a question, the teacher listens intently and waits until the student finishes before responding. The teacher knows that interrupting a student before he or she finishes asking the question would send the message that the teacher does not consider the student's question important. Then a concerned teacher will answer the student's question directly and patiently. For example, many effective teachers ask a follow-up question such as, "Does that answer your question?" or "Do you have any other questions you want to ask?" Good teachers are not afraid to say, "I don't know the answer to your question, but perhaps we can find out the answer." Additionally, successful teachers demonstrate their respect for students by learning their students' names during the first week of class. No student wants to be thought of as a number or a box on a seating chart. These teachers call on students by name and involve them in class discussion. In sum, effective teachers know that showing respect for students will relieve anxiety in the classroom.

Sometimes the writer moves the topic sentence to the end for dramatic effect.

> Joan has sweaty palms when she enters her math class. Her heart beats faster and faster as she moves toward her seat. She remembers that she is getting back her chapter test today, and she knows she did not do as well as she should have. She studied hard for a week before the test, but her mind went blank on some of the questions. She remembers feeling the same way in elementary school in Mrs. Smith's class. Mrs. Smith always told her, "You're not trying hard enough. You're lazy; that's what your problem is." Joan looks at the other students sitting calmly in their seats. Is she the only one who feels this way? What Joan does not know is that many students like her suffer the symptoms of math anxiety.

In other paragraphs the topic sentence is not directly stated.

> Visitors to downtown Tampa can begin their tour at the Tampa Museum of Art, which offers its patrons a collection of Greek amphora and other ancient vases as well as a spectacular view of the Hillsborough River. Within walking distance of the museum is the Center for the Performing Arts where theatergoers can purchase tickets for a variety of musicals, plays, and concerts. Downtown tourists should not leave without taking in a movie at the Tampa Theater. Built in the style of an Italian Renaissance palace, this theater is nothing like the suburban cineplex.

The implied topic sentence for the above paragraph can be stated a number of ways. Here is one possibility: "Visitors to downtown Tampa need not worry about boredom."

EXERCISE 2.7

Write a topic sentence for each of the following paragraphs. Be sure that your topic sentence is comprehensive enough to reflect all of the details in the paragraph.

1. Appetizers at the Sum Ho Chinese Restaurant are priced reasonably. Egg rolls are $1.00 each. The cost of soups ranges from egg drop soup at $.85 a bowl to hot and sour soup at $1.50 per bowl. The entrees range from $4.95 for Chinese vegetables to $14.95 for Peking duck. Two popular entrees, Cashew Chicken and Sweet and Sour Pork, are just $5.95 each. Desserts are limited but still inexpensive. A bowl of ice cream costs $1.00, and a serving of fried bananas with honey is $1.95.

_____

_____

2. Some people use home computers to keep track of their checking accounts. Software is available that will allow users to record deposits, withdrawals, and checks, and then determine their balance in their checking accounts. These users can also monitor withdrawals and deposits to their savings accounts. Those home computer users with stock investments can use financial software programs to record changes in the net asset value of their stocks so they can determine their stocks' worth on any given day. Finally, these programs can evaluate an individual's net worth, including any assets and liabilities.

_____

_____

3. A fifth-grade boy at a local elementary school brought a small handgun to class. When another student told the teacher the boy had a gun, the teacher turned to the boy and said, "Why are you carrying a gun?" The boy's reply was, "A kid on the playground yesterday told me he was going to shoot me." A six-year-old girl carried a small pistol inside her purse. When the principal asked her how she got the gun, she told him she had picked it up off the breakfast table at her house because a girl on her bus had threatened to kill her.

_____

_____

4. According to a report by the Environmental Protection Agency, secondhand cigarette smoke has caused a dramatic increase in the number of respiratory infections in babies. An estimated 150,000 to 300,000 respiratory infections occur in babies in just one year. These infections lead to as many as 15,000 hospitalizations annually. Secondhand smoke also aggravates the symptoms of the estimated 1 million children with asthma and causes new cases of asthma among previously unaffected children.

_____

_____

5. According to a report by the Office of Juvenile Justice and Delinquency Prevention of the U.S. Justice Department, the number of American teens arrested for murder increased 85 percent from 1987 to 1991. In 1991 30 percent of juvenile arrests for murder involved a juvenile victim. Juveniles also accounted for 17 percent of arrests for violent crimes in 1991. Furthermore, according to the FBI, in 1991 over 2,200 murder victims were under 18. That figure represents an average of more than six juveniles killed every day.

_____

_____

FOCUS ON SUPPORTING DETAILS

When you write a topic sentence, you enter into an implied contract with the reader. Your reader will also expect you to provide enough evidence to convince him or her that you are knowledgeable about the topic. Supporting details can come from a number of sources including first-hand experience, reading, and common knowledge.

If you have difficulty coming up with enough support, you can try brainstorming, freewriting, list making, or clustering using key words from your topic sentence. Depending on your subject, you can also ask yourself the same questions an inquiring reader will be asking: *who, what, when, where, how,* and *why?*

In Exercise 2.7, example 1, the first major point of support is the appetizers. As the reader you are probably thinking, *"What* appetizers? *How much* do they cost?" The writer then proceeds to discuss the prices of three specific appetizers—egg rolls, egg drop soup, and hot and sour soup—to support the major point. The second major point is the cost of the entrees. Again the reader is undoubtedly curious about *what* the entrees are and *how much* they cost, and again the writer names specific dishes to support the major point. The same is true with the last major point—the desserts.

Supporting details in topic sentence paragraphs must be organized for a reader. Most paragraphs are ordered in one of three ways:

- Time order
- Spatial order
- Order of importance

Time order is sometimes referred to as chronological order. When using time order, writers arrange the paragraph's supporting details in the order in which they happened or in a step-by-step arrangement. Time order is commonly used in narrative paragraphs that relate a series of events or in paragraphs that include step-by-step directions. Once a time order has been established, it is important that the writer make sure that no important events or steps are omitted or out of place. Otherwise, the reader is likely to be confused. You will be using time order to develop your narrative paragraph in Chapter 4.

Another way to arrange a paragraph's supporting details is *spatial order.* Paragraphs that relate an observation or a description are often arranged using spatial order. When using spatial order, writers organize the supporting details in a spatial pattern. For example, a writer describing a photograph may begin at the top on the photo and end at the bottom or begin on the lefthand side of the photo and end on the righthand side. As long as the writer proceeds in a clear direction, the reader should be able to follow the writer's description. You can find more information about spatial order in Chapter 5.

A third way to organize a paragraph's supporting details is *order of importance*. This method is commonly used in formal writing (as opposed to paragraphs that tell stories or relate a description). Using this organizational pattern, you arrange your supporting details from least important to most important. These ideas can be examples, reasons, or facts that support your topic sentence. Placing the most important idea last emphasizes its importance. Your reader is more likely to remember the last supporting detail of your paragraph than the first. Chapter 3 will give you practice in arranging your details according to their importance.

EXERCISE 2.8

Consider the following topic sentences. Place the letters **CO** in the blank to the left of the topic sentences that would be developed using details arranged in chronological order. Use **SO** for the topic sentences that would be developed in spatial order, and **OI** for those topic sentences whose supporting details would be arranged in order of importance.

_____   1.   The first morning of the river rafting trip was a disaster.

_____   2.   The atrium of the office building was beautiful.

_____   3.   An important advantage of owning a small car is reduced maintenance costs.

_____   4.   A city-imposed curfew for teenagers under 16 is unworkable.

_____   5.   Before beginning a quilt, the quilter must carefully choose the overall design.

_____   6.   College classes should not have mandatory attendance policies.

_____   7.   The 5″ by 7″ photograph features a beautiful field of wildflowers.

_____   8.   My first day as a college student was one of adventure.

_____   9.   One disadvantage of attending a community college is the lack of dormitory rooms.

_____ 10.   The cover of this textbook is visually appealing.

FOCUS ON TRANSITION

The word *transition* comes from the Latin word *transitus* meaning *to move across*. Instructors of writing use the term transition to refer to those techniques used by a writer to help the reader move easily through the supporting details of a composition. Readers are thankful for writers who take the time to provide transition in their compositions because it makes the reading experience enjoyable. The reader has confidence in the writer's ability to provide clear direction through the supporting details that form the heart of the composition.

Three techniques that writers use to provide transition are:

- Transitional words and phrases
- Repetition of key words from the topic sentence
- Use of synonyms for key words from the topic sentence

Transitional Words and Phrases

Knowledgeable readers immediately recognize the use of certain words as signals. Readers know, for example, that the use of the transitional word *also* signals that an idea is being added, and the transitional phrase *on the other hand* means the next idea will provide a contrast to the one preceding it.

As writers, you want your transitional expressions to sound smooth and not stilted. You may need to experiment with transitional phrases and expressions that are new to you. It is easy to use the same transition words again and again with little variation. Some of these commonly used words include *first, second, third, then, next, also,* and *finally.* However, writers who want to keep their readers' interest know that they cannot remain dependent on these words in every composition.

Table 2.2 provides a list of common transitional words and phrases. In the lefthand column is the purpose for which they are generally used. You will need to keep this purpose in mind and match it to the sentence in which the transitional expression appears. Any use of transitional words and phrases must be logical, or the purpose for using transition is defeated.

Transitional words and phrases can appear at the beginning or the end of the sentence, in the middle of the sentence, or between coordinated independent clauses. Students are sometimes worried about using transitional expressions because they are unsure how to punctuate them. The section on commas in Chapter 3 will address the punctuation of these expressions when they are at the beginning or in the middle of a sentence. Chapter 4 addresses the punctuation of transitional expressions when they are used to coordinate independent clauses.

Repetition of Key Words from Topic Sentence

Writers use this method of transition to remind the reader of the focus of the paragraph at frequent intervals. Some students are reluctant to use this method because they have been taught never to repeat an idea. However, the repetition of key words is not the same as repeating an idea. Writers need to keep their readers on track, and this method accomplishes that task.

Using Synonyms

Sometimes the repetition of key words can become ineffective. When the writer wants another option, synonyms can substitute for key words. These synonyms, of course, must be used correctly in context.

TABLE 2.2	Common Transitional Words and Phrases
Purpose	*Transitional Word/Phrase*
To add an idea	first, second, third, also, then, next, in addition, moreover, furthermore, besides, additionally
To compare one idea to another	also, too, in the same way, similarly, likewise, in like manner, both . . . and, not only . . . but also, either . . . or
To contrast one idea with another	however, nevertheless, yet, on the one hand, on the other hand, in contrast, to the contrary, contrarily, unlike, conversely
To give an example	for example, for instance, as an illustration, to illustrate, as a case in point, in particular, in general
To emphasize an idea	above all, especially, in fact, surely, most importantly, equally important
To concede a point	granted, certainly, of course, no doubt, surely, naturally, although this may be true
To qualify a point	perhaps, probably, for the most part
To indicate an effect	therefore, as a result, thus, indeed, consequently, accordingly, hence, as a consequence, for this reason, because of this
To place in time	before, meanwhile, afterward, at the same time, to begin with, subsequently, previously, at last, at present, briefly, currently, eventually, finally, gradually, immediately, in the future, then, now, later, suddenly, earlier, formerly, shortly, at that time, in the meantime, in the past, until now
To indicate spatial relationships	here, above, beside, below, beyond, further, there, inside, outside, nearby, next to, on the far side, to the east (north, south, or west), behind, adjacent to, in the background, opposite to, to the right, to the left
To summarize	overall, all in all, finally, in brief, in other words, lastly, on the whole, to sum up, in sum

EXERCISE 2.9

In the following paragraph, circle (or highlight) transitional phrases and expressions. Then go back through the paragraph and underline key words repeated from the topic sentence.

One characteristic of a good teacher is excellent preparation. To begin with, a good teacher prepares ahead of time for the next day. For instance, if her class is supposed to have a reading assignment, she also reads the material in case there are any questions. Also a well prepared instructor devises an outline of what she will teach the next day. In addition, a good teacher always gives sufficient notes and provides a review prior to a test. For example, she gives her class ample time to study notes, ask questions, and consult for extra help. Furthermore, she budgets her time well in order to cover the required curriculum. For instance, she does not get behind on her assignments and does not cram work in all at once. When budgeting her class time, she always follows up on specific dates when information is to be covered. Finally, a well prepared teacher keeps each student informed of his or her progress throughout the course. If the student is doing great work, the teacher will comment to the student and give him or her confidence to continue. On the other hand, if a student is not doing well in the course, the teacher detects the problem and takes whatever means are necessary to help the student and see that he or she is taking the right steps toward improvement. An excellent teacher prepares herself daily to meet her students' educational needs.

FOCUS ON THE CONCLUDING SENTENCE

Every writer knows the importance of a strong ending. The concluding sentence provides you the opportunity to reinforce the main idea of your paragraph and to create a sentence that will make a lasting impression on your reader.

Before you write your concluding sentence, reread your topic sentence. You do not want to repeat your topic sentence as your concluding sentence but instead compose a concluding sentence that will bring the paragraph to a forceful close.

Write a concluding sentence for each of the narrowed topics you chose in Exercise 2.6 on page 31. Recopy your topic sentence in the spaces provided.

EXERCISE 2.10

1. Topic: Characteristics of an Ideal Job

    Topic sentence: _____

    Concluding sentence: _____

2. Topic: What I Would Do If I Won a Lottery

    Topic sentence: _____

    Concluding sentence: _____

3. Topic: A Great Place to Vacation

    Topic sentence: _____

    Concluding sentence: _____

4. Topic: Qualities of a True Friend

Topic sentence: _____

Concluding sentence: _____

5. Topic: Advantages of a College Education

Topic sentence: _____

Concluding sentence: _____

FOCUS ON GRAMMAR

Writing clear, effective paragraphs depends on your ability to write clear, effective sentences. The "Focus on Grammar" sections in this chapter and in subsequent chapters are designed to provide you with an introduction to the basic rules of the Standard American English dialect and exercises to reinforce specific grammatical skills. This chapter focuses on the central unit of all written communication—the sentence.

Sentences cannot exist without two key elements:

- Verbs
- Subjects

In order to write effective sentences, you need to be able to identify subjects and verbs and understand their functions.

Identifying Verbs

Verbs are the heartbeat of all sentences in the English language. Verbs are words that express action (*action verbs*) or link the subject of the sentence to the words following the verb (*linking verbs*). Being able to identify verbs will improve the strength of your sentences.

Action verbs are easy to identify because the reader or writer can visualize the expressed action. The following are some common action verbs; however, there are many more that you use every day.

walk	lie	love	plan	say
take	play	come	start	lead
eat	work	go	finish	help
sit	study	leave	want	need
stand	sleep	arrive	tell	think

An action verb can appear alone in the sentence, or it can be accompanied by one or more *helping verbs* (sometimes called *auxiliary verbs*). Helping verbs are invaluable because they allow writers flexibility in expressing the action taking place in the sentence. The words below are common helping verbs. Therefore, their appearance in a sentence is often an indication that they are accompanying another verb.

can	must	have	am
could	shall	had	do
may	should	is	does
might	be	are	did
will	been	was	
would	has	were	

In the sentences below notice how the meaning of the action verb changes when helping verbs appear.

I **walk** home from work.

I **can walk** home from work.

I **could walk** home from work.

I **may walk** home from work.

I **might walk** home from work.

I **will walk** home from work.

I **would walk** home from work.

I **must walk** home from work.

I **do walk** home from work.

I **shall walk** home from work.

I **should walk** home from work.

I **will be walking** home from work.

I **have been walking** home from work.

I **have walked** home from work.

I **had walked** home from work.

I **am walking** home from work.

I **was walking** home from work.

I **did walk** home from work.

As you will notice in the sentences above, more than one helping verb sometimes appears with the action verb.

Helping verbs are sometimes separated from the main verb by such words as

not	never	also	usually	even
always	sometimes	often	generally	

These words are *not* considered part of the verb.

Helping verbs can also be separated from the main verb in questions.

Have you **done** your homework?

Will you **answer** this question for me?

Have you **eaten** dinner yet?

Another general classification of verbs is linking verbs. Some common linking verbs are:

am	be	have been	shall have been
is	been	had been	should have been
are	will be	would be	
was	shall be	should be	
were	has been	will have been	

You will notice that these verbs also appear in the list of helping verbs. However, each of these verbs can also be a linking verb when it appears as the only verb in the sentence.

Linking verbs do not express action but do link the subject to the words that follow the verb and describe or rename the subject. Note that in the following sentences the meaning of the sentence is affected depending on which linking verb is used. In the first group of sentences the word *absent* describes the subject. In the second group of sentences the word *president* renames the subject.

She **is** absent.	He **is** president of the club.
She **was** absent.	He **was** president of the club.
She **will be** absent.	He **will be** president of the club.
She **shall be** absent.	He **shall be** president of the club.
She **has been** absent.	He **had been** president of the club.

Like action verbs, linking verbs provide writers with the flexibility needed to communicate ideas effectively.

A few verbs, including *look, feel,* and *smell,* can be either action verbs or linking verbs, depending on their context.

Before crossing the street, the young child **looked** carefully in both directions. (action verb)

Standing in front of the classroom, the teacher **looked** confident. (linking verb)

The cool weather **feels** good after last sumer's heat. (linking verb)

I **feel** something under my feet. (action verb)

The cat **smelled** the chicken cooking on the stove. (action verb)

The cheesecake in the oven **smells** wonderful. (linking verb)

Like subjects, verbs can be compound and joined together by *and, or, either . . . or,* or *neither . . . nor.* In compound verbs, the parts of the verb are often separated.

The audience **giggled** and **squirmed** through the audiovisual presentation.

The student **can walk** to school or **take** the bus.

Either **do** the laundry or **wear** dirty clothes!

You **should** neither **slump** in your chair nor **sit** too straight.

In the following sentences underline the verbs.

1. One proposal to reduce the number of firearms in America is gun-swap programs.

2. These gun-swap programs offer various incentives in exchange for guns.

3. For example, in New York City citizens were offered a gift certificate for toys in exchange for turning in a firearm at a police station.

4. During a 14-day period in December 1993, approximately 1200 firearms were brought to police stations in the city.

5. In Los Angeles guns could be swapped for tickets to concerts and sporting events.

6. Approximately 400 firearms were exchanged in Los Angeles' gun-swap program.

7. Other cities are thinking about a gun-swap program.

8. Various civil rights organizations and church groups have supported these programs and encouraged local sponsors.

9. Can gun-swap programs really make a difference in firearms reduction?

10. What incentives will be needed for these programs to continue?

11. Communities must either try innovative ways of firearm reduction or accept the number of firearms in America's streets and homes.

Identifying Subjects

Subjects are nouns or pronouns that tell *who* or *what* is performing the action expressed in the sentence or *who* or *what* is being discussed. *Nouns* are words that identify persons, places, or things. *Pronouns* that you can use as subjects are *I, you, he, she, it, we,* or *they.*

You can identify subjects as *complete subjects* or *simple subjects.* A complete subject is the noun or pronoun and the descriptive words surrounding it that form the subject. For instance, in the sentence

A day in the mountains is my idea of heaven.

the complete subject is *a day in the mountains.*

A simple subject is the main noun or pronoun found in the complete subject. In the sentence above the simple subject is *day.*

Subjects can appear in various locations in the sentence. You can often locate a subject in the opening words of a sentence. Placing the subject at the beginning of the sentence lets the reader or audience know immediately who or what is being discussed. Consider the following sentence:

The students in the classroom are waiting for the instructor to appear.

To find the subject of this sentence (or the subject of any sentence), ask yourself the question, "Who _____ ?"or "What _____?" and fill in the blank with the remainder of the sentence. "Who are waiting for the instructor to appear?" The answer to the question is the complete subject, *The students in the classroom*, or the simple subject, *students*.

A subject can also appear near the end of the sentence. Sentences in which subjects are located in the closing words are called *inverted sentences*. The root of the word *inverted* is the Latin word *vert*, which means *to turn*. Inverted sentences are turned around so that the subject, which would generally appear at the beginning of the sentence, instead appears after the verb. Some common inverted sentences are:

- Sentences beginning with the word *there*
- Sentences beginning with the word *here*
- Questions

Consider these sentences:

There are the long-awaited packages.

Here are our coworkers waiting to open the packages.

When will the rest of the packages arrive?

The easiest way to locate the subject of an inverted sentence is to turn the sentence around so that the subject appears first.

The long-awaited packages are there.

Our coworkers are waiting to open the packages here.

The rest of the packages will arrive when?

Now the subjects are clear. In the first sentence the simple subject is *packages* (What are there?). In the second sentence the question (Who are waiting to open the packages?) leads to the simple subject *coworkers*. In the third sentence (What will arrive when?) the complete subject is *the rest of the packages*, and the simple subject is *rest*.

Using these two techniques—turning around the sentence and asking yourself who or what questions—will help you find difficult-to-spot subjects of inverted sentences.

Some sentences have "you understood" subjects. These sentences are *imperative* sentences, which express a command. The following are examples of imperative sentences:

Go home.

Please write legibly.

Avoid consuming too much fat.

The subject of each of the above is "you," but this subject does not appear. Instead, it is understood that the command expressed in the sentence is directed toward someone.

(You) Go home.

(You) Please write legibly.

(You) Avoid consuming too much fat.

Generally, imperative sentences do not appear in formal writing (except for letters) because imperative commands are best understood in a specific context.

Some sentences feature more than one subject. When more than one subject is present in a sentence, the subject is *compound*. Compound subjects are joined by the words *and, or, either . . . or,* or *neither . . . nor.* In the following sentences the compound subjects and connecting words are in bold print.

Jenny and Leah both made honor roll last semester.

Len or Nan will be joining us for dinner.

Either Joe or John will make the presentation.

Neither the state government nor the federal government is doing enough to address crime.

In the following sentences circle the simple subjects and underline the verbs. **Hint:** Locate the verb first. Then ask yourself a "Who?" or "What?" question to locate the subject.

EXERCISE 2.12

1. Another proposal to reduce the number of guns in the United States is an increase in gun dealers' licensing fees.

2. There are more gun dealers in the United States than McDonald's restaurants, according to one study.

3. Every one of the gun dealers must pay a licensing fee to the federal government.

4. Gun dealers currently purchase a three-year license for $200 or $66 a year.

5. This fee had previously been just $10 a year.

6. Most business owners in this country pay higher licensing fees.

7. This increase in the licensing fee might discourage some people from becoming gun dealers.

8. A recent suggestion is raising that fee to a minimum of $600.

9. Think about this question.

10. Would raising this fee affect the number of handguns in circulation?

11. Imagine the estimated 200 million guns currently in America's streets and homes.

12. American citizens and government officials should carefully consider this proposal.

Identifying Phrases

In addition to subjects and verbs, one of the basic building blocks of sentences is the *phrase*, defined as a group of words that does *not* contain a subject *and* a verb. Two common types of phrases are:

- Prepositional phrases
- Infinitive phrases

The most common type of phrase is the prepositional phrase. Just as musical notes bring life to a song, prepositional phrases add details to sentences that might otherwise be dull. Being able to locate prepositional phrases in your sentences will help you identify subjects and verbs because subjects and verbs are *not* found in prepositional phrases.

A prepositional phrase begins with a word known as a *preposition* and ends with a noun or pronoun called the *object of the preposition*. In order to recognize prepositional phrases, you need to know prepositions. The following is a list of common prepositions:

about	beside	on
above	between	over
across	by	since
after	down	through
against	during	to
along	for	toward
among	from	under
around	in	until
at	inside	up
before	like	with
behind	of	without
beneath	off	

Sometimes prepositions can be made up of more than one word:

according to	except for	along with
because of	in addition to	out of

Here are some examples of prepositional phrases:

Preposition	Object
across	the field
through	the woods
under	the sink
according to	the source
except for	him
along with	the others

Another type of phrase is the infinitive phrase. This phrase consists of the word *to* followed by a verb. Infinitive phrases also can include a noun or pronoun object. The following are infinitive phrases:

Infinitive	Object
to see	him
to look	
to compose	a letter
to jump	
to simplify	a problem
to direct	

Infinitive phrases are sometimes confused with prepositional phrases. However, prepositional phrases consist of the preposition *to* followed by a noun or pronoun (object of the preposition) while in an infinitive phrase the word *to* is followed by a verb.

to the store **(prepositional phrase)**

to reduce the fraction **(infinitive phrase)**

Both prepositional and infinitive phrases can have compound objects connected by *and* or *or.*

Preposition	Compound Object	Infinitive	Compound Object
from	school and work	to edit	punctuation and spelling

Being able to identify phrases will help you locate hard-to-spot subjects and verbs. If you have trouble recognizing phrases, try reading the sentence aloud. The words in a grammatical phrase, like the notes in a musical phrase, work together to form an expression. As you read the sentence aloud, listen for the beginning and ending of the phrase.

Using the first sentence of Exercise 2.12, notice how identification of prepositional and infinitive phrases (placed in parentheses marks) exposes the subject and verb.

| | Prepositional | Prepositional |
| Infinitive phrase | phrase | phrase |

Another proposal (to reduce the number) (of guns) (in the United

Prepositional phrase

States) is an increase (in gun dealers' licensing fees).

After these phrases have been identified, the simple subject *proposal* and verb *is* are easily located.

EXERCISE 2.13

In Exercises 2.11 and 2.12, place parentheses around infinitive and prepositional phrases. Then place the letters **PP** over the prepositional phrases and the letters **IP** over the infinitive phrases. Check to be sure that none of the subjects and verbs you have previously identified are located in these phrases.

Identifying Clauses

A clause is a group of words containing at least one subject *and* at least one verb. Clauses form the backbone of all sentences. There are two types of clauses: independent (main) and dependent (subordinate).

An independent clause expresses a complete idea and is the heart of any sentence. Without the subject and verb located in the independent clause, the message of the sentence would be lost. An independent clause, consisting of at least one subject, at least one verb, and any accompanying phrases, can form a sentence by itself. However, it can also be linked to one or more dependent clauses.

A dependent clause also contains a subject and a verb, but it must be joined to an independent clause in order for its meaning to be clear. Suppose you were reporting to your local newspaper about an accident you had witnessed, and you wrote,

Because the driver and passenger were injured

Your words include a compound subject *driver and passenger* and a verb *were injured*, so you have written a clause. However, the message of your clause *Because the driver and passenger were injured* is not complete. What happened *because the driver and passenger were injured*? The clause you have written is *dependent* and must be joined in an independent clause if the message is to be complete. If you had written the sentence,

Because the driver and passenger were injured, I called an ambulance to the scene.

your message would have been clear. The words *I called an ambulance to the scene* form an independent clause and complete the meaning expressed in the dependent clause. You could also have written the sentence this way:

> I called an ambulance to the scene because the driver and passenger were injured.

A dependent clause can come before or after the independent clause.

Dependent clauses have a distinct feature that independent clauses lack. Dependent clauses generally begin with words known as *subordinating conjunctions*. Some important subordinating conjunctions are

after	if	unless
although	in order that	until
as	once	when
as if	rather than	whenever
as though	since	where
because	so that	wherever
before	than	whether
even though	though	while

Writers use a subordinating conjunction to show a relationship between the idea in the independent clause and the idea in the dependent clause.

TABLE 2.3	Subordinating Conjunctions and Their Meanings	
Subordinating Conjunction		*Meaning*
after as before once since	until when whenever while	indicates time relationship
although as if as though if even if	even though though unless whether	indicates contrasting or conditional relationship
where wherever		indicates location relationship
in order that so that	that	indicates expression of purpose
because since		indicates cause-effect relationship

Notice that some of these words also appeared in the list of prepositions. Look at these two groups of words:

after the party

after the party was over

Which group of words forms a phrase? Which group of words forms a clause?

The words *after the party* form a prepositional phrase. The word *after* is a preposition, and the word *party* is the object. The words *after the party was over* form a dependent clause because both a subject and verb are present. The word *after* is a subordinating conjunction followed by a subject *party* and the verb *was*. Remember that if you have a subject and a verb present, the group of words forms a clause.

Subordinating conjunctions are very powerful words in sentences. They have the key function of joining dependent and independent clauses. A subordinating conjunction is also the only word that distinguishes an independent clause from a dependent clause. Removing the subordinating conjunction from a dependent clause results in an independent clause.

When the guests left the party (dependent clause)

The guests left the party. (independent clause)

Dependent clauses can also begin with these words:

that	whom	which
who	whomever	whichever
whoever	whose	

These words are known as *relative pronouns*. Like subordinating conjunctions, they join the dependent clause to the independent clause. However, when the relative pronoun *who, which,* or *that* begins a dependent clause, it also serves as the subject of the clause.

dependent clause

She is the one (who won the election).

dependent clause

The Pinehaven Resort, (which is my favorite vacation resort), is charming.

dependent clause

The report (that was sent to top management) was well documented.

Fill in the following blanks as directed.

EXERCISE 2.14

1. Write a prepositional phrase: _____

2. Write an infinitive phrase: _____

3. Write a dependent clause: _____

4. Write an independent clause: _____

5. Write a sentence consisting of one dependent clause followed by one independent clause: _____

   _____

6. Write a sentence consisting of one independent clause followed by one dependent clause: _____

   _____

In the blanks, identify each of the following as an independent clause (**IC**), a dependent clause followed by independent clause (**DC/IC**), or an independent clause followed by dependent clause (**IC/DC**). Underline simple subjects once, verbs twice, and circle subordinating conjunctions. (**Hint:** Cross through phrases if you have trouble locating simple subjects and verbs.)

EXERCISE 2.15

_____ 1. Some criminal justice experts are not enthusiastic about gun swaps.

_____ 2. Because there are so many guns on America's streets, gun-swap programs will not result in a significant firearms reduction.

_____ 3. Many of the guns have not been used for years.

_____ 4. Some guns do not function properly.

_____ 5. Some gun owners may even use the money from the gun swap to purchase a new gun.

_____ 6. Police personnel must be used to process the guns that are swapped in exchange for money or certificates.

_____ 7. Is this use of manpower effective in crime reduction?

_____ 8. Other means of gun control would be more effective.

_____ 9. If gun owners were required to renew their licenses every four years, police officials could monitor the number of legal gun owners.

_____ 10. Criminal justice experts should work with communities to find effective ways to reduce the number of guns in our streets and homes.

Now that you have learned some ways to generate ideas for your compositions, structure your paragraphs, and strengthen your sentences, you are ready to develop paragraphs for different purposes. As your paragraph development and composition skills improve, you will be ready for longer compositions, such as the essay, and will be on your way to becoming a successful writer both in the classroom and on the job.

Writers as Spiders

One of the greatest benefits for "spiders" is the access to online writing centers. These writing lab sites provide online handouts on grammar and writing, including some of the topics presented in this chapter. For example, three helpful writing center sites that offer information about paragraph development (as well as many other topics in this book) are

http://aix1.uottawa.ca/academic/arts/writcent/hypergrammar/
    grammar.html

http://webserver.maclab.comp.uvic.ca/writersguide/Pages/
    MasterToc.html

http://owl.english.purdue.edu/Files/118.html

Each of these writing center web sites offers hyperlinks to other web pages (look for underlined print, usually blue). By clicking on these hyperlinks, you can connect with other pages with additional information. Then you can use the "back" or "forward" command to navigate between pages, or you can go to a new location.

Some web sites offer online exercises for you to check your knowledge of paragraph development. For additional exercises on identifying topic sentences, see

http://www.bell.k12.ca.us/BellHS/Departments/English/
    idtopicsentence.html

If you need more practice with supporting details, visit

http://www.bell.k12.ca.us/BellHS/Departments/English/
    supportingdetails.html

For more information about identifying subjects and verbs, try

http://leo.stcloud.msus.edu/grammar/verbsub.html

These pages offer assistance with phrases and clauses:

http://aix1.uottawa.ca/academic/arts/writcent/hypergrammar/
   bldphr.html

http://aix1.uottawa.ca/academic/arts/writcent/hypergrammar/
   bldcls.html

If you want still more information about any of the topics in this chapter, don't forget to use the search engines. The more specific your search, the more you will likely be satisfied with the results. For instance, instead of searching for *paragraph,* try *paragraph + composition* or *topic sentence.* Each search engine will provide tips to make your searches more efficient.

CHAPTER 3

Focus on Development by Example

FOCUS ON PURPOSE

One of the most common ways to develop a paragraph is to use examples to illustrate the topic sentence. When you write a paragraph using examples, you use first-hand experiences, logical reasoning, illustrations, and/or statistics to support your main idea and show your reader that you are knowledgeable about the subject. If your examples are convincing, then you will awaken your reader's curiosity about what you know and how you know it, and your reader will want to finish your paragraph and learn from your writing.

Successful students recognize the importance of using details to support their ideas. For example, your college instructors will often ask you to respond to test questions by citing examples. In a humanities class, a test question might be "Give three examples of Greek sculptures from the Hellenic period," or in a composition class "List three ways to arrange ideas in a paragraph." If you can recall the answer and communicate it clearly through the use of supporting examples, you will likely receive a high grade.

Successful businessmen and women also rely on their ability to use examples effectively. Salespeople must illustrate their products' effectiveness if they are to convince consumers to make purchases. Companies must design sales brochures that provide illustrations of their products' success or cite testimonials by consumers who have used their products.

The ability to support a main idea with relevant details is thus a keystone for success both in the classroom and in the workplace.

FOCUS ON CHOOSING A TOPIC

Effective development-by-example paragraphs begin with a general topic of interest to the writer. Any of the following topics from the beginning of Chapter 2 could be developed by the use of supporting examples:

- Challenges Facing College Students Who Work
- Characteristics of an Effective Leader
- Problems Facing Today's Adolescent
- Characteristics of a Good Parent
- Benefits of Regular Exercise

You could also use any of the general topics from Exercise 2.6:

- Characteristics of an Ideal Job
- What I Would Do If I Won a Lottery
- A Great Place to Vacation
- Qualities of a True Friend
- Advantages of a College Education

Here are some other general topics:

- College Skills that Will Prepare Me for My Future Career
- Advantages of Being an Only (or Eldest, Youngest, Middle) Child
- Disadvantages of Being an Only (or Eldest, Youngest, Middle) Child
- Advantages of Owning a Pet

Remember that before you write an effective topic sentence, you must narrow your *general topic* to a *limited topic*. The general topics above are appropriate for an essay-length writing assignment, but it would be difficult for you to discuss comprehensively any of these topics in a single paragraph. To limit your topic, you can use any of the methods discussed in Chapter 2 — brainstorming, listing, clustering, or freewriting — or you can use one of the narrowed topics you developed in Exercise 2.6.

FOCUS ON ORGANIZING

The Topic Sentence

Once you have chosen a limited topic, you are ready to draft your topic sentence. Remember that the purposes of the topic sentence are

- To direct the reader's attention to the subject of your paragraph
- To narrow the paragraph's focus to a supportable main idea

Topic sentences that are too broad or unfocused will result in ineffective paragraphs. If your topic sentence is too general, you will be unable to provide enough supporting details to convince the reader of your knowledge of the subject. Here are some examples of weak topic sentences:

Unfocused: Good parents possess many qualities.

Unfocused: If I won the lottery, I would fulfill all my dreams of a luxurious lifestyle.

Unfocused: A great place to vacation is Europe.

How would you be able to discuss in a single paragraph (or even an essay or a book) all the qualities of a good parent, all your dreams of a luxurious lifestyle, or all the marvelous vacation spots in Europe? The following topic sentences are strong in comparison:

Focused: Good parents are patient.

Focused: If I won the lottery, I would buy the sports car of my dreams.

Focused: A great vacation spot is the small French ski village of Chamonix.

The Supporting Details

Once you have written your topic sentence, you are ready to add supporting details to form the body of the paragraph. You must make sure the supporting details you use are

- Sufficient
- Related
- Arranged
- Engaging

How many supporting details are *sufficient* for a development-by-example paragraph? The answer depends on your topic sentence, your knowledge of the subject, and your reader's interest in your topic. In general, you need at least two major points to support your topic sentence. Sometimes three or four are needed. If you think you need more than four major points to support your topic sentence, then you need to reevaluate the focus of your topic sentence. If you have difficulty coming up with enough supporting details, ask yourself how, why, and what questions or try brainstorming, clustering, and/or freewriting.

Suppose you are developing a paragraph with the topic sentence *Good parents are patient*. You (and later your reader) will be thinking, "How are good parents patient?" or "Why are good parents patient?" If the supporting details are sufficient, the reader's curiosity will be satisfied. If the supporting details are insufficient, the reader will have doubts about your knowledge of the topic.

Consider the following paragraph:

> Good parents are patient. They demonstrate their patience when their children are learning new skills. When their children ask them to help with their homework, they also remain calm. Furthermore, they listen patiently when their children tell them about problems at school.

Are the major points of this paragraph sufficient? Do they satisfy a reader? You are probably thinking, "What new skills are their children learning?" or "How do they remain calm when their children ask them to help with homework?" or "What problems at school are their children discussing?" The fact that this paragraph makes you want to know more is a key indication that the details in this paragraph are not sufficient.

One way to help ensure that the reader will find the supporting details sufficient is to add at least two minor points to support each major point. These minor points provide further illustrations to help the reader understand the importance of each major point. Here is the revised paragraph:

> Good parents are patient. They demonstrate their patience when their children are learning new skills. For instance, when their children try to tie their shoelaces but fail, impatient parents sometimes scream, "Can't you do anything right?" Good parents, on the other hand, encourage their children by saying, "Try again. You'll get it right." When their children ask them to help with their homework, good parents remain calm. They may be tempted to say, "I've been through school already. It's your turn." However, caring parents respond, "I don't know if I can help, but I'll try." Furthermore, they listen patiently when their children tell them about problems at school. If one of their children tells them that he or she failed a math test, impatient parents may yell, "I knew you were no good in math." Patient parents, though, may respond, "Have you talked with your teacher about the test?" Good parents patiently think through their responses to their children's actions.

This time the writer has taken care to provide specific examples of the responses of impatient parents versus the responses of patient parents. The result is a "full-bodied" paragraph likely to satisfy the reader.

In sum, a paragraph sufficiently developed with supporting examples can be graphically illustrated as shown in Figure 3.1 on page 59.

EXERCISE 3.1

Read each of the following paragraphs. If you are satisfied with the number of details in the paragraph, write **Sufficient** in the blanks following the paragraph. If you are not satisfied with the supporting details, write **Insufficient** and then write a few supporting details that could be added to the paragraph for support.

1.   College students who work sometimes have difficulty scheduling study time. Some students have an opportunity to study while at work. Other students must study after a full day of school and work. Exhaustion can interfere with study time.

_____

_____

2. An effective teacher uses a syllabus to explain the grading policy of the course. This syllabus, which she distributes during the first week of class, states the grades that will be assigned in the course. Also stated are the percentages corresponding with each grade. For example, A equals 90–100, B equals 80–89, etc. Furthermore, the syllabus describes how each type of assignment is calculated into the course grade. For instance, tests equal 30%, midterm equals 20%, papers equal 30%, and final exam equals 20%. In this way all her students will know her grading policies from the beginning of the course.

_____

_____

3. An ideal job offers employees excellent medical insurance coverage. Doctors' visits should be included in the plan. If a co-payment is required for regular doctor's visits, the amount of the co-payment should be reasonable. The medical insurance plan should also pay for yearly checkups as a preventive measure. Emergency room visits should be covered under the plan as well. Any deductible for emergency room visits should be minimal. The plan should also clarify whether trips to out-of-town emergency rooms are reimbursed. Furthermore, the plan should include generous hospitalization coverage. Any deductible should be clearly stated. Finally, the plan should identify how much of the daily room costs are covered. A comprehensive medical insurance plan is a major factor in job satisfaction.

_____

_____

4. A great vacation spot is Helen, a small town in the North Georgia Mountains. The Chattahoochee River, which runs through the town, offers great opportunities for river lovers. The center of town features many shops and restaurants.

_____

_____

5. Going on a daily walk is great exercise. Walking improves cardiovascular fitness. Walking also develops leg muscles. Finally, walking helps to rid the body of stress.

_____

_____

Not only must the supporting details be sufficient, but they must also be clearly *related* to the topic sentence. Your topic sentence is like a road map for your reader. Whenever you leave the road you have set out upon and move in some unexpected direction, the reader, who is trying to follow your train of thought, will be confused. These unexpected directions are called *digressions*, and

Topic Sentence
    Major point #1
        Minor point #1a
        Minor point #1b
    Major point #2
        Minor point #2a
        Minor point #2b
    Major point #3
        Minor point #3a
        Minor point #3b
Concluding sentence

(A)

Figure 3.1
Arrangement of supporting details.
(A) General structure;
(B) Supporting details for paragraph on good parents.

Topic Sentence: Good parents are patient.
    Major point #1: Demonstrate patience when children learn new skills
        Minor point #1a: Impatient parents' response
        Minor point #1b: Patient parents' response
    Major point #2: When children have problems at school
        Minor point #2a: Impatient parents' reply
        Minor point #2b: Patient parents' reply
Concluding sentence: Good parents patiently think through their responses to their children's actions

(B)

they happen easily. You can check for digressions by checking frequently to be sure that each major point is clearly related to your focus. Try rereading your topic sentence every time you add a major point. Doing so will remind you of the focus of your paragraph and will keep your writing on track and organized.

In the following paragraph the author digresses from the topic sentence. Read carefully to determine where the digressions begin and end. Use the numbers placed before each sentence to answer the questions following the paragraph.

EXERCISE 3.2

(1) Mesa Verde National Park outside Durango, Colorado, is a great vacation destination. (2) This park contains the ruins of the cliff dwellings of the

Anasazi Indians, who mysteriously abandoned the area circa 1300 A.D. (3) These cliff dwellings, some of which are several stories tall, appear in recesses in the canyon walls. (4) The dwellings can be reached via a trail from the Visitors Center. (5) The Visitors Center's bathrooms are not as clean as they could be. (6) It is hard to understand why the federal government cannot make sure that the bathrooms are cleaned hourly. (7) One of the most interesting cliff dwellings is Spruce Tree House, which was discovered in 1888 by two brothers who wandered into the canyon looking for lost cattle. (8) This dwelling has over 114 living rooms and may have housed a population of 100 Anasazis. (9) Of particular note are the kivas, which are dug-out, round areas. (10) At Spruce Tree House the kivas are located below the floor level and must be reached by ladders. (11) These kivas were probably used for religious rites and were almost certainly limited to men only. (12) What were the women doing at the time? (13) They were probably left to do all the childcare and housework while the men were taking steam baths in the kivas and gossiping. (14) Spruce Tree House is just one of the many fabulous ruins in this park visited by over 610,000 people each year. (15) A visit to Mesa Verde National Park is guaranteed to be unforgettable.

Where does the first digression begin? _____

Where does the first digression end? _____

Where does the second digression begin? _____

Where does the second digression end? _____

Your supporting details must also be *arranged*. The supporting details of development-by-example paragraphs are generally arranged according to the order of their importance. Specifically, the details should be arranged from least important to most important Readers generally remember most clearly what they read last rather than first, so your last supporting details will likely receive the most attention from your reader.

EXERCISE 3.3

In Exercise 2.6 you developed a narrowed topic and a topic sentence based on five general topics. For each of the topic sentences you generated in Exercise 2.6, add three major points and two minor points for each major point. Use phrases rather than complete sentences for these supporting details. Check to be sure that all major points are related to the topic sentence and are arranged from least important to most important. Use the first example as a model.

1. Topic: Characteristics of an Ideal Job

Narrowed topic: medical insurance coverage

Topic sentence: An ideal job offers employees excellent medical insurance coverage.

Major point #1: <u>emergency room visits</u>

    Minor point #1a: <u>amount of deductible</u>

    Minor point #1b: <u>coverage of out-of-town emergency rooms</u>

Major point #2: <u>doctors' visits</u>

    Minor point #2a: <u>co-payment for regular visits</u>

    Minor point #2b: <u>coverage of yearly checkups</u>

Major point #3: <u>hospital visits</u>

    Minor point #3a: <u>amount of deductible</u>

    Minor point #3b: <u>coverage of cost of room</u>

2.   Topic: What I Would Do If I Won a Lottery

Narrowed topic: _____

Topic sentence: _____

Major point #1: _____

    Minor point #1a: _____

    Minor point #1b: _____

Major point #2: _____

    Minor point #2a: _____

    Minor point #2b: _____

Major point #3: _____

    Minor point #3a: _____

    Minor point #3b: _____

3.   Topic: A Great Place to Vacation

Narrowed topic: _____

Topic sentence: _____

Major point #1: _____

    Minor point #1a: _____

    Minor point #1b: _____

Major point #2: _____

    Minor point #2a: _____

    Minor point #2b: _____

Major point #3: _____

   Minor point #3a: _____

   Minor point #3b: _____

4.   Topic: Qualities of a True Friend

Narrowed topic: _____

Topic sentence: _____

Major point #1: _____

   Minor point #1a: _____

   Minor point #1b: _____

Major point #2: _____

   Minor point #2a: _____

   Minor point #2b: _____

Major point #3: _____

   Minor point #3a: _____

   Minor point #3b: _____

5.   Topic: Advantages of a College Education

Narrowed topic: _____

Topic sentence: _____

Major point #1: _____

   Minor point #1a: _____

   Minor point #1b: _____

Major point #2: _____

   Minor point #2a: _____

   Minor point #2b: _____

Major point #3: _____

   Minor point #3a: _____

   Minor point #3b: _____

Finally, your supporting details must be *engaging*. You do not want your reader to be bored by your examples, nor do you want to present your reader with obvious points. Your reader is setting aside time to read your paragraph, and you want to make sure the time is well spent.

Consider these two paragraphs:

College students who work often get tired. Between the hours at work and the hours at home, there is never enough time to rest. Sometimes they fall asleep in class the next day. They need to be sure to allow enough time to sleep. Often they do not have enough time to eat balanced meals, so they stop at the local fast food drive-through window. A lack of sleep and a poor diet make it difficult to concentrate in class.

College students who work often suffer from exhaustion. Between the hours they spend at work, the hours they spend in the classroom, and the hours they spend at home, it is difficult to get seven or eight hours of sleep each night. As a result, they may have a difficult time concentrating on the teachers' lectures the next day or, worse, they may fall asleep at their desks. Their exhaustion can also be a result of a poor diet. Students who leave work only to rush to their classes do not always have enough time to eat balanced meals. Consequently, they stop too many times at the local fast-food drive-through window. Weeks of hamburgers, tacos, and French fries leave the working student with little energy. When exhaustion sets in, the student will find it difficult to concentrate in class or do well on tests. Low self-esteem is often a result. If they are to perform well in their classes, working college students must take steps to prevent exhaustion.

Which of the two paragraphs do you find more engaging? Why? Keep in mind that what is interesting to one reader is not necessarily interesting to another. Also a long paragraph does not always equal a good paragraph. Some long paragraphs are repetitious and/or rambling. While you cannot always know what a reader will find interesting, you can work diligently as a writer to inform (and sometimes entertain) your reader.

FOCUS ON TRANSITION

Once you have determined which supporting details you will use to develop your paragraph, you are ready to add transitional words and phrases to help your reader move through your paragraph. In general, you should consider using a transitional expression when you move from your first major point to your second major point, and again when you add your last major point. Try to avoid relying on the "tried-and-true" transitional expressions: *first, second,* and *third*. Instead, consider using one of these transitional expressions when you are adding a new point: *also, then, moreover, besides, next, in addition, furthermore, additionally*.

You should also use a transitional expression when you move from your first major point to the details that support that point, and perhaps when you provide supporting details for your other major point. Some possible choices include *for example, for instance, as a case in point, as an illustration,* or *to illustrate.*

Finally, although it is not necessary, you may want to provide a transitional expression to mark the concluding sentence of your paragraph. Avoid the obvious *in conclusion.* Instead, try one of the following: *overall, all in all, finally, in brief, in other words, lastly, on the whole, to sum up,* or *in sum.*

Note the transitional expressions (in bold print) that appeared in the paragraph on good parents:

> Good parents are patient. They demonstrate their patience when their children are learning new skills. **For instance,** when their children try to tie their shoelaces but fail, impatient parents sometimes scream, "Can't you do anything right?" Good parents, **on the other hand,** encourage their children by saying, "Try again. You'll get it right." When their children ask them to help with their homework, good parents remain calm. They may be tempted to say, "I've been through school already. It's your turn." **However,** caring parents respond, "I don't know if I can help, but I'll try." **Furthermore,** they listen patiently when their children tell them about problems at school. If one of their children tells them that he or she failed a math test, impatient parents may yell, "I knew you were no good in math." Patient parents, **though,** may respond, "Have you talked with your teacher about the test?" Good parents patiently think through their responses to their children's actions.

EXERCISE 3.4

Read the following paragraph. Then insert a transitional expression in each blank. After you finish, locate this paragraph in Chapter 2 (look just after Exercise 2.6). Your choice of transitional expressions does not have to be identical to those in the original paragraph but should be similar.

An effective teacher shows respect for her students in the classroom. When a student asks a question, the teacher listens intently and waits until the student finishes. The teacher knows that interrupting a student before he or she finishes asking the question would send the message that the teacher does not consider the student's question important. _____, a concerned teacher will answer the student's question directly and patiently. _____, many effective teachers ask a followup question such as, "Does that answer your question?" or "Do you have any other questions you want to ask?" Good teachers are not afraid to say, " I don't know the answer to your question, but perhaps we can find out the answer." _____, successful teachers demonstrate their respect for students by learning their students' names during the first week of class. No student wants to be thought of as a number or a box on a seating chart. These teachers call on students by name and involve them in class discussion. _____, effective teachers know that showing respect for students will relieve anxiety in the classroom.

FOCUS ON GRAMMAR

Fragments

A *fragment* is a word group that looks like a sentence but does not express a complete thought. Fragments begin with capital letters and end with periods—conventions that signal complete sentences. The reader, who expects a complete thought, is, therefore, confused when the writer's words are incomplete. Because fragments distract your reader from the message that you are communicating, you want to avoid them.

Three common types of fragments are

- Dependent clause fragments
- *-ing* fragments
- Example fragments

Dependent Clause Fragments. In Chapter 2, you learned the difference between dependent (subordinate) clauses and independent clauses. You also learned that while independent clauses can function alone, dependent clauses must be joined to independent clauses in order to form a complete thought. If a dependent clause is separated from an independent clause, the result is a fragment.

Consider this sentence:

If they are to perform well in their classes, working college students must take steps to prevent exhaustion.

The dependent clause is *if they are to perform well in their classes*. This clause begins with a subordinating conjunction *if*, which is followed by the subject *they* and the verb *are*. The independent clause that follows, *working college students must take steps to prevent exhaustion*, also has a simple subject *students* and a verb *must take*. Both types of clauses—dependent and independent—have subjects *and* verbs. The difference is that dependent clauses begin with subordinating conjunctions and depend on an independent clause to complete their meaning. Without this independent clause, the dependent clause alone would be a fragment. However, once it is joined to an independent clause, its meaning is complete.

Fragment: If they are to perform well in their classes.

Independent clause: Working college students must take steps to prevent exhaustion.

Dependent clause followed by independent clause: If they are to perform well in their classes, working college students must take steps to prevent exhaustion.

Independent clause followed by dependent clause: Working college students must take steps to prevent exhaustion if they are to perform well in their classes.

Notice that it does not matter whether the dependent clause comes before or after the independent clause. In fact, some sentences begin and end with subordinate clauses with the independent clause sandwiched in between:

Fragment: When a student asks a question.

Independent clause: The teacher listens and waits intently.

Fragment: Until the student finishes speaking.

Dependent clause followed by independent clause followed by another dependent clause: When a student asks a question, the teacher listens and waits intently until the student finishes speaking.

EXERCISE 3.5

In the paragraph below circle or highlight the dependent clause fragments. Then draw an arrow to the independent clause to which the fragment should be connected.

A true friend is trustworthy. If I share a secret with her about a coworker. I do not have to worry about her repeating my secret. Last year I experienced a problem with my supervisor. When I mentioned this problem to one of my "friends." She went straight to my supervisor's office and repeated what I had said. This betrayal of loyalty is not characteristic of true friendship. When I have a problem communicating with my children. I sometimes express my frustration to a friend. A true friend will set aside what she is doing. Because she knows it is important for me to have an outlet for my frustration. I know a true friend will not be disloyal and talk about me behind my back. If she does. I will no longer be able to trust her. Because true friends are hard to find. A friend who is trustworthy is a treasure. Who is worthy of my trust in return.

-ing *Fragments.* Some fragments are not clauses but phrases. One common type of phrase fragment is the *-ing* fragment, so-called because it includes (often at the beginning) a word that ends in *-ing*. Here are some examples:

Having stayed up too late last night

The judge delaying the trial for another week

One good way to test for any type of fragment is to read the suspected fragment aloud. Read each of the above fragments aloud. They sound incomplete because they are incomplete. The first fragment lacks a subject and a complete verb. Who stayed up too late last night? One way to correct this fragment is to add a subject and drop the *-ing* word:

Sue stayed up too late last night.

Another way is to connect the fragment to an independent clause:

> Having stayed up too late last night, Sue had trouble staying awake in class.

The second fragment lacks a complete verb. An *-ing* word alone cannot be the complete verb of a sentence. One way to correct this fragment is to add a helping verb:

> The judge is delaying the trial for another week.

Another way to correct the fragment is to change the verb to the past tense:

> The judge delayed the trial for another week.

In the paragraph below circle or highlight the *-ing* fragments. Then rewrite each fragment to form a complete sentence.

EXERCISE 3.6

Being the oldest child of five. I had the greatest number of household responsibilities. Whenever my parents needed help with work around the house, I was the one they asked. Washing the clothes, vacuuming the house, doing the dishes, keeping the room clean. All these were my chores. My parents knowing they could trust me to do the work well. Often I was also the babysitter for my two brothers and two sisters. My mother working two jobs and my dad staying late at the office. Many nights I cooked dinner and supervised my sisters' and brothers' homework. Resenting the time I spent doing housework. Overall, these responsibilities prepared me for adulthood.

Example Fragments. An example fragment occurs when the writer cuts off an example from the point that it illustrates. These fragments occur easily in development-by-example paragraphs. Example fragments commonly begin with *such as, for example,* or *for instance:*

> Some of my favorite books are classics. **Such as** *Wuthering Heights, A Tale of Two Cities,* and *Pride and Prejudice.*

> One can keep in good physical shape by participating in aerobic activity. **For example,** jogging, swimming, or aerobic dance.

> If I win the lottery, I want to visit several sites in Florence, Italy. **For instance,** the Florence Cathedral, the Florence Baptistry, the Uffizi Museum, and, most importantly, the grave of my uncle.

To correct an example fragment, join the fragment to the sentence it illustrates. If the example is lengthy, you can use a dash for emphasis.

> Some of my favorite books are classics **such as** *Wuthering Heights, A Tale of Two Cities,* and *Pride and Prejudice.*

One can keep in good physical shape by participating in aerobic activity, **for example,** jogging, swimming, or aerobic dance.

If I win the lottery, I want to visit several sites in Florence, Italy—**for instance,** the Florence Cathedral, the Florence Baptistry, the Uffizi Museum, and, most importantly, the grave of my uncle.

EXERCISE 3.7

In the paragraph below, circle the fragments and draw an arrow to the sentence to which they should be connected.

If I win the lottery. I want to visit several sites in Florence, Italy. Including the Florence Cathedral. I want to stand in the middle of the cathedral and gaze at Brunelleschi's dome. I also want to walk in the passageway between the inner dome and the outer dome and admire Brunelleschi's architectural feats. Such as the use of herringbone brickwork to support the weight of the dome. Then I want to see Ghiberti's doors on the Florence Baptistry and admire the figures cast in gilded bronze. For example, Abraham, Isaac, Ghiberti himself, and Ghiberti's son. Touring the Uffizi Museum. I can gaze admiringly on the great works of Botticelli. Such as *Primavera* (*Allegory of Spring*) and *The Birth of Venus* (which I call *Venus on the Half Shell*). Finally, I would love to place flowers on my uncle's grave. He was shot down over Italy two weeks before the end of World War II. I want to see the place where he has rested all these years. When my winning numbers come in. I will be packed and ready to catch a plane to Florence.

EXERCISE 3.8

Circle or highlight the fragments in the paragraph below and draw an arrow to the independent clause to which the fragment should be connected.

Because of its abundant entertainment opportunities. Tampa, Florida, is a great vacation destination. The city is rich in museums. For example, the Tampa Museum of Art, the Florida Aquarium, and the Museum of Science and Industry. The newest of these museums is the Florida Aquarium. Featuring aquatic life from the seashore, the inland hammocks, and the coral reefs. A recently renovated museum is the Museum of Science and Industry. Which features a new theater and interactive exhibits on a variety of scientific and environmental subjects. Exhibits at the Tampa Museum of Art change regularly. The city also offers access to nearby beaches. Many located in adjacent Pinellas County. Water activities such as jet skiing, water skiing, and boating abound. A tropical climate makes these activities accessible nearly every month of the year. When considering a vacation destination spot. Vacationers should keep in mind the city of Tampa.

Follow the directions for Exercise 3.8.

The waterfalls in the North Georgia mountains offer an abundance of delights for summer hikers. For instance, Minnehaha Falls, located near Rabun Beach Recreation Area in Rabun County, is just a short, moderately easy hike from Bear Gap Road. Although finding the unpaved Bear Gap Road and the trailhead to the waterfalls can be an adventure. Once there, the falls are enticing stair steps of rock and water. A log at the foot of the falls is easily accessible for hikers. Who may have sore feet and a meditative spirit. Anna Ruby Falls in Unicoi State Park is a double waterfall. An unusual site in these Georgia Hills. The falls, named after the daughter of a farmer who discovered them, are located at the end of a paved, one-quarter mile hike from a parking lot managed by the U.S. Forest Service. In the summer hikers can enjoy the cool walk along Smith Creek. Listening to the creek tumble over logs and large boulders. For those who are clever enough to bring along a picnic lunch. There are several rocks in the stream suitable for a picnic spread. Although these waterfalls in the North Georgia mountains are enjoyable any time of year. A summer hiker will especially appreciate the cool water on a hot day.

Some beginning college students, afraid that their sentences will be too long, divide them. However, instead of making their writing clear, they create fragments and "muddy the waters." Other students swear a teacher once told them, "Never begin a sentence with *because*." Yet many effective sentences begin with *because*.

To check your paragraph for fragments, read each group of words beginning with a capital letter and ending with a period. If the group of words sounds incomplete, ask yourself these questions:

- Is there a subject?
- Is there a complete verb?
- Is there a subordinating conjunction?

If the answer to the first question or second question is *no*, then the group of words is a fragment. If the answer to all three questions is *yes*, then the group of words is a dependent clause and must be joined to an independent clause to form a sentence.

FOCUS ON PUNCTUATION

Commas

Students ask more questions about commas than about any other form of punctuation. For example, in the last section you may have been wondering, "What punctuation do I use to join a dependent clause to an independent clause?" You may have also wondered what punctuation to use when you include transitional expressions.

Writers both use and misuse commas. Many beginning college writers insert commas in sentences whenever they think they hear a pause. Sometimes this method works; often it does not. However, commas do provide a signal for readers who need to catch a breath.

Whenever possible, writers should use commas when conventions, or rules, call for their use. The following rules relate to the most common uses of the comma. This list of rules does not govern all uses of the comma. However, studying this list can help you build confidence in your ability to use the comma correctly and effectively.

Comma Rule 1: Use a comma before a coordinating conjunction (*and, but, or, nor, for, so, yet*) joining two independent clauses (each with a subject and a verb). These coordinating conjunctions (sometimes called **FANBOYS**—**F**or, **A**nd, **N**or, **B**ut, **O**r, **Y**et, **S**o) are the only words used with a comma to connect two independent clauses.

My mother wants me to come see her this weekend, **and** I plan to go.

My daughter can walk to school, **or** she can ride her bike.

I do not like eating raw fish, **nor** do I want to see a fish head on my plate.

Joe cannot read music, **yet** he is a talented musician.

Kathy knows the rules, **so** why is she cheating at this game?

The Jones family did not take a vacation this year, **for** they decided to pay off their credit cards instead.

I would have enjoyed the concert, **but** I left my tickets at home.

Coordinating conjunctions (*junc* = join, *con* = together) indicate specific relationships between two or more independent clauses, as shown in Table 3.1.

TABLE 3.1 Coordinating Conjunctions and Their Meanings	
Coordinating Conjunction	*Meaning*
for	because, the reason why, the cause
and	in addition, along with
nor	introduces a negative alternative
but	however, on the other hand, the opposite
or	introduces an alternative
yet	nevertheless, however, in spite of
so	as a result, therefore

The key to understanding this comma rule is to realize that the comma followed by the coordinating conjunction is a signal to the reader that another subject and another verb will follow in the second part of the sentence. The words before the comma form a complete thought, and so do the words after the conjunction.

Caution: Do not use a comma before a conjunction when that conjunction is not followed by an independent clause. The sentence above with the conjunction *or* could have been written this way:

My daughter can walk to school or ride her bike.

A comma is usually not necessary unless both a subject *and* a verb follow the conjunction.

Comma Rule 2: Use a comma to separate transitional expressions or lengthy prepositional phrases at the beginning of a sentence.

Furthermore, incidents of teenage violence are not expected to decrease next year.

In addition, students need a cafeteria rather than a lounge with snack and soda machines.

During the winter season from November to March, motel rooms are expensive along the Florida coast.

A comma is used following transitional words (over four letters in length) and transitional phrases used at the beginning of a sentence. Commas are generally considered optional following short transitional words such as *also,* *then,* and *next:*

Then we went home.

Comma Rule 3: Use a comma to separate an introductory dependent clause from the independent clause that follows it.

Because traffic was heavy this morning, I was late to class.

When families have trouble communicating, counseling can sometimes help.

Comma Rule 4: Use commas to set off nonessential (sometimes called nonrestrictive) clauses beginning with *who* or *which.*

Martin Luther King, Jr., **who was a famous civil rights leader,** was born January 15, 1929.

The 1989 four-door sedan, **which I bought used,** has been a wonderful car.

In the first example the clause *who was a famous civil rights leader* is nonessential because the words in the clause are not necessary (not essential) to identify Martin Luther King, Jr. The clause adds information about Martin Luther King, Jr., but the words in the clause do not identify him.

In the second example the model of the car (a 1989 four-door sedan) is identified in the subject. The words *which I bought used* are not necessary to identify the car. Therefore, the clause is nonessential and set off with commas.

Caution: If the words in a clause beginning with *who* or *which* are necessary for identification of the noun preceding the clause, commas are omitted. *That* is usually used in place of *which* in such essential (sometimes called restrictive) clauses.

She was the student **who was late for class.**

Which student? The words *who was late for class* are essential for clear meaning. Therefore, commas are not present.

Comma Rule 5: Use a comma to separate three or more items in a series.

Chili contains **beans, meat, onions, and peppers.**

Comma Rule 6: Use commas to set off transitional words and phrases that interrupt the flow of the sentence.

He will, **however,** be home by midnight.

She will not, **therefore,** come to visit us this weekend.

We must, **nevertheless,** try to understand her situation.

This student, **for example,** will not be able to attend class.

Comma Rule 7: Use a comma to separate coordinate adjectives.

The **tall, skinny** man walked gracefully down the street.

The adjectives *tall* and *skinny* are considered coordinate because they can be reversed without changing the meaning of the sentence:

The **skinny, tall** man walked gracefully down the street.

Caution: If the two adjectives cannot be reversed, no comma is used between them.

The seven-foot tall man walked gracefully down the street.

Comma Rule 8: Use a comma to separate items in dates and addresses.

My mother was born on **Saturday, April 17, 1922,** in **Saluda, South Carolina.**

Sue resides at **4922 Brook Creek Road, Tiger, Georgia 30357.**

The student moved from **Buffalo, New York,** to **San Francisco, California.**

Be careful to use a comma after the last item if the date or address appears in the middle of the sentence. Do not, however, use a comma before a zip code.

Comma Rule 9: Use commas to separate units of three within numbers.

Neanderthal man lived approximately **300,000** years ago while Cro-Magnon man lived approximately **50,000** years ago.

If you have been frustrated about punctuation in the past, use these rules as guidelines in your writing. Remember that the rules above do not govern all uses of the comma. For example, commas used with direct quotations, introductory subordinate clauses, and appositives are discussed in Chapter 4.

The more you read and the more you write, the more confident you will feel about using commas in your compositions and the less you will have to think about the rules.

Insert commas where needed.

EXERCISE 3.10

Rembrandt Harmenszoon van Rijn who was one of the most gifted artists of all time was born July 15 1606 in Leiden Holland. His father was a miller and his mother was a baker's daughter. By the age of 17 or 18 he had learned everything that his teacher had to offer so his father sent him to Amsterdam to a teacher named Pieter Lastman. Rembrandt however only studied with Lastman for six months. Then he went back to his hometown and became an independent master. His hometown was the second largest in Holland with about 50000 residents. This energetic bustling town was home to a university and a lively prosperous marketplace. Rembrandt later moved to Amsterdam in 1631 or 1632. While he was living in Amsterdam his career began to flourish and he married in 1634. Art students today are amazed by Rembrandt's productivity. His known works total approximately 2300 and include 1400 drawings 300 etchings and 600 paintings. His works include 90 self-portraits as well as religious paintings landscapes and group portraits. His most famous works include *The Anatomy Lesson of Dr. Tulp Return of the Prodigal Son* and *Night Watch*.

Did you insert 23 commas in the exercise above? Follow the same directions for this exercise as you did for Exercise 3.10.

Much of Rembrandt's life was full of sadness even though he enjoyed a brief happy marriage to Saskia van Uylenburgh. The years between 1635 and 1642 brought him much suffering. During this seven-year period his mother sister-in-law and three infant children died. This period ended with the death of Saskia just a few weeks before she turned 30. The years after his wife's death were very difficult for Rembrandt loved his wife dearly. She left him with his beloved only child named Titus. Later Rembrandt fell in love with his housekeeper named Hendrickje Stoffels. This gentle loving woman bore him a daughter and she outlived both Rembrandt and her mother. Hendrickje however died at the age of 37. Titus also died before his father and his death deeply saddened the aging artist. Rembrandt died on October 4 1669 at the age of 63.

Place commas where they are needed in the following passage.

Pocahontas the daughter of Powhatan and the wife of a British soldier is a popular figure in American history. Movies children's books and legends have all contributed to her fame. However the facts about her life are very different from the fictionalized details in some of the movies and books that bear her name. Pocahontas was born near the first American colony in Jamestown Virginia. Although some tales give the impression that Pocahontas was romantically involved with Captain John Smith she was just twelve years old when he arrived in Jamestown. After Captain Smith returned to England he wrote a book telling of his exploits. In this book he claimed that Pocahontas once saw that he was about to be beaten to death ran to his side put her head across his body and stopped her tribesmen from killing him. No other account of this heroic deed exists. Ironically Pocahontas later married an Englishman John Rolfe and went with Rolfe to England. A portrait of her in Elizabethan dress survives today. Sadly she did not live long. She died when she was in her early twenties.

Apostrophes

Another common punctuation mark is the apostrophe. Many students omit apostrophes. These omissions can be confusing for a knowledgeable reader. The rules governing apostrophes are as follows:

Apostrophe Rule 1: Use an apostrophe to form a contraction.

I am = I'm	we are = we're	we have = we've
it is = it's	you are = you're	you have = you've
she is = she's	they are = they're	they have = they've
he is = he's	do not = don't	will not = won't
is not = isn't	did not = didn't	are not = aren't
would not = wouldn't	was not = wasn't	should not = shouldn't
were not = weren't	cannot = can't	

Listed above are commonly found contractions. The two words on the left of the equal mark are contracted, or shortened, to form one word. Contractions are used frequently in informal speech and writing. The apostrophe appears at the place where a letter is omitted.

Apostrophe Rule 2: Use an apostrophe to show possession on nouns.

lady**'s** gloves (Think: The gloves belong to the *lady*.)

ladie**s'** gloves (The gloves belong to the *ladies*.)

man**'s** room (The room belongs to the *man*.)

men**'s** room (The room belongs to the *men*.)

Leah**'s** son (The son belongs to *Leah*.)

Jame**s'** son (The son belongs to *James*.)

boy**'s** toys (The toys belong to the *boy*.)

boy**s'** toys (The toys belong to the *boys*.)

student**'s** assignments (The assignments belong to the *student*.)

Each of the italicized words above represents the owner. The use of the apostrophe gives writers a shortcut. Instead of writing, *The gloves belong to the ladies*, the writer can write the *ladies' gloves*. To show possession,

- Add **'s** if the word representing the owner does not end in **-s**
- Add just the apostrophe if the word representing the owner already ends in **-s**

Students must also keep in mind that pronouns (*my, mine, your, yours, his, her, hers, its, our, ours, their, theirs*) show possession without the apostrophe. In addition, not every word that ends in **-s** requires an apostrophe; there must be something being possessed and a possessor.

If you follow the guidelines in the above paragraphs, you will master the use of the apostrophe and gain confidence in mastering punctuation.

EXERCISE 3.13

Insert apostrophes where they are needed.

It's easy to contrast Rembrandts career with that of his contemporary, Jan Vermeer. One of the major differences between these two artists work is the subjects of their paintings. Rembrandts subjects were often religious, such as his painting of Jesus parable of the prodigal son. This painting entitled, In *The Return of the Prodigal Son,* shows the sons return to his fathers household. The son is kneeling as his fathers arms encompass him. The expression on his fathers face is compassionate; hes celebrating his long-lost sons return. Vermeer, on the other hand, painted very few paintings with religious subjects. He was more interested in commonplace subjects, particularly scenes of everyday Dutch life. One of Vermeers most famous paintings is *A Lady Weighing Gold.* In this painting a lady stands at a wooden table with a pair of scales in her right hand. Shes weighing her gold, and the scales arent perfectly in balance. On the table are the ladys pearls and a couple of the ladys gold necklaces. The look on the womans face is serene as she gazes at her scales.

EXERCISE 3.14

The above paragraph needs 17 apostrophes. If you inserted more than that number, you are probably placing apostrophes on words where they are not needed. In the following paragraph insert apostrophes as needed.

Another difference between Rembrandts and Vermeers paintings is the use of color. In *The Return of the Prodigal Son* the fathers cloak is red as is the cloak of the figure on the canvas right side. The rest of the figures—the son and three shadowy figures in the background—are clothed in shades of brown and black. The background is dark, and its difficult to determine specific objects. On the other hand, in Vermeers *A Lady Weighing Gold,* the womans cloak is a velvety blue, and the cloaks lining and the sleeves lining are white ermine. The ladys veil is also white. The paintings background is not dark but is illuminated by light from a window located in the upper left-hand corner. Light from a window is a common device in Vermeers work. The windows light shines on the table, which holds the ladys prized possessions. Behind the womans figure is a framed painting on a religious subject. Many of Vermeers paintings feature a framed object in the background; often this object is a map. Although Rembrandt and Vermeer were both seventeenth-century artists, their choices of subjects and use of color are distinctively different.

EXERCISE 3.15

Place apostrophes where they are needed in the following passage.

Peter Paul Rubens was the greatest Flemish painter of the seventeenth century. Rubens was born June 28, 1577, in Westphalia, Germany. Rubens father had moved to Germany after being exiled from Flanders. However, after his fathers death in 1587, his mothers desire to move back to Flanders led her to relocate the family in Antwerp. In addition to painting, Rubens lifelong interests included diplomacy and travel. In 1600, he went to Italy to serve in a diplomatic post and study Italian art. Rubens liked to paint in a highly dramatic, colorful style. For example, in his painting, *Descent from the Cross,* Marys figure is dressed in a bright red cloak. The other figures clothing is not colorful at all. The paintings background is dark, but Jesus figure is brightly illuminated as he is removed from the cross. Through the dramatic contrasts between light and dark, the viewers attention is drawn to the central figures of Jesus and his mother, and the viewer can sense the paintings pathos.

Furthermore, Rubens figures are often robust and passionately bold. In 1630, four years after his first wifes death, Rubens married a sixteen-year-old girl, Helena. To celebrate his love for her, he painted *The Garden of Love*. The paintings dimensions are large—6'6" by 9'3½"—another characteristic of his paintings. On the canvas left side are two figures. One is a self-portrait of Rubens in a large, black Flemish hat holding his wifes hand and back gently as if they are dancing. Pushing them into the garden is a small, rounded cupid. In the center of the painting are many female figures awaiting their lovers in the garden. Above them are various cupids with arrows pointing toward the paintings center. In the paintings background is the porch of the house. Art historians believe this was the outside of Rubens home, which still stands today. The viewers impression is that all of the figures appear to be enjoying the gardens delights. The artists purpose is clear—he desires a happy marriage in the new house he has bought for his bride.

Student Samples

Development by Example

College Skills for Future Success

Developing math skills in college will help prepare me for a career as a registered nurse. As a licensed practical nurse, I have to calculate almost every day, whether it be a simple math problem or a complicated formula. Prior to my completing elementary algebra and a math topics course, whenever I needed to figure out dosages, the process took me a long time. I had to break down each part of the problem and then bring all these parts together to reach the correct answer. After completing my math courses, I was able to

➥

incorporate what I had learned on my job, thereby saving myself a lot of time. In addition, most medications in pill form are usually prepackaged, but the nurse must measure liquids. Most conversions, such as how many millileters make an ounce, are simple. However, when dealing with continuous flows such as intravenous infusions and artificial feedings, the nurse needs to calculate the rate of flow. For example, if the doctor orders 1000 ml to infuse over 12 hours, the nurse needs to calculate how many drops will equal a milliliter, how many milliliters per minute, and then how many milliliters per hour. Being able to obtain correct answers with an easier method is beneficial to both the nurse and the patients. My successful completion of college math classes has made these skills possible for me.

—Kathryn Figueroa

Rainy Days

Rainy days are my favorite times to catch up on indoor activities. A couple of weeks ago, it slowly started to rain. From my bedroom I could hear the winds picking up and tiny rain drops tickling the glass, bouncing off, and running down the side of the house. Then dark clouds rolled over the skies above. Within a few minutes I was sleeping like a baby. Not only do rainy days make me sleepy, but they also set my mind at ease so I can do my homework. Just last semester I had a critical analysis due on the novel *Oliver Twist*. Like every other student I waited until the last minute to get started. Fortunately, that weekend before my paper was due, it rained, which forced me to concentrate on my paper since I couldn't participate in any outdoor activities. In addition to catching up on my homework on rainy days, I enjoy reading gloomy books because the mood is already set. During the storms around Christmas last year, I bought a scary book about dragons. The dark, windy atmosphere outside drew me into the book as if I were one of the characters, and I finished the book in a day. I look forward to rainy days so I can catch up on my sleep, homework, and reading.

—Sozan Klonaris

FOCUS ON PEER REVIEW

After you have chosen a topic, written a focused topic sentence, and developed it with supporting details, you are ready for peer review of your draft. Use the following questions as a guide:

1. What is the topic sentence of the paragraph? Is the topic sentence focused enough to be developed in a single paragraph?

2. What are the two or three major points the writer uses to support the topic sentence?

3. Is each of the major points sufficiently developed with additional supporting details?

4. Is each of the major points clearly related to the topic sentence? If not, which ideas digress from the topic sentence?

5. Is each minor point clearly related to the major point it is intended to support? If not, where does a digression occur?

6. Are the supporting details arranged from least to most important? If not, how are they arranged?

7. Are the supporting details interesting? If not, what details could be added to enliven the paragraph?

8. What transitional words or phrases does the writer use?

9. Does the concluding sentence reinforce the topic sentence? If not, why?

10. Are all sentences clearly worded? If not, where are the unclear sentences located?

11. Are there any fragments? If so, where?

12. Are any commas missing? Are any commas inserted where they are not needed? If so, where?

13. Are any apostrophes missing or inserted where they do not belong? If so, where?

14. Are there any other grammatical or punctuation errors? Where?

15. Are any words misspelled? If so, where?

16. The strengths of this paragraph are _____.

17. The weaknesses of this paragraph are _____.

Without lively details to support your topic sentences, your paragraphs can lose their vitality. However, when you support your topic sentence with carefully selected examples, your reader will respect your knowledge of the subject and will be more likely to receive your message

Writers as Spiders

One way to review the concepts you have learned in the first three chapters is to visit some web sites. For a comprehensive look at composing paragraphs, consult

http://97.com/pi/writing-center/118.html

If you need more exercises on fragments, try these pages:

http://www.esc.edu/htmlpages/Writer/pandg/exg11men.htm
http://owl.english.purdue.edu/Files/67E.html

Many writing center sites offer reviews of punctuation rules. The U.S. government is also interested in helping writers with editing their documents. Here is a government site (NASA) that offers assistance on commas.

http://sti.larc.nasa.gov/html/Chapt3/Comma.html

For helpful comma exercises that will reinforce the rules you learned in this chapter, visit

http://owl.english.purdue.edu/Files/6.html
http://owl.english.purdue.edu/Files/7.html
http://owl.english.purdue.edu/Files/8.html
http://owl.english.purdue.edu/Files/9.html

For hints to use when you are proofreading for commas, check out

http://owl.english.purdue.edu/Files/117.html

You can locate information about apostrophes as well as exercises at the following web site:

http://owl.english.purdue.edu/Files/13.html

Most browsers offer bookmark features that will let you "mark" web sites for easy reference. You may want to add these sites to your bookmark collection so you will have them readily available to answer questions regarding punctuation of your paragraphs and essays.

Web Exercise

Visit this web site:

http://www.spjc.cc.fl.us/0/research/home.html

After you have read this page, write a paragraph focusing on the advantages of using one of the search engines featured on this page. Develop this paragraph using order of importance (see Chapter 2). Make sure that you place the advantage you consider most important last in your paragraph.

CHAPTER 4

Focus on Narration

Focus on Purpose

The purpose of a narrative paragraph is to relate to a reader a memorable personal experience. When you write a narrative, you are joining a long list of storytellers from the Paleolithic people who drew animal figures on the ceilings of the caves in Lascaux, France, to the modern-day griots who preserve the stories of their African tribes. These storytellers are part of a narrative tradition that extends back to the earliest beginnings of humankind.

Today, as in the past, narratives—both oral and written—are vital to our cultural existence. By developing narrative skills you are increasing the chances of your success as a college student and as a working professional.

In the college classroom you will have many chances to use the narrative skills you develop in this chapter. For instance, many American history textbooks include slave narratives written during the early years of our country's history. These first-hand accounts, which incorporate many of the narrative techniques you will learn about in this chapter, offer invaluable insights into the daily lives of slaves. In a psychology class your textbook will feature case studies that illustrate a particular concept. Your teacher may even require that you write a case study to narrate a sequence of events you have observed.

Narrative skills are also important in many career fields. Nurses and doctors must write accurate, specific case histories of their patients. Police officers must write arrest reports. Journalists rely heavily on narrative skills when they are writing interviews.

Focus on Choosing a Topic

Effective narratives, whether they are written by beginning college students or by career professionals, have certain features in common. One is a clearly focused topic. Here are some possible topics for your narrative paragraph:

- Choose a moment when you were proud of yourself for having accomplished a goal.
- Write about a memorable experience you had while on vacation.
- Remember a time when you had luck when you least expected it.

- Reflect on an important decision you have made in your life.
- Focus on a memory from childhood.
- Write about a valuable lesson you learned.
- Write about an unforgettable experience.

As you choose a topic for your paragraph, remember that in a narrative you are recording a snapshot of your past—both for yourself and for your reader. Because your paragraph is a snapshot and not an entire photo album, you will need a narrow focus. Otherwise, you will not be able to include the specific details necessary for an effective narrative. For instance, you will probably not be able to write an engaging paragraph about your family's two-week vacation last summer. You are more likely to write effectively if you select a specific event that occurred during your trip.

FOCUS ON ORGANIZING

The Topic Sentence

Once you have focused on a topic, you are ready to write your topic sentence. As in other paragraphs, the topic sentence will announce the focus of your paragraph to your reader. You also want to write a topic sentence that will make your reader want to read more. Generally, the topic sentence briefly answers key questions for the reader.

- *Who was involved in the event?* You should write your narrative, including the topic sentence, in first person singular (*I, me, my*), or first person plural (*we, us, our*) if others are involved.
- *When did the event occur?* Establishing a timeframe in the topic sentence helps the reader to focus his or her attention on the event. Also, the reader will understand immediately whether you are relating an event in the recent or distant past.
- *Where did the event occur?* In many narratives the setting of the event is critical. If you state the general setting in the topic sentence, the reader will have an easier time picturing the scene than if you wait to provide all the details of the setting in the body of your narrative.
- *What is the focus of your narrative?* Are you writing about a moment when you were proud? Are you recalling a childhood memory? Are you relating a recent decision you have made? While the topic sentence should announce the focus of your narrative, you may want to create some suspense by withholding the final outcome until later in the paragraph.

Some topic sentences of narrative paragraphs are too unfocused to be effective:

Unfocused: I can remember many good times on the playground of Saluda Elementary School.

83

Unfocused: I spent many summer Sundays after church eating "dinner on the grounds" with my family.

Effective narrative paragraphs begin with a focused topic sentence that can be developed in a single paragraph.

Focused: At my sixth-grade picnic softball game, I learned a valuable lesson about sportsmanship.

Focused: The summer of my twelfth year I spent a memorable Fourth of July afternoon enjoying "dinner on the grounds" with my family.

EXERCISE 4.1

Read each of the following sentences. If you think that the sentence would make a good topic sentence for a narrative, place a check in the blank to the left. If you think that this sentence is too broad or too unfocused, place an **X** in the blank.

_____ **1.** I will never forget all the good times I had on my trip last summer.

_____ **2.** I can still remember the first moments of my first day in first grade

_____ **3.** On August 25, 1983, in a casino in Las Vegas, I learned a valuable lesson.

_____ **4.** One afternoon last summer my family and I took an unforgettable rafting trip on North Carolina's Nantahala River.

_____ **5.** During my senior year in high school I made many decisions that would affect the rest of my life.

The Supporting Details

In the body of the narrative paragraph, just as in all paragraphs, you will support your topic sentence with specific details. In a narrative these details are arranged in chronological order so that you can recreate the experience for your reader. The problem is that at first you may not remember the details in the order in which they occurred, or you may omit details that are essential to the narrative. In order to help you recall the details before you begin to write them in paragraph form, try listing all the details you can remember. Then arrange these details in chronological order. A flow chart such as this one can help:

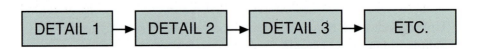

Then, as other details occur to you, you can add them in. Using a flow chart helps to reinforce the idea that the best narratives move smoothly from one detail to another.

After you complete your flowchart, you may discover that some of the details do not seem relevant or necessary. Ask yourself, "Does that detail support my topic sentence and help me recreate the event for my reader?" If the answer is "no," then omit it from your chart. Irrelevant details distract and frustrate the reader.

FOCUS ON TRANSITION

Once you have decided which details to include, you are ready to write the body of the narrative. As you write, be sure to include transition words that will help your reader move through the event with you. Such words as *then, afterwards, before, next, later, at last,* and *finally* are often helpful. For other suggested transitional expressions, see Table 2.2 on page 38.

In the following narrative paragraph, circle or highlight the sentences that are unrelated to the topic sentence. Underline transitional words.

EXERCISE 4.2

On a steamy, hot summer day when I was 10 years old, I was frightened for my life. My mother had taken me along while she visited a sick friend who lived a few miles outside town. Since I had no interest in going inside the sick woman's unairconditioned house for a visit, I decided to stay outside and wait for my mother. Then I saw a beautiful field next door to the house. All I wanted to do that morning was wander around in that field, so I did. Earlier that morning I remember having cereal for breakfast. My sister and brother were away at camp. As I ran in circles in the middle of the field, I heard an incredible roar from above. I looked up and saw a small jet plane diving straight for me. My uncle used to make jet planes from models. First, I froze; then I cried out, "Mama! Where are you?" The plane continued its nose-first descent. Suddenly, the pilot pulled the plane out of its descent. I ran into the house and straight into my mother's arms. Later my mother told me that the Air National Guard had been practicing strafing runs in that area on that day and that I had probably been used for target practice. I wonder how the Air National Guard differs from the Army National Guard. I will always remember the day I learned the meaning of the word—PANIC!!

The Concluding Sentence

In a narrative paragraph it is essential that you write a concluding sentence that emphasizes the main point of your narrative. If you write about a sequence of events but do not make a point about your reaction to them, then you are doing diary writing. This type of writing is not likely to engage your reader's interest. You should write your concluding sentence in such a way that the reader cannot fail to understand the purpose for your narrative. Otherwise, your reader may finish reading your paper and think, "So what?"

Like your topic sentence, your concluding sentence should be focused on the main idea of your narrative:

> **Unfocused:** I wish I could return to my elementary school days.
>
> **Unfocused:** I have never enjoyed any Sunday dinners as much as I did those.
>
> **Focused:** My sixth-grade classmates taught me the meaning of the word "sportsmanship."
>
> **Focused:** Even now on a hot summer Sunday afternoon, I can still taste those wonderful home-cooked dishes.

FOCUS ON DICTION

Good storytellers use a variety of techniques to keep their narratives interesting. Many of these techniques involve word choice.

Action Verbs and Adverbs

The strength of the verb is important in any sentence in any paragraph but especially in a narrative paragraph. Strong action verbs (verbs that indicate movement) will keep your readers focused on the action.

A student narrating his first approach to his girlfriend's house writes,

> A stereo inside her house was blaring the popular song, "Kiss."

The use of the word *blaring* is far livelier than if the student had substituted the word *playing*.

Another student writing about a near accident asserts,

> I used my turn signal as I aggressively dodged into the next lane.

Again the words *aggressively dodged into the next lane* are much more interesting than "I changed lanes." In the example above note the addition of the adverb aggressively to the verb *dodged*. Many narrative writers use -ly words (adverbs) to change (or modify) verbs. This student did not just *dodge* the accident; she *aggressively dodged* it! Adverbs energize action verbs.

Finally, a student, describing a bike ride, states,

> The houses sped by me; my ponytail whipped my face, and my eyelashes were pasted to my eyebrows.

Each of the above examples shows the interest a writer can create through the use of lively diction. When you write your paragraph, try using a thesaurus (a dictionary of synonyms and antonyms) to vary your choice of verbs and adverbs.

Revise the sentences below by changing the verbs (in bold print) and adding adverbs. You may use a thesaurus and/or a dictionary. Be ready to explain to your instructor how the meaning of the sentence changes when the verb is replaced and an adverb is added.

1. I **watched** as he **walked** across the street.

    _____

2. My friend **talked** about her plans for the summer.

    _____

3. My teacher **gave** the homework assignment on the board.

    _____

4. When I **left** the room, my dog **followed.**

    _____

5. As I **looked** at the camera, the photographer **took** my picture.

    _____

6. The mother **saw** her son as he **played** in the sandbox.

    _____

7. As the hikers **entered** the cave, they **looked** around them cautiously.

    _____

8. The students **waited** anxiously while the teacher **handed out** the test papers.

    _____

9. As the children **arrived,** the clown **gave** them some candy and balloons.

    _____

10. When I t**urned** into my driveway, I **saw** that my company had arrived.

    _____

Adjectives

Another technique is to use many adjectives (words that describe nouns) so that the reader can "see" the scene as you recreate the event. Using adjectives that denote color is particularly helpful. In the following passage a student writes about the moment she discovered there was no Santa. Notice how she combines the use of action verbs, adverbs, and adjectives for maximum effect.

I tiptoed quietly onto the soft, faded, avocado carpet of the immense room, ducked quickly into the dark, cavernous closet, closed the door, and pulled the string for the light. . . . I froze, staring at the box for what seemed an eternity. . . . I snapped the light off and scurried out of the closet and up to the refuge of my room.

Debra Bates

Recalling sensory details through the use of adjectives will help the reader relive the experience through your narrative. Using descriptive words to appeal to the senses of smell, sight, touch, hearing, and taste is a favorite stylistic device of narrators. In the following sentence a student describes her memories of her childhood home:

Lilac bushes bloomed in the spring, and their sweet scent mingled with the harsh odor of ammonia when my mom opened the house and began her spring cleaning.

Debra Bates

Another student, describing her trip to the beach with a friend, writes:

As we opened the car doors and sank into the plush seats, the heavy smell of cleaning fluid permeated our nostrils.

Jennifer Munz

Similes

One way to increase the impact of a descriptive passage is to write a simile, a comparison between two unlike things using *like, as,* or *than.* Using a simile helps the writer to connect an event in the narrative with something with which the reader is familiar. One student, writing about her first trip to the dentist, states that after administering the anesthetic,

The dentist came and gently picked up my cheek as if it resembled my English bulldog's flappy jaws.

Cassandra Vukcevic

Later, she adds that the hygienist's scraping "sounded like fingernails screeching down a chalkboard."

Another student conveys to the reader her panic at the thought of her boyfriend's proposing to her:

All these thoughts went spinning through my head like a toy top that was soon going to stop and fall over on its side. . . . He was pacing the floor like an expectant parent.

Laura Knight

This student uses a simile so she can explain a movement of an elderly driver:

His shaky, round hand rose from his tightly gripped steering wheel, and he began waving it back and forth like the old electric Santa Claus seen in the dime store window.

Lisa Bolyard

Finally, a student describes his anxiety as he approaches a girl to ask her for a date:

I was as tense and nervous as a turtle on a busy highway.

Jon Stapleton

Metaphors

In addition to using similes to create images in the minds of their readers, narrative writers use metaphors, comparisons between two unlike things that do not use the words *like*, *as*, or *than*.

Sometimes a student will extend a metaphor over several sentences to enliven his or her writing. Read the following passage to determine what comparisons the student is making as he describes himself as a boy killing a snake in his backyard:

I was hired by the King of Zendar to slay an evil serpent that terrorized the kingdom and the surrounding villages. I chose my weapon carefully. It very closely resembled a shovel, but it was really a special spear given to me by King Arthur several years ago when I rescued his daughter from the black knight. . . . I entered the serpent's lair. . . . He had a notorious reputation for striking his prey from behind, sinking his fangs deep into their flesh, instantly contaminating their bloodstream with his deadly venom, and watching as they died a slow death and their bodies writhed in excruciating pain. . . . Suddenly he appeared before me—his slick, jet-black scales glistening in the bright sun, his forked, blood-red tongue whipping in and out of his grinning lips as his lackluster eyes glared at me.

Jeff McIntosh

The author ends his tale by using a simile to describe his guilt after he has killed the snake:

> All I could feel was this overpowering sense of pure guilt drowning me like a skyscraper casting its shadow on a small daisy struggling to rise up from a crack in the sidewalk.

All of these techniques—action verbs, adverbs, adjectives, similes, and extended metaphors—will help you keep your reader entertained.

EXERCISE 4.4

Complete the following sentences to create similes:

1. I was as frightened as

   _____

2. I was as happy as

   _____

3. Walking into class that day was like

   _____

4. All I can remember was feeling like

   _____

5. Writing a paragraph is like

   _____

6. The thunderstorm sounded like

   _____

7. When I rode the roller coaster, my stomach felt as if

   _____

8. I felt as free as

   _____

9. The cool water rushing over my hands was like

   _____

10. The chili peppers in the burrito tasted like

    _____

FOCUS ON GRAMMAR

Students who write narrative paragraphs often find themselves needing to vary the types of sentences they write. Otherwise, it may seem to the author that every sentence starts out, "Then I . . ." In order to vary your sentences, you must also know how to punctuate a number of different types of sentences. In Chapter 2, you learned to identify the differences between clauses and phrases. In this chapter you will learn to join clauses together through the processes of coordination and subordination.

The term *coordination* refers to the process of joining independent clause to independent clause. Of course, a writer generally separates independent clauses from one another with periods. But what if you want to connect independent clauses some other way? What alternatives are available? The term *subordination* refers to the process of joining one or more dependent (or subordinate) clauses to an independent clause. What if you want to subordinate? How do you punctuate the sentence?

Coordination

A writer uses coordination to join together independent clauses of equal importance. Suppose you want to coordinate these independent clauses:

> I needed to leave the house in a hurry. I could not find my keys.

or these:

> My daughter was sick. I had to miss class.

You have several alternatives to using a period between these independent clauses.

Alternative 1. Join the two independent clauses with a comma followed by a coordinating conjunction—*for, and, nor, but, or, yet,* or *so* (FANBOYS).

> I needed to leave the house in a hurry, **but** I could not find my keys.
>
> My daughter was sick, **so** I had to miss class.

Caution: Remember that when you use a comma before a coordinating conjunction, you are signaling the reader that a subject and a verb will appear in the next clause (see Comma Rule 1 in Chapter 3).

Alternative 2. Join the two independent clauses with a semicolon.

> I needed to leave the house in a hurry; I could not find my keys.
>
> My daughter was sick; I had to miss class.

Caution: In the English language, a semicolon has the same strength as a period. Therefore, you should not place a semicolon between clauses unless you could also use a period there. Also, independent clauses joined together with a semicolon must be closely related in meaning, equal in importance, and short.

Alternative 3. Join two independent clauses with a semicolon followed by a conjunctive adverb. The most common conjunctive adverbs are *however, therefore, moreover, furthermore, consequently, otherwise, instead, nevertheless, thus, also, then*, and *meanwhile*.

I needed to leave the house in a hurry; **however** I could not find my keys.

My daughter was sick; **therefore** I had to miss class.

John was caught in traffic; **consequently,** he was late for work.

Table 4.1 illustrates how conjunctive adverbs show a specific relationship between the two independent clauses.

Caution: The conjunctive adverbs listed in Alternative 3 can also be used as interrupters in sentences. In this case, they are set off by commas (see Comma Rule 6 in Chapter 3).

I needed to leave the house in a hurry; I could not, however, find my keys.

My daughter was sick; I, therefore, had to miss class.

Coordinating independent clauses is like providing a traffic light at the intersection of two major roads. Strong signals are needed. To bring the reader to a full stop, a writer uses a period. (In England a period is called a *full stop*.) To slow the reader down but not stop him or her completely, the writer uses a comma followed by a coordinating conjunction, a semicolon, or a semicolon followed by a conjunctive adverb.

TABLE 4.1	Conjunctive Adverbs and Their Meanings
Conjunctive Adverb	*Meaning*
however nevertheless	express a contrast
consequently therefore thus	express a result
otherwise instead	express an alternative
then meanwhile	express a time relationship
moreover furthermore also	add a closely related idea

In the following sentences, underline the independent clauses. (**Hint:** If you have trouble finding where the independent clauses begin and end, try reading the sentences aloud and listening for each complete thought.) Write the letters **CO** in the blank for sentences that contain two coordinated independent clauses. Write the letter **N** in the blank for sentences that contain only one independent clause.

_____ **1.** One autumn night my brother, my sister, and I waited impatiently for my father to come home from work.

_____ **2.** Our hopes were high; we wanted to go to the state fair.

_____ **3.** We did not want to beg, for whining would only make him angry.

_____ **4.** We decided, instead, to put on sad faces and wait for him to notice.

_____ **5.** The plan worked, and soon my father noticed our unhappiness.

_____ **6.** Then he told us to go get in the car; he had a surprise for us.

_____ **7.** We ran outside and saw "State Fair or Bust" written on the car windows.

_____ **8.** My father has been dead for almost 20 years, yet every Father's Day I remember his kindness on that autumn night.

Subordination

In Chapter 2, you learned to recognize a dependent (subordinate) clause. When a writer subordinates, he or she places the idea of less importance in a dependent clause and the idea of greatest importance in the independent clause. This chapter will show you how to join one or more dependent clauses to an independent clause.

Alternative 4. Begin the sentence with a dependent clause, insert a comma, and then write an independent clause.

> Although I wanted to leave the house in a hurry, I could not find my keys.
>
> Because my daughter was sick, I had to miss class.

Caution: The comma following the introductory dependent clause is **not** optional. If you have difficulty deciding where to insert the comma, try reading the sentence aloud. You may be able to hear where the comma should go. Remember that the comma after the beginning dependent clause is not for the writer's benefit, but for the reader's. The comma is a signal to the reader to pause briefly before continuing the reading of the sentence.

Alternative 5. Begin the sentence with an independent clause and then write a dependent clause.

> I could not find my keys although I wanted to leave the house in a hurry.

> I had to miss class because my daughter was sick.

Caution: No comma appears between the clauses. The subordinating conjunctions, *although* in the first example and *because* in the second, are so powerful that no punctuation is needed; the subordinating conjunction does the work of joining the clauses. Because no comma appears, the reader will read the sentence in a continuous flow of words.

EXERCISE 4.6

In the following exercise underline the independent clauses once and the dependent clauses twice. Place the letter **C** in the blank for sentences that contain two coordinated independent clauses. If the sentence contains one subordinate clause and one independent clause, place the letter **S** in the blank. Place the letter **X** in the blank for sentences that contain only one independent clause.

_____ 1. One of my earliest memories must have occurred when I was about two or three years old.

_____ 2. I was visiting my grandmother as I did many summer afternoons.

_____ 3. That afternoon I was very hungry, and I begged my grandmother for something to eat and drink.

_____ 4. My grandmother packed a picnic lunch for two, and off we went.

_____ 5. We walked to a field and found a shade tree.

_____ 6. After we sat down under the shade tree, I looked up and saw the sun shining on my grandmother's long, flowing, ebony hair.

_____ 7. I don't remember much else about that picnic, but I do remember the look of love on my grandmother's face.

_____ 8. My grandmother is in a nursing home now; I visit her whenever I can.

_____ 9. When I look at my grandmother now, her hair is gray.

_____ 10. Her skin is wrinkled, too, but I still can see her sitting under that tree with a hungry toddler.

Run-ons

Run-ons, sometimes called *fused sentences*, occur when the writer writes two sentences and fails to place a period, a semicolon, or a comma with a coordinating conjunction between them. Run-ons sometimes occur in narrative paragraphs because the writer gets so caught up in the pace of the story that he or she overlooks the intersection of two complete sentences. Run-ons are confusing to the reader, who is looking for some signal that a new sentence is following.

Imagine if you were reading a narrative, and you came upon the following run-on:

I could not see the car was approaching too quickly.

It would be easy to misread the writer's ideas by reading *I could not see the car* and then stumbling through the rest of the sentence. Readers find run-ons frustrating because they make the task of reading difficult as sentences, like cars in a traffic accident, collide into each other.

As a writer, then, you need to edit your paragraphs carefully so you can eliminate run-ons. You might try reading your paragraphs backwards (sentence by sentence) so that you can check for run-ons without getting carried away by the narrative action. After you locate a run-on, correct it by using a period or coordinating or subordinating the clauses:

I could not see. The car was approaching too quickly.

I could not see, and the car was approaching too quickly. **(Alternative 1)**

I could not see; the car was approaching too quickly. **(Alternative 2)**

Notice that these two ideas work best when they are separated by a period or coordinated with a semicolon. It is not always possible to subordinate two ideas and write a clear sentence. When you correct the run-ons on your paper and in the following exercises, check to see that you have preserved the original meaning of the ideas.

In the following narrative, place a slash mark (/) where a run-on occurs. Then correct the run-on by inserting a period followed by a capital letter or using any of the alternatives given in this chapter.

EXERCISE 4.7

It was a hot night in New York City. My husband and I decided to sit out on the fire escape by my sister's apartment. We had been chatting awhile when we noticed a disagreement erupt between two homeless men on the street below. They were arguing quite loudly soon after they began to scuffle. A few minutes later their girlfriends got involved. The women were screaming and punching each other. By this time a crowd of people had gathered below at the same time an eighteen-wheel produce truck pulled up to the stoplight on the corner. Suddenly, both women pulled each other to the ground. The light turned green the wheels of the truck slowly started to move. Both women heard the truck only one could get up. My husband and I started screaming as did the rest of the crowd it was too late. The truck had rolled over the woman in the street.

EXERCISE 4.8

Did you locate 5 run-ons in Exercise 4.7? The rest of the narrative follows. Follow the same directions as in Exercise 4.7.

I screamed into the apartment for my mother to call 911. I grabbed a sheet then I ran downstairs to see if I could help. Crying uncontrollably, the injured woman lay in the street. When I reached her, I put the sheet on top of her and sat on the street next to her. I held her hand I tried to reassure her that she would be all right. Finally, the ambulance and police arrived. They took the woman to a hospital nearby she died on the way. My husband and I were taken to the police station to make a statement. After four hours of grueling police interrogation, we were allowed to go home we were both very sad because the police did not know how to contact the woman's family. I often think of this woman and wonder if her family knows that she is dead. I hope someone attended her funeral her name was Sharon.

Jennifer Andresen

EXERCISE 4.9

In the following narrative, place a slash mark (/) where a run-on occurs. Then correct the run-on.

One of my most exciting experiences occurred two years ago when five of my friends and I went whitewater rafting on the Nantahala River in North Carolina. Our rafting trip began with safety instructions our instructor told us to keep our feet securely tucked under the seat at all times. Then we were told that if we fell out of the raft into the swiftly moving current, we should not try to walk to shore even though the water would only be a few feet deep instead we were to do a "whitewater swim." A "whitewater swim" involves floating feet first down the river using the lifejacket to keep afloat. One of my friends had been whitewater rafting many times he decided to be our raft guide. The guide sits in the back of the raft his responsibility is to steer the raft around rocks and other obstacles in the river. We soon departed down the river we were confident that we would have a successful trip. The water was beautiful on that summer day the sun glistened playfully on its surface. At first we responded well to the challenges that the river offered us then we began to relax and quickly forgot the safety instructions. Suddenly, a small ripple in the water became our guide's undoing. The drop in the river at first appeared shallow it was, in fact, much deeper than we thought. The back of the raft came down in this "hole" in the river it landed on a rock submerged just a few inches below the water. The raft acted like a trampoline, bouncing our guide several feet in the air and into the water. Trying to be a hero, our guide attempted to walk to the edge of the river. Fortunately, he slipped on a rock, fell into the water, and began a "whitewater swim." The rest of us took the raft to the bank realizing he was not hurt, we laughed as he climbed back into the raft. The next time we go rafting, we will listen to the safety instructions—and not our "experienced" guide.

Comma Splices

One of the most common grammatical errors is the comma splice. A comma splice occurs when a writer uses a comma alone to join two independent clauses. In other words, the writer uses a comma at the point where the independent clauses intersect but omits the coordinating conjunction (*and, but, or, nor, so,* or *yet*) that must accompany the comma (see Coordination, Alternative 1, p. 91).

Comma splices often occur in narrative paragraphs—many times before an independent clause that begins with a personal pronoun (*I, he, she, it, we, you, they*). Consider the comma splices below:

I could feel my heart beating like a drum, I was scared to death.

I tried desperately to locate my brother, he was nowhere to be found.

If you read these sentences aloud, you can see how the writer might get so carried away with the narrative that he or she might forget about joining together independent clauses. Because comma splices are confusing to many readers, it is important that you be able to spot comma splices and edit them out of your paragraphs.

In the English language, a comma is not considered strong enough punctuation to prevent the head-on collision of two independent clauses. The reader needs a stronger traffic signal. A comma splice can be corrected by using a period or by coordinating or subordinating the clauses. Use the alternative that you think best expresses the ideas.

I could feel my heart bleeding like a drum, **(comma splice)** I was scared to death.

I could feel my heart beating like a drum, **and** I was scared to death. **(Alternative 1)**

I could feel my heart beating like a drum; I was scared to death. **(Alternative 2)**

I tried desperately to locate my brother; **however,** he was nowhere to be found. **(Alternative 3)**

Even though I tried desperately to locate my brother, he was nowhere to be found. **(Alternative 4)**

My brother was nowhere to be found **even though** I tried desperately to locate him. **(Alternative 5)**

In the narrative below place a slash mark (/) where a comma splice occurs. After you have identified the comma splices, correct them by removing the comma and inserting a period followed by a capital letter or by coordinating or subordinating the clauses.

If I had not been wearing my seatbelt when I was in my first accident, I probably would not be here today. Mike, my boyfriend, and I had just finished a late dinner at his house, we got in our cars and headed to my house to watch movies. Mike went first, I followed him. I lost sight of Mike's car when there was suddenly very little visibility. Heavy smoke covered the road as I approached a curve. Just as I went around the curve, there was Mike. I tried to stop and turned my car to the side of the road, it was too late. At the speed of forty-five miles per hour my car slammed into the back of Mike's. When I realized what had happened, I was scared. The impact had pushed the dash of my car into my knees, blood was all over my face and clothes. I managed to unbuckle the seatbelt and get out of the car. Mike was still inside his car. He could not open his door because the frame of his car had buckled. I saw him climbing out of the window. Mike was all right. There was no one around to help. Mike picked me up and headed for a house down the road. The owners of the house heard the crash and called 911, help was on the way.

Exercise 4.10 featured 6 comma splices. See how many you can find as the narrative continues. Follow the directions for Exercise 4.10

It seemed like we waited for hours for the highway patrol and ambulance to arrive on the scene. As the paramedics took us inside the ambulance, I realized my knees and legs were hurting. The paramedics determined my nose had been broken, the dash of the car had cut and scratched my legs. Mike was told he would be okay but would probably be sore for a few days. The highway patrol arrived and filled out a report. I was not ticketed for the accident, the conditions were hazardous. Then I had to notify my parents. The officer telephoned my mother and explained the situation. Because of his expertise, my mother stayed calm, she soon arrived to comfort me. Now the first thing I do every time I get into the car is buckle my seatbelt. The accident happened almost three years ago, the memory of the collision, however, is still vivid. The officer at the scene of the incident said, "If you had not had the seatbelt on, you probably would not have survived the crash." Because of the speed I was traveling, I would have been thrown through the windshield upon contact with Mike's vehicle. Accidents occur without warning, there is not enough time to fasten the seatbelt when the driver realizes he or she is about to crash. I learned that wrecks can occur on even the most untraveled roads and when they are least expected. My advice is "buckle up."

Kerri Carlisle

In the narrative below, place a slash mark (/) wherever a comma splice occurs. Then correct each comma splice.

EXERCISE 4.12

One of the most memorable sites on our Nantahala River rafting trip was a five-foot waterfall at the end of the rafting run. A quarter-mile before the waterfall, the guides pulled the rafts to the right bank of the river, they exited the rafts and hiked along the bank to observe the river as the current approached the waterfall. The guides then determined how to steer the rafts to "run" the waterfall successfully. The most experienced member of the team gave advice to the guides. The river bent to the right, therefore, all guides should steer to the left. If the guides steered the rafts to hug the left bank as it approached the right-hand bend in the river, then the rafts would be in the best position to descend the waterfall. From the bank of the river, the approach to the waterfall looked easy to our guide, however, back in the raft in the strong, swift current, he began to lose confidence. Split-second, decisive action was required to stay on course, the current was strong and demanding. Somehow our crew managed to get to the left bank, however, there was no time to sigh with relief. Then we were heading directly into a sea of foam, it seemed to drop off into nowhere. The crew had to work as a team, we all had to respond instinctively. Somehow we managed to hit the center of the waterfall, for a split second we were in a free fall in foam. Within seconds the plunge was over, the river slowed more quickly than the pounding of our hearts. I will never forget that trip, I'm ready to go again any time.

FOCUS ON PUNCTUATION

Quotation Marks with Dialogue

Many students like to use dialogue when they write narratives. The use of dialogue (conversation between people) is effective because it helps make the narrative come alive for the reader. The only hesitation student writers have about the use of dialogue is that many are unsure how to punctuate direct quotations.

If you wish to include dialogue in your narrative, keep the following rules in mind:

◆   Begin the exact words of the speaker with quotation marks followed by a capital letter. If you plan to follow the speaker's exact words with the name of the speaker and a verb (*said, stated,* or *exclaimed,* etc.), then end the speaker's words with a comma (if the words form a statement), a question mark (if the words pose a question), or an exclamation point (if the words indicate surprise) followed by quotation marks and the rest of the sentence. If you begin the next sentence with the author's exact words, you must open quotation marks at the beginning of the sentence and close the quotation marks at the end of the speaker's words.

"What are you planning to take with you on the trip?" she asked her children as they ran out the door.

"I can't believe this trunk is already packed full!" he shouted in a voice full of frustration.

"I've got more stuff to pack in the trunk," she responded. "You'll just have to make room."

◆   If you plan to introduce the sentence with the name of the speaker and the verb, then follow this introduction with a comma followed by quotation marks and the exact words of the speaker. Remember to end the sentence with the appropriate punctuation. Also keep in mind that periods, questions marks, and exclamation points should appear inside quotation marks.

She asked her children as they ran out the door, "What are you planning to take with you on the trip?"

He shouted in a voice full of frustration, "I can't believe this trunk is already packed full!"

She responded, "I've got more stuff to pack in the trunk. You'll just have to make room."

Commas with Appositives

In your narrative you may want to provide the names of some of the people involved in the story. For instance, instead of saying "my friend" did this or "my friend" did that, you can name your friend so that the reader will be able to follow your story easily. When you introduce your friend for the first time, you will probably be using an appositive. An appositive is a noun, often a proper noun, that renames or identifies the noun immediately preceding it in the sentence. A comma should appear immediately before and after the appositive.

My friends, Denise and Tiffany, went with us on vacation that year.

My teacher, Ms. Jones, responded quickly to my question.

In the narrative below, punctuate the dialogue as needed and place commas around appositives.

Last summer my husband Dan and my daughters Jenny and Leah took a day trip to the Smoky Mountains. Just inside the national park was our first stop Fontana Lake. The green-colored lake looked so inviting on that hot day that my husband decided to go for a swim and proceeded to take off his shirt. Watch out we cried. That water sure looks cold. Don't worry he replied. I'll be all right. We sat on the bank in the shade and continued to yell at him. I screamed You don't know how deep that water is. You're going to break your neck. He replied You're just jealous. Then we saw him jump into the water. Yikes he screamed. We looked to see him scrambling back to the shore like a clown shot from a cannon. What's wrong we cried. When he reached the shoreline, he grabbed his shirt and ran through the poison ivy to the car. When we crawled into the car with him, we felt the heat blasting through the vents. Where's the air conditioning we cried. I'll never complain about being hot again Dan whined. Then we all laughed until we cried.

Student Samples—Narration

A Summer Adventure

On a beautiful summer's morning last August, I had an incredible first-time experience exploring the "Windy City" of Chicago with my children. My journey began at the first blush of day. I packed up the car and proceeded towards the city. I knew we were approaching the city as traffic turned into confusion. Cars were overheating, people were yelling, and taxi drivers were abusing their horns. After the flow of traffic subsided, I found a parking place on the waterfront. What a picture-perfect scenario! We could see the beautiful sailboats rocking on Lake Michigan as the waves rolled along from passing boats. Across the way stood rows of tall buildings. My oldest daughter, Nicole, said, "They look like soldiers standing at attention" as she stood engrossed with the view of the city. My destination was the most famous toy store in Chicago. Along the way, we passed expensive stores and fancy restaurants. Finally, I spotted the toy store, but first we had to cross the street. The pedestrians were huddled together, and then the sign said, "Walk." I could feel the

➡

earth tremble as if a herd of buffalo were passing by. The kids were astonished as we entered the toy store. The walls were covered with thousands of toys. After playing for two hours, the children were ready to head home. I knew my trip was complete when my youngest daughter, Ariell, looked at me with her big, blue eyes and thanked me for bringing her to the city. As we drove away, the "Windy City" faded into the mist of the clouds.

—Michelle Greene

The Thrill of the Ride

On a hot, sticky summer day when I was seven years old, I awoke excitedly. It was the opening day of the Jackson County Fair. For months I had been impatiently awaiting the fair's arrival. Maybe this year I would be tall enough to ride the roller coaster. I felt like a little caboose trying to measure up to the gigantic locomotive. I was the first person dressed and ready to go that morning. However, it seemed like an eternity before everyone else was ready. Finally, we were on our way. When we arrived at the fair, I felt the same tingling sensations as I had coming down the stairs each Christmas morning. The first place I headed was the ticket window. Afterwards, I walked toward the roller coaster. I could feel my stomach tighten; it was as if someone had grabbed my belt and was vigorously pulling at it. I stood in line, peering at the yellow and red yardstick. I was still too far back to see if I measured up. Suddenly, the ride stopped, and the line slowly eased forward. I must have been daydreaming because before I knew it, I was next. As I walked up to the cart, the man running the ride said, "Wait a minute! I have to see if you're tall enough." My heart felt like it had dropped to my feet. I turned and gazed at the stick; then I slowly walked toward it. When I reached the yardstick, I turned around and held my chin up as far as it would go. When the man shouted, "Come on," I was as happy as a squirrel in an oak tree. That day I rode every ride at least twice. The thrill of being able to ride was greater than the thrill of the ride itself. I remember my mom always telling me to keep my chin up, but I never realized it could serve a purpose.

—Rebecca Smith

FOCUS ON PEER REVIEW

Now that you have chosen a topic and reviewed organizational, diction, and grammar skills, you are ready to write an experimental draft of your narrative paragraph and participate in peer review using the following guide questions:

1. Does the topic sentence of the paragraph focus on a specific memory or event? Tell why or why not.

2. Does the topic sentence establish the following: when the incident took place, where the incident took place, and who was involved? If not, which of the above is missing?

3. Is there anything missing from the topic sentence that you think should be included? Is this lack of information likely to affect the reader's comprehension of the paragraph?

4. Does the writer use first person (*I, me, my, mine, myself, we, us, our, ourselves*) consistently? If the writer uses second person point of view (*you, your, yourself, yourselves*) anywhere in the paragraph, please indicate by circling each use. Can this sentence be rewritten using first person point of view?

5. Check the development of the body of the paragraph. Is something happening? Is the writer detailing related experiences clearly?

6. Does the writer include any information that does not seem directly related to the purpose of the paragraph? If so, indicate where the writer gets off the track.

7. Does the concluding sentence emphasize the purpose for the narrative and satisfy the reader?

8. List the transitional expressions the author uses.

9. List four or five action verbs in the paragraph.

10. List five or six descriptive words (adjectives) that the writer uses.

11. List any similes or metaphors the writer uses.

12. Does the writer use dialogue? If so, is it effective? If not, where might the writer use dialogue to improve the paragraph?

13. Note any misspelled words or punctuation problems. Place a check mark at the end of each line with an error that needs attention.

14. Are there any fragments, run-ons, or comma splices? If so, indicate where they occur.

15. What I like most about this paragraph is _____.

16. What I think needs more work is _____.

Using the student samples as models, and the advice of your peer editor, keep working until you have written a paragraph that represents your best work. Who knows who might read your paragraph years from now? What will you think of your story in twenty or thirty years? What will your children and grandchildren think? Videotapes and photographs create important visual memories, but writing narratives is a wonderful way to preserve the stories of our lives for future generations.

Writers as Spiders

As you have learned in this chapter, narration is a powerful form of expression. Many libraries and other organizations are preserving historical narratives on the World Wide Web. These narratives include holocaust narratives, slave narratives, and Chicago fire narratives, to name a few.

Web Exercise

For a fascinating look at a narrative by a former slave and fierce abolitionist, consult

http://www.compu-help.com/liberty/douglastext.html

After you reach the site, scroll down to the end of Chapter 1. Read carefully the last two paragraphs, in which Frederick Douglas tells about the first time he witnessed the beating of a slave. Then answer the following questions:

1. What is the focus of this memory?

2. Who is involved in this event?

3. What are some descriptive words (action verbs, adjectives) that the author uses as he recreates this event?

4. What is the effect of the dialogue used in this passage?

5. What is the author's attitude toward this experience?

Another intriguing narrative is "My Experience of the Chicago Fire," twelve-year-old Fannie Belle Becker's account of the Chicago fire she survived in 1871. This account appears as it was written, including grammatical and spelling errors. You can reach this site at

http://www.chicagohs.org/fire/witnesses/becker.html

After you finish reading this narrative, answer these questions:

1. What is the focus of this memory?

2. Of all the things that Fannie carries from the house, which seems most important to her? Why?

3. What are some action verbs that Fannie uses to recreate this event?

4. What is the author's attitude toward this event?

5. Since a child wrote this narrative, there are a number of sentence structure errors including run-ons and comma splices. Identify one run-on and one comma splice

Additional Help

For a humorous look at the art of writing similes, see

http://advance.byu.edu/people/jeff/funny/simile.html

If you need additional help with avoiding comma splices and run-ons, check out

http://leo.stcloud.msus.edu/punct/csfsro.html

You can find exercises on comma splices and run-ons at

http://owl.english.purdue.edu/Files/12.html

At this site you will discover information on using quotation marks in dialogue:

http://owl.english.purdue.edu/Files/14.html

Exercises on this topic can be found here:

http://owl.english.purdue.edu/Files/15.html

CHAPTER 5

Focus on Observation

FOCUS ON PURPOSE

The purpose of an observation paragraph is to share with a reader your description of a person, an animal, an object, or a place. Active readers are curious about the world around them, and writers are eager to record their observations.

History would certainly not be the same were it not for sharp observers. In the first century A.D. the Jewish historian, Josephus, recorded many of the Roman military conquests in what is now the Middle East. Most dramatically, Josephus was present during the Roman siege of the Jewish Zealots at Masada circa 72 A.D. Today's knowledge of this lengthy siege and the eventual deaths of all but a handful of the Zealots is largely due to Josephus' journals. In science accurate observations are also critical. In 1928 when Alexander Fleming observed a mold on a culture containing some common germs, he noted that the germs were disappearing. His discovery led to the development of penicillin.

Keen observation skills are essential today in the classroom and in the workplace. College students enrolled in humanities classes develop observation skills as they study great works of art. In science labs students must focus observations sharply in order to complete their labs accurately and efficiently.

Observation techniques are also critical in any career. Physicians must observe their patients closely and accurately to make correct diagnoses. Assembly line workers must constantly observe their products to assure quality control. Supervisors schedule interviews in order to observe job applicants before they are hired. During the interview job applicants have a chance to make observations about their potential work environment.

If you are to be a successful student and worker, you will often need to record your observations in writing. This chapter will help you learn to sharpen your observation skills and communicate your observations to a reader.

FOCUS ON CHOOSING A TOPIC

When you choose a subject for an observation paragraph, you must narrow your focus, or you will not be able to complete your observation within the limits of one paragraph. Think of yourself as a photographer. Use the zoom lens on your camera to focus on one person, one object, or one place. Following are some suggested topics:

- **Choose a favorite photograph.** How would you describe the photograph to someone who has not seen it? What is the subject of the photograph? What makes up the foreground? What is in the background? Why is this photograph important to you? Try to choose a photo that is not crowded with people or scenery so that you can complete your observations in one paragraph.
- **Observe a person.** If you were a portrait painter, what physical characteristics of this person would you emphasize? If you were describing this person's features to someone who was blind, which observations would you include? Why do you think this person is interesting?
- **Think about a place where you like to spend time.** Then take your imaginary zoom lens and zoom in on one area. How would you describe this place to someone who has never been there? Why do you enjoy spending time there?
- **Select a prized possession.** What are its physical characteristics? How would you describe this object to someone who has never seen it? Why does this object hold a special meaning for you?
- **Observe an animal.** What is its size? Its shape? What are its movements? Why do you choose this particular animal to observe?
- **Select a favorite painting.** What is the subject of the artist's painting? What objects compose the painting? What colors did the author use? What shapes? What overall impression does the painting convey to the viewer?

When you choose your topic, keep in mind that you will be using words to help the reader see what you have observed. You will need to keep a narrow focus so that you can provide all the details necessary to form an image in your reader's mind.

Focus on Organizing

The Topic Sentence

Now that you have chosen a topic, you can write the topic sentence. The topic sentence of an observation paragraph announces the focus of your observation to the reader. An effective topic sentence also communicates to the reader your overall impression of your subject. The topic sentence, then, should answer these questions:

- **Whom or what did you observe?** Be as specific as you can when you name the focus of your observation. The use of a specific, rather than a general, name will help the reader form an immediate impression.

107

- **Why is this observation memorable?** Include in the topic sentence the dominant impression that this observation made on you, the observer.

EXERCISE 5.1

Read each of the following sentences. Place a check in the blank for the sentences you think would make good topic sentences for observation paragraphs. If the sentence is too broad or too unfocused to be effective, place an **X** in the blank.

_____ 1. My two-year-old daughter, Frances, is beautiful when she sleeps.

_____ 2. The students in Ms. Campbell's English class are all interesting.

_____ 3. My favorite photograph is a picture of me taken when I was a carefree toddler.

_____ 4. This photograph of twenty-five family members at last year's reunion is a personal favorite.

_____ 5. The gold pocket watch lying on the table intrigues me.

_____ 6. All the guests at my sister's wedding enjoyed themselves at the reception.

_____ 7. The young boy playing in the sand looks intently at his sand castle.

_____ 8. The mountains look majestic in the distance.

_____ 9. The waterfall is lovely in the early morning light.

_____10. The students, waiting for class to begin, are gathering outside the classroom door.

The Supporting Details

In the body of the observation paragraph, you will include the specific details necessary to communicate your observations to a reader. Before you can do that, you must record and organize your observations. Observe your subject for at least five consecutive minutes—more if the subject is not active. Repeated observations are recommended because it is easy to miss important details during a single observation.

During your observations you should take notes. These notes are for your use, not your reader's, so you should jot them down in a way that is helpful for you. Some students prefer to jot down their observations in random order as quickly and as fully as possible. Try taking a page and dividing it into two columns, one headed "objective" and one "subjective." On the objective side note your factual observations: what you see, what you hear, what you touch—any physical description of the object, person, or place. Also note any changes in the subject that occur during your observation. On the subjective side note your feelings or opinions about what you are observing.

What are you thinking about as you make the observation? Does this observation remind you of any other similar observations? What is your attitude toward the subject of your observation?

A student made the following notes as she watched a young boy, Evan, ride his rocking horse.

Objective	**Subjective**
black mane	horse always happy
oval eyes	horse enjoys rocking
four eyelashes	horse awaiting his favorite cowboy, Evan
black felt ears	horse's ears looking like devil horns
red mouth	Evan releasing his death grip to wave as he rocks
9-inch red saddle	horse's eyes looking like eggs
5-inch black yarn tail	
black harness	
made from pine wood	
natural color	
26 inches tall	
30.5 inches long	
9-inch legs	
16-inch long body	
black reins	
silver carpet tacks	
Evan rocking back and forth	
Evan gripping the horse's handle	
horse's eyes never closing	
horse always standing	

Note that in these notes there are more observations on the objective side than on the subjective side. It is not necessary to take an equal number of notes on each side. The number and type of notes you take will vary greatly according to your subject. These notes are a starting point for your observation paragraph. At the end of this chapter is a sample paragraph developed from these observations.

Write the letter **O** in the blank to the left of those sentences that present objective observations and the letter **S** in the blank to the left of those sentences that make subjective observations.

EXERCISE 5.2

_____ **1.** My dog, Cinnamon, is a sweet but quirky Chow.

_____ **2.** He has a purple tongue, a Chow characteristic.

_____ **3.** He also has the red fur typical of many Chows.

_____ **4.** When his fifty-pound, stocky frame struts around the backyard, his red fur contrasts beautifully with the green grass.

_____ **5.** Unlike many Chows, Cinnamon has a friendly temperament and enjoys being around people.

_____ **6.** He does have some strange habits, though.

_____ **7.** He runs in circles in the backyard whenever he is energetic.

_____ **8.** He will not eat dry dog food; he would rather starve.

_____ **9.** When I feed him, he licks the empty can before he begins his dinner.

_____ **10.** For all his eccentric habits, he is a lovable pet.

Once you have completed your observation notes, you need to arrange your observations in an order that will appeal to your reader. The supporting details of observations of places or objects are generally arranged in spatial order. For instance, if you are observing a photograph, you can begin with the top of the photograph and then work your way to the center of the picture and finally to the details in the bottom half. Or you can begin by discussing the details to the left followed by the details in the center and the details on the right. Observations of people or animals include details that describe physical characteristics and/or personality traits. These details should also be arranged for the convenience of the reader. An observation of a person, for instance, often starts with a physical description of hair color, facial features, and other prominent physical characteristics. Most observations feature both objective and subjective details. It does not matter where you begin and end your description as long as the reader can follow the order.

The Concluding Sentence

The concluding sentence of your observation paragraph should reinforce the focus of your observation and the general impression you want to leave in the mind of the reader. Before you write your concluding sentence, reread your topic sentence. Does your concluding sentence bring the reader back to where you begin?

FOCUS ON TRANSITION

When you have decided how to arrange the details of your observation, you are ready to write the body of your paragraph. As you write, be sure to include transitional words and phrases to help your reader visualize the object, person, or place you are observing. The following transitional expressions will be helpful when you observe an object or a place; *here, there, above, below, at the top, at the bottom, nearby, next to, to the right,* and *to the left*. See Chapter 2 for other possible expressions.

EXERCISE 5.3

Read the following paragraph, and highlight or circle the transitional expressions.

The twenty-one-inch nutcracker stands guard on the fireplace's mantel. At the top sits a sable-colored, Cossack-style helmet made of fake fur. Below the helmet protrudes his gray hair. His face is colorful. His dark black eyebrows are striking. Below are his black eyes, petite nose, black mustache, and red mouth ready to crack a nut at any opportunity. To the left, his bent arm holds a pole topped by a red flag. To the right his arm rests by his side. His military-style jacket is green. To the right and left of his jacket are five white buttons. His red pants match the red of the flag and the jacket's cuffs. At the bottom his black boots stand on a red base. The nutcracker's figure is imposing.

FOCUS ON DICTION

Effective writers use a number of techniques to communicate their observations to their readers. These include the use of sensory details and specific, rather than general, nouns. These techniques help the reader to see your observation through your eyes.

Sensory Details

Sensory details appeal to the reader's senses of smell, sight, touch, hearing, and taste. A writer can create these details through the use of action verbs, adverbs, adjectives, similes, and metaphors—techniques that were introduced in Chapter 4.

In the following passage a student uses a simile as she observes her two-year-old daughter dancing:

Her legs and arms began swinging and bouncing in sync to the music as if she were the new guest star for Soul Train.

Later in the observation she uses another simile to describe her daughter's smell after she has been playing in her food:

The odor reeked like that of stinky, molded forgotten leftovers in the refrigerator.

Casey Vukcevic

EXERCISE 5.4

In the following passage a student uses sensory details to communicate his discovery of a pocket knife as he rummages through boxes in his bedroom closet. Circle the action verbs and underline the similes.

After I rummaged through several dust-covered boxes of childhood delights, I encountered a shoebox that was taped shut. I ripped the yellow, discolored tape, lifted the box's lid, and found, among some "Where's the Beef?" pins and assorted action figures, a pocket knife. . . . As I stared at the knife, it snatched my attention like a hawk snagging a rodent and held it like a hawk's talons gripping a squirming mouse. . . . The knife was about four inches long with the blades tucked away inside. The casing was made out of bone or some revolutionary plastic. This bone-like material was chocolate-brown, and the texture was both bumpy like stucco and smooth like a pearl. I flipped out my favorite blade, which was still rust-free and razor-sharp. Unfortunately, I sliced my finger, too. The knife evoked crystal-clear memories of my father, which were etched like granite in my mind. When my father gave me that knife, he told me it could be mine if I always handled it the way I had been taught. Who knows? Maybe I can give it to my son one day. Maybe he'll discover it one day in his closet, and it will produce similar memories of me.

Jeff McIntosh

General versus Specific Nouns

Understanding the difference between a general noun and a specific noun can help any student writer. You should use specific nouns liberally in observation paragraphs to help the reader form a mental image of the subject being observed.

A general noun names a group or class of people, places, or things. Examples of general nouns are such words as *park, man, child, cat,* and *clothing.* Notice that the word *park* could refer to one of many different parks in your community, county, state, nation, and world. The words *man, child, cat,* and *clothing* similarly represent a general class. In contrast, a specific noun is an exact, sometimes proper, name for a person, place, or thing. In the columns below note the differences between the general nouns and the specific nouns.

General Noun	Specific Noun
park	Yosemite National Park
man	John Smith
child	Stephen Patrick Campbell
cat	Siamese cat
clothing	t-shirt

Notice what a difference the use of specific nouns combined with action verbs and adjectives makes in the following descriptions of a toddler:

General nouns: She started to play by stripping off her **clothes.** She then located a basket of **laundry** and plundered through the **clothes.** One leg at a time she carefully put on her **shorts.** She completed the outfit with a **shirt.**

Specific nouns: She started to play by stripping off her **denim, mid-shin shorts** with a **white, lace-trimmed ruffle** and her **white, midrift tank top.** She then found a basket of **unfolded laundry** and plundered through the clothes until she discovered the ideal **"bum" outfit.** One leg at a time she carefully put on a **navy blue, oversized pair of shorts** with **yellow x's inside mauve squares.** She completed the outfit with a **large, inside-out, grungy, well-worn T-shirt** that hung to her ankles.

Casey Vukcevic

In the following passage the writer uses adjectives, adverbs, action verbs, and specific nouns to invite her reader into her backyard where she is watching an alligator:

Its head lay on the bank while the remainder of its elongated, diamond-shaped body rested in the murky, turtle-infested water. . . . I noticed how the varying shades of browns and blacks changed as the water lapped at its powerful legs and tail. The water seemed desperate to cover the gator's scaly protrusions which have been artistically placed along its muscular body.

Kathy Deist

The above passage is much more effective than if the writer had used general nouns as follows:

Its head lay on the bank while its body rested in the water. I noticed how the shades changed as the water lapped at its powerful body. The water seemed desperate to cover the scales placed along its body.

Revise the following sentences by changing the general nouns (in **bold** print) to specific nouns. You may add adjectives or other descriptive words as well.

EXERCISE 5.5

1. Yesterday I observed a beautiful sunset at the **park.**

   _____

2. The sky was streaked with **color.**

   _____

3. **Birds** flew overhead as their silhouettes stood out against the darkening sky.

   _____

4. Children romped on the **playground equipment.**

_____

5. The light wind gently blew the **trees.**

_____

6. The scent of **flowers** hovered in the air.

_____

7. **People** strolled hand-in-hand along the sidewalks.

_____

8. **Animals** scurried along the ground.

_____

9. I could hear **noises** in the distance, but they did not interrupt my thoughts.

_____

10. I waited a long time as I sat quietly watching the **sight.**

_____

FOCUS ON GRAMMAR

Students who write effective observation paragraphs must be conscious of verb tense. Some students want their readers to join in their observations, so they write about them as if they are happening at the time the observations are being made. These writers use the *present tense* of the verb. Other writers communicate their observations to their readers after they have occurred. These writers use the *past tense.*

Subject–Verb Agreement

The grammatical term *tense* refers to the time of the action expressed in the verb. In the Standard American English (SAE) dialect (see Chapter 1), the prsent tense of the verb has certain characteristics depending on the subject that is used with it. The principle of *subject–verb agreement* states that verbs must agree with their subjects in number.

♦ If the subject is *he, she, it,* or any singular subject, the verb must also be singular (representing one). A singular verb in the third person ends in *-s.* This *-s* ending is referred to as an *-s marker.* The subject and verb in the following sentence agree in number because both are singular.

The **girl** with her bucket full of sand **plays** on the beach.

The subject *girl* is singular, so the present tense verb *plays* ends in -*s*. If you know that the subject is singular and in the third person (not *I* or *you*), read the sentence substituting *he, she,* or *it,* and you will get the correct verb.

The girl plays on the beach.

She plays on the beach.

◆ If the subject is *we, they,* or any plural subject, the verb in the present tense must be plural. Plural verbs do not end in -*s*. The subject and verb are said to *agree* because both are plural (representing more than one).

The **girls** with their buckets full of sand **play** on the beach.

This time the subject *girls* is plural, so the verb *play* does not end in -*s*. If you know that the subject is plural, read the sentence substituting the word *they* for the subject, and you will be able to read the sentence correctly.

They play on the beach . . .

There are no exceptions to the -*s* marker on a third person singular verb. Many students get confused because they associate the letter -*s* with plural words. Plural subjects (unless they are irregular nouns or pronouns) do end in -*s*, but plural verbs do not. The letter -*s* on a verb **always** makes it singular (see Table 5.1).

In Table 5.2, note that first person singular (the subject *I*), second person singular (the subject *you*), and first, second, and third person plural subjects all have present tense verbs that do not end in -*s*. The **only** time the -*s* marker appears on a present tense verb is with a third person, singular subject.

Many students and English teachers alike have wondered why the -*s* marker exists on third person, singular, present-tense verbs. Whatever the reason, the presence of the -*s* marker makes mastering subject–verb agreement difficult for those who are learning English as a second language.

Almost every writer at one time or another has problems with subject–verb agreement when the subject is difficult to find and the correct verb is thus difficult to hear. In these situations students, after hearing the correct answer according to SAE, often exclaim, "That sentence just doesn't sound right!"

TABLE 5.1	**Noun and Present Tense Verb Endings**		
Noun	*Endings*	*Verb*	*Endings*
Singular	Plural	Singular	Plural
-no s	-s	-s (in third person)	-no s
table	*tables*	*is*	*are*

TABLE 5.2	Present Tense Verb Endings		
Singular		**Plural**	
First person	I walk	First person	we walk
Second person	you walk	Second person	you walk
Third person	he, she, it (or any singular subject) walks	Third person	they (or any plural subject) walk

In the following situations the subject is often hard to spot and the correct verb difficult to determine. In every case the verb is in the present tense.

Case 1: When the subject is separated from the verb by one or more phrases, the subject—not the noun in the phrase—determines the verb.

        subject   phrase   phrase   verb

The **students** (in the front row) (of the classroom) **take** good notes.

In the above sentence the subject is *students* because the word *students* answers the question, "Who takes good notes?" The two phrases that come between the subject and the verbs are prepositional phrases (see Chapter 2). Because the subject is plural, the verb *take* does not end in *-s*.

    subject   phrase   verb

One (of the team members) **waits** for the coach.

Here the subject of the sentence is harder to find. Keep in mind that the subject of the sentence will not appear in a prepositional phrase. Therefore, the answer to "Who waits for the coach?" is *one*—not *team members*. Since *one* is singular and in the third person, the verb *waits* ends in the *-s* marker.

    subject   phrase   verb

John (as well as his brothers) **wants** to go with us.

     subject   phrase   verb

His **brothers** (along with John) **want** to go with us.

In the first sentence, the phrase *as well as his brothers* does not affect the verb. However, the placement of the phrase next to the subject makes the correct verb hard to determine. In the second sentence, the phrase *along with John* does not affect the verb.

In all the instances above, the subject, not the noun in the prepositional phrase, determines the verb. This arrangement—**subject (prepositional phrase) verb**—is commonplace in both student and professional writing; thus, it is essential that student writers master this pattern.

Case 2: When the word *and* joins two or more subjects, the subjects are considered plural, and the verb (in the present tense) must also be plural (no *-s*).

subject   +   subject   verb
Laura and Kathy work hard to achieve their goals.

In this example the subject *Laura* is joined with the subject *Kathy* by *and*. The word *and* functions as an addition sign. Therefore, the subjects *Laura and Kathy* are plural. If you substitute the pronoun *they* for the subjects, you can determine that the verb is plural: *They work.*

The same rule applies in the following cases:

Mark and his wife, Gail, enjoy going to the movies.

The **student** in the last seat of the first row **and** the **student** in the first seat of the last row **are** brother and sister.

Caution: Occasionally an exception to this rule occurs when two subjects connected by *and* create a subject that cannot be separated into two units because it acts as an individual subject:

Rock and roll is my favorite type of music.

Bacon and eggs is my family's favorite breakfast.

Case 3: When two or more subjects are joined together by *or, nor, either . . . or,* or *neither . . . nor,* the subject closest to the verb determines whether the verb is singular or plural. If the subject closest to the verb is singular, then the verb is singular (ends in *-s*). If the subject closest to the verb is plural, then the verb is plural (does not end in *-s*).

Jan or her sisters are coming with us.

In this sentence two subjects *Jan* and *sisters* are linked by the word *or.* Since the subject *sisters* is closest to the verb and the word *sisters* is plural, the verb is plural (does not end in *-s*).

However, if the sentence had been written,

Her sisters or Jan is coming with us.

the verb would be singular (with the *-s* marker) since the subject *Jan* is closest to the verb.

The same principle applies to these sentences:

Jan **nor** *her sisters* **are** coming with us.

Her sisters **nor** *Jan* **is** coming with us.

Either Jan **or** *her sisters* **are** coming with us.

Either her sisters **or** *Jan* **is** coming with us.

Neither Jan **nor** *her sisters* **are** coming with us.

Neither her sisters **nor** *Jan* **is** coming with us.

Notice how in each of the above sentences the subject in italics controls whether the verb is singular or plural. While the word *and* between two subjects makes the subjects plural, the use of *or, nor, either . . . or,* or *neither . . . nor* to join two subjects means that only the subject closest to the verb will control the verb.

Case 4: When the subject of the sentence is singular but represents a group of people acting as a whole, the verb is singular. These subjects are called *collective nouns* and include such words as *class, committee, company, crew, family, group, jury,* and *team.*

The **jury** announces the verdict.

The **team** plays tomorrow night for the championship.

The **committee** appoints the chairperson.

The **family** plans to take a three-week vacation.

Case 5: In a sentence beginning with *there* or *here*, the subject following the verb determines whether the verb is singular or plural.

There **go** the **girls.**

Here **is** today's **newspaper.**

The best way to determine the correct verb is to change the sentence so that the subject comes first:

The **girls go** there.

Today's **newspaper is** here.

Caution: Be careful when you begin a sentence with the contraction *there's.* Remember that *there's* stands for *there is.* Even though the sentence *There's the girls* can be acceptable in casual conversation, the sentence should be written this way in Standard American English dialect: *There are the girls.*

Case 6: If a sentence begins with one or more prepositional phrases followed immediately by a verb, the subject following the verb controls whether the verb is singular or plural.

On the wall **are** several **posters** of famous musicians.

Beneath her bed **are** her **shoes,** her **socks,** and her **schoolbooks.**

Underneath the table **is** the **cat** eating leftovers.

The above sentences are said to be *inverted* because the subjects follow the verbs. As in Case 5, the easiest way to get the correct verb is to turn the sentence around so that the subject comes before the verb.

Several **posters** of famous musicians **are** on the wall.

Her **shoes,** her **socks,** and her s**choolbooks are** beneath her bed.

The **cat** eating leftovers **is** underneath the table.

These inverted sentences are commonly found in observation paragraphs. Therefore, recognizing inverted sentence patterns is important.

Case 7: When the subject of the sentence is an indefinite pronoun, the verb is singular or plural depending on which indefinite pronoun is used. The indefinite pronouns listed below are singular.

any**one**	any**body**	
every**one**	every**body**	either (of)
some**one**	some**body**	neither (of)
no **one**	no**body**	each (of)

These pronouns can be easily memorized if you will learn them as they appear above—all the *-one* words, all the *-body* words, and the last three: *either, neither, each*. Also, the word *of* appears following *either, neither,* and *each* because these indefinite pronouns are usually followed by a preposition phrase beginning with *of*. You need to memorize indefinite pronouns because even students who generally use Standard American English dialect have occasional problems with indefinite pronouns used as subjects.

Anyone loves pepperoni pizza.

Anybody loves pepperoni pizza.

Everyone loves pepperoni pizza.

Someone loves pepperoni pizza.

No one loves pepperoni pizza.

Everybody loves pepperoni pizza.

Somebody loves pepperoni pizza.

Nobody loves pepperoni pizza.

Either of the girls **loves** pepperoni pizza.

Neither of the guys **loves** pepperoni pizza.

Each of the children **loves** pepperoni pizza.

Notice how the verb is singular (ends in *-s*) in each of the above sentences. While the *-s* on the first six verbs is easy to hear and to write, it is much more difficult to hear and write the -*s* when the pronoun *either* (of), *neither* (of), or *each* (of) is used as the subject. If you have trouble determining the correct verb, substitute the word *one* for any of the indefinite pronouns above.

One loves pepperoni pizza.

One of the girls **loves** pepperoni pizza.

One of the guys **loves** pepperoni pizza.

One of the children **loves** pepperoni pizza.

The indefinite pronouns, *none* and *some*, are sometimes singular or sometimes plural depending on the context of the sentence:

None of the food **was** left on the plates.

None of the students **come** late to class.

Some of the food **was** left on the plates.

Some of the students **come** late to class.

If you have trouble with *none* or *some*, substitute *no* for *none of the* or omit the words *of the* following the word some:

No food was left on the plates.

No students come late to class.

Some food was left on the plates.

Some students come late to class.

The best way to master subject–verb agreement is practice through your writing. Mastery of subject–verb agreement is essential for all writers who compose for an educated reader. Those readers who use the Standard American English dialect expect to see its correct use by the writers with whom they come in contact.

EXERCISE 5.6

Read the following observation paragraph and look for subject–verb agreement errors. If you see a verb that does not agree with its subject, cross through the verb and write the correct form of the verb.

My fourteen-year-old daughter's bedroom is a colorful mess. Immediately to the left of the door is a yellow hanging rack with a white, shoulder-length purse and a backpack hanging from its knobs. Clothes and games as well as toy boxes is crammed in the closet. Neither the toys nor the clothing are in any apparent order. On one side of the room are a desk and a bookcase. Each of her desk drawers are stuffed with papers.

The bookcase with two rows of books, various magazines and forty-eight paperbacks rest on top of the desk. Her collection of stuffed animals including rabbits, bears, and kangaroos is showcased on top of the bookcase. Papers, pencils, earrings, and other junk litters her desk top.

How many subject–verb agreement errors did you find in Exercise 5.6? There are 5 errors. Below is the rest of the observation paragraph. Follow the directions for Exercise 5.6.

EXERCISE 5.7

Adjacent to the desk area is her single bed with a light oak spindle headboard. Geometrical designs in hot neon colors decorates her white background bedspread. A seven-inch, hot pink troll doll and a white, lace-trimmed heart pillow is visible at the top of the bed near the headboard. Her five-drawer chest beside her bed is stuffed with jeans, T-shirts, socks—all hanging out of the drawers. A black drawing table with an adjustable light and a two-drawer nightstand makes up the rest of the room. Neither the top of her drawing table nor the surface of the nightstand are clear. On the top of the nightstand is the cage for her pet cockatiel, Tweeters. The contents of Tweeter's cage litters the nightstand's surface as well as the dull, brown carpet. There's school awards and posters of a famous cat hanging on the off-white wall. My daughter's room is never very clean, but it is definitely colorful.

Read the following passages carefully, and look for subject–verb agreement errors. If you see a verb that does not agree with its subject, cross through the verb and write in the correct form of the verb.

EXERCISE 5.8

The photograph of two children dressed in Halloween costumes rest on my bedside table. Both of the children appear to be girls, one about 7 and the other about 4. On the left side of the photograph stand the older girl dressed in a clown's costume. The costume consist of a multi-colored clown's wig, large, blue clown glasses, a yellow and red polka-dot bow tie, and a multi-colored harlequin costume. Not one of the items appear out of place. Her face is full of expression as she poses for the camera. Her right hand rest on her hip. On the right is the other child dressed like a bunny. Pink bunny ears cover the top of her head. A black mask as well as a pink mask with bunny teeth cover her face. She is dressed in a white leotard with a white bunny tail. Each of these children appear happy. There's many objects hanging on the wall in the background including a clock. This picture, however, is timeless.

Follow the directions for Exercise 5.8.

EXERCISE 5.9

The red sports car is intriguing as it sits in the car lot. Its sleek exterior design and its aerodynamic style attracts my attention. Each of its exterior features are graceful including its wide tires with shiny aluminum wheels and sculpted, curved lines. The tinted windows as well as the glistening paint adds to the sporty effect. In the interior is many attractive features including roominess in both the front and the back. A six-footer would have no trouble comfortably driving this car, and three screaming kids could easily fit in the back seat. The leather-covered seats and precision dashboard add to the beauty of the interior. The specs on this car points to its potential power on the road. A 210-horsepower, 24-valve, V-6 engine offers power while front-passenger air bags and anti-lock brakes provides safety. Unfortunately, on the window is the prices for all the special options this car offers its lucky owner. This sleek beauty along with all its attractions is a treat for the eye but not for the wallet.

Past Tense

A verb expressing action that has already occurred is said to be in the *past tense*. The narrative paragraph you wrote in Chapter 4 was probably written using past tense verbs. Past tense verbs are easily recognizable because most of them end in *-ed*. These verbs with *-ed* past tense endings are called *regular verbs*. As shown in Table 5.3, the endings of past tense verbs are not affected by the number of the subject. If the subject is singular, plural, first person, second person, or third person, the ending is still *-ed*.

Another form of a verb, called the *past participle*, is used with a helping verb, *have* or *has*. When you use this verb form, the *-s* marker reappears on the helping verb *has* in the third person singular, but the *-ed* ending appears consistently on the main verb.

Unfortunately, not all past tense verbs and past participles end in *-ed*. Some verbs, called *irregular verbs*, dramatically change their spelling when they appear in past tense or the past participle form.

The most common irregular verb is the verb *be*. You should familiarize yourself with this verb's parts since it is the most commonly used irregular verb in the English language.

An irregular verb commonly used in observation paragraphs is the verb *lie* (meaning "to recline"). Table 5.8 shows the past tense of the verb *lie*.

TABLE 5.3	Present Tense Endings — Regular Verbs		
Singular		**Plural**	
First person	I walked	First person	we walked
Second person	you walked	Second person	you walked
Third person	he, she, it (or any singular subject) walked	Third person	they (or any plural subject) walked

TABLE 5.4   Past Participle Verb Form

Singular		Plural	
First person	I have walked	First person	I have walked
Second person	you have walked	Second person	you have walked
Third person	he, she, it (or any singular subject) has walked	Third person	they have walked

TABLE 5.5   Present Tense of Verb *Be*

Singular		Plural	
First person	I am	First person	we are
Second person	you are	Second person	you are
Third person	he, she, it (or any singular subject) is	Third person	they (or any plural subject) are

TABLE 5.6   Past Tense of Verb *Be*

Singular		Plural	
First person	I was	First person	we were
Second person	you were	Second person	you were
Third person	he, she, it (or any singular subject) was	Third person	they (or any plural subject) were

TABLE 5.7   Past Participle of Verb *Be*

Singular		Plural	
First person	I have been	First person	we have been
Second person	you have been	Second person	you have been
Third person	he, she, it (or any singular subject) has been	Third person	they (or any plural subject) have been

TABLE 5.8	Past Tense of Verb *Lie*		
Singular		**Plural**	
First person	I lay	First person	we lay
Second person	you lay	Second person	you lay
Third person	he, she, it (or any singular subject) lay	Third person	they (or any plural subject) lay

Today Ruth **lies** in the sun working on her tan. **(present tense)**

Yesterday Ruth **lay** in the sun for an hour as she worked on her tan. **(past tense)**

The verb of the first sentence *lies* is in the present tense. The verb of the second sentence *lay* is in the past tense. The past participle form of *lie* is a surprise to many students (Table 5.9).

Thus, in SAE dialect the following sentences are correct:

I **have lain** on the couch every afternoon this week.

Every day Ruth **has lain** in the sun to work on her tan.

Caution: Many students confuse the present tense verb form *lie* ("to recline") with the present tense verb form *lay* ("to place"). In casual conversation, a person may say, "I want to *lay* down for a nap." However, the sentence should not be written that way. The correct SAE form is, "I want to *lie* down for a nap."

One way to clear up the confusion is to remember that the present tense verb form *lay* will always be followed by a noun (in the first example, *wallet*, and in the second example, *books*):

Every night he **lays** his wallet on his nightstand.

Today Beth **lays** the books carefully on the desk.

TABLE 5.9	Past Participle of Verb *Lie*		
Singular		**Plural**	
First person	I have lain	First person	we have lain
Second person	you have lain	Second person	you have lain
Third person	he, she, it (or any singular subject) has lain	Third person	they (or any plural subject) have lain

TABLE 5.10	Past Tense of Verb *Lay*		
Singular		**Plural**	
First person	I laid	First person	we laid
Second person	you laid	Second person	you laid
Third person	he, she, it (or any singular subject) laid	Third person	they (or any plural subject) laid

Another way to avoid this confusion is to check by substituting the present tense form of the verb *place* for the verb *lay:*

Every night he **places** his wallet on his nightstand.

Today Beth **places** the books carefully on the desk.

Table 5.10 shows the past tense forms of the verb *lay:*

Last night he **laid** his wallet on his nightstand.

Yesterday she **laid** the books carefully on the desk.

Notice that in the above sentences the verb *placed* can be substituted for the past tense verb *laid.* You can always check your use of the verb *laid* by using this substitution.

In Table 5.11 you will see that the past tense form and past participle form are the same word *laid.*

The sentences below illustrate the use of the past participle form:

Every night he **has laid** his wallet on his nightstand.

Every day she **has laid** the books carefully on the desk. (Think "Every day she *has placed* the books carefully on the desk.")

The verbs, *be, lie,* and *lay* are just three examples of potentially troublesome irregular verbs. If you are unsure of the correct form for the past tense

TABLE 5.11	Past Participle of Verb *Lay*		
Singular		**Plural**	
First person	I have laid	First person	we have laid
Second person	you have laid	Second person	you have laid
Third person	he, she, it (or any singular subject) has laid	Third person	they (or any plural subject) have laid

and past participle of an irregular form, look up the present tense form in a dictionary to find the past tense and past participle forms. If you do not see these forms given, then you can assume the verb is regular and adds *-ed* in the past tense and past participle form. After you have found the verb in the dictionary, you can use the following sentences to be sure you understand the use of each verb part:

Today I _____ . **(present tense)**

Today she _____ . **(present tense**—add *-s* marker for third person)

Yesterday I _____. **(past tense)**

Every day I have _____. **(past participle)**

Every day she has _____. **(past participle)**

EXERCISE 5.10

Use your dictionary to locate the past tense and past participle forms of the following irregular verbs.

		Past Tense	**Past Participle**
1.	arise	_____	_____
2.	beat	_____	_____
3.	burst	_____	_____
4.	dive	_____	_____
5.	fling	_____	_____
6.	raise	_____	_____
7.	rise	_____	_____
8.	spring	_____	_____
9.	swim	_____	_____
10.	tear	_____	_____

Shifts in Tense

Writers of effective paragraphs, including effective observation paragraphs, maintain consistent verb tense. They know that sudden changes (shifts) from present tense to past tense or from past tense to present tense can confuse the reader. Many writers discover that they must reread their paragraphs several times in order to locate tense shifts, which happen easily. Editing your paragraphs for tense shifts will strengthen your knowledge of verb forms.

In the following paragraph, change all verbs to the present tense. Remember to check for the *-s* marker if the verb is third person singular.

In my son's aquarium one particular fish, known as Bluey, provided a fascinating show of beauty and awe-inspiring violence. He was a betta splendons, commonly known as a Siamese fighting fish. His color was a vivid blue with imperceptible, iridescent gold flecks. The blue faded to a deep purple in the valley at the base of his tail. His scales were so tiny that he appeared cloaked in a soft, velvety robe. Bluey's body was less than an inch-and-a-half long; his tail was another inch-and-a-half of veil-like fins. These fins hung, when he was still, like the wet hair of a mermaid. This tail was the most remarkable trait of a betta. Like a crepe paper streamer, it floated behind him as an afterthought. As he rose toward the top of the tank, the light illuminated his tail, and it changed to a deep, blood red. It was not as long as it once was, having been nipped away by a challenging subordinate. Bluey's head was shaped like the prow of a graceful sailing ship of old. His eyes appeared to be small, dark buttons attached to either side of his head. His tidy mouth was turned up in indignation—a princely pout. The milky-white area was separated by the start of his gills, which spread apart into a V-shape and disappeared into black on the lower side of his head. Immediately behind each gill was a small, fan-shaped fin, which appeared to be the fish's main source of propulsion. As he swam, the fins moved back and forth with a twisting motion to the top and bottom and appeared translucent, except for the slight bit of blue that trimmed the edges. Just behind and below these fins were two long strands of midnight-blue fins that resemble a mustache. This refined, elegant fish ruled the tank.

Debra Bates

In the paragraph below change all present tense verbs to the past tense.

As I write this paragraph, my two-year-old cat, Sammy, lies on the floor beside me. I lay him on the floor because I know he wants to sit on my lap, but I do not want to write with a cat in my lap. He lies on his back with his two white paws straight in the air. His tail lies between his legs and rests on the carpet. From my desk I see his white fur exposed on his chest. Then I notice that the rest of his body is black except for his front paws and a triangle above his nose. Suddenly his ears perk up, and he flips his body over, stands up, and runs down the stairs. For him, this observation is definitely finished.

Sentence Combining

A series of short, choppy sentences can ruin the effect of an observation. Suppose Debra had written about her son's fish:

> The area was below his mouth. The area was white. The color was like milk. The area was separated by the start of his gills. The gills spread apart into a V-shape. They disappeared into black. The black was on the lower side of his head.

instead of

> The milky-white area below his mouth was separated by the start of his gills, which spread apart into a V-shape and disappeared into the back of his head.

Like Debra, a good writer combines ideas by using adjectives, phrases, and the principles of coordination and subordination (see Chapter 4).

EXERCISE 5.13

Combine each group of sentences below into one sentence. Use adjectives, appositive phrases, coordination, and/or subordination to write each sentence as clearly as possible. Keep in mind that several combinations are possible. Use the first example as a model.

1. The lizard in the window is a male.
   The lizard has a patch.
   The patch is on his throat.
   The patch is bright.
   The patch is orange.
   The patch is shaped like a fan.

   The male lizard in the window has a bright, orange, fan-shaped patch on his throat.

2. The other lizard is female.
   The female has a few small spots.
   The spots are white.
   The female has stripes.
   The stripes are thin.
   The stripes are white.
   The stripes run down her back.

   _____

   _____

3. The male extends his patch.
   The male needs to show dominance.
   The male wants to attract the female.

   _____

   _____

4. The female darts at the male.
   The female dashes back to cover.
   The female warns the male of an intruder.
   The female signals the male.
   The female is in the mood for love.

   _____

   _____

5. Each lizard's foot has five toes.
   Three toes face forward.
   Two toes face backward.
   Each foot acts separately.
   Each foot balances the lizard.

   _____

   _____

6. Each lizard has a tiny hole.
   The hole is like a tunnel.
   The tunnel goes through its head.

   _____

   _____

7. An observer can see the hole.
   The observer must sit very still.
   The lizard must pass between the observer and the light source.

   _____

   _____

8. These lizards are quick.
   These lizards are light.
   These lizards are fun to watch.
   These lizards are reminiscent of dinosaurs.
   The dinosaurs are mysterious.

   _____

   _____

Adapted from an observation by Mary Fowlds

FOCUS ON PUNCTUATION

Hyphens with Compound Adjectives

Because observation paragraphs involve much descriptive writing, you will need to use many adjectives to enliven your writing. Some of these adjectives will likely be compound—that is, made up of more than one word. When these compound adjectives appear before a noun, a hyphen is used to separate them.

For example, in Exercise 5.9 the writer uses the phrase "*awe-inspiring violence.*" *Awe-inspiring* is a compound adjective. A good way to test for a compound adjective is to see if the meaning changes if one of the parts is omitted. The phrase "awe violence" does not make sense, nor does the "inspiring violence." The words *awe* and *inspiring* are dependent upon each other and are hyphenated to form a compound adjective. The same test applies to these compound adjectives also found in Exercise 5.11:

veil-like fins

fan-shaped fins

midnight-blue fins

and to these compound adjectives in Exercise 5.4:

dust-covered boxes

bone-like material

rust-free

razor-sharp

crystal-clear

Hyphens are also used to write out numbers between twenty-one and ninety-nine and some amounts. In Exercise 5.6, the author refers to her fourteen-year-old daughter, and in Exercise 5.11, the writer refers to the fish's body length of an inch-and-a-half. Here are some other examples:

one-hundred twenty-two miles long

one-quarter inch wide

If you are uncertain when to use a hyphen, a good dictionary can help.

Caution: Do not confuse a hyphen with a dash. A dash (—) is longer than a hyphen (-) and is used for a different purpose (see Chapter 6).

EXERCISE 5.14

In the following observation paragraph, insert hyphens as needed.

As I watch two fourteen year old boys playing together in a backyard swimming pool, I am reminded of the bottle nose dolphins that play along the shoreline. There really is a sense of innocence that surrounds their play. The boys are both about five feet, four inches tall and weigh approximately one hundred twenty five pounds. They have different coloring. One boy has golden brown hair while the second boy has chestnut brown hair and almost black brown eyes. They are definitely boys; their straight, up and down shapes have no curves. As I sit watching, the boys pretend they are dinosaurs from millions of years ago. Watching the boys cavort in the pool reminds me of my own childhood and the hours my siblings and I spent in our parents' backyard swimming pool. It is hard to watch a child become an adolescent. I wonder if the two boys would be embarrassed if their peers saw them pretending to be dinosaurs. The innocence I see in their play will not be there for long. I love the innocence children house within themselves.

—Dorie Wilcox

Insert hyphens as needed.

EXERCISE 5.15

Both girls had long, brown hair. One was wearing a solid, forest green shirt that only covered about two thirds of her upper body. She had a matching scrunchy holding her hair in a ponytail along with matching colored socks and nail polish. I doubt that her neon orange pager was in her color scheme when she spent two hours staring in the closet trying to figure out what would look best on her five feet, eight inch, one hundred and thirty five pound body. The other girl wore white tennis shoes with loose blue jeans. She had on a huge, multi colored shirt that looked as if she had just been in a paint fight with someone and apparently lost. Hanging from her ears were huge, lime green loops that looked like trial issues of the hula hoop. My overall impression of her was that she looked as if her friend had decided to go out and stopped by to see if she wanted to go. She probably took five minutes to pick up the shirt and jeans off the floor, put them on, look in the mirror, and say, "What do you think?" to her friend.

—Andy Warren

Student Samples—Observation

A Cowboy and His Horse

The 26-inch tall rocking horse anxiously awaits his favorite cowboy's arrival. At the top of his head is a wavy black mane. His pointy, black felt ears stand straight like devil horns. Under his ears lie four long eyelashes resting on oval white and black eyes. Tucked underneath the silver-tacked black harness in his bright red mouth.

➡

His red felt saddle with silver tacks softly cushions his back. His natural, pine-colored, 16-inch long body ends with his five-inch black yarn tail. Resting on the 30½ inch rocker are his four 9-inch legs and black hooves. Along with the two handles on his head he also has a footrest on his right and left side. His favorite cowboy, Evan, climbs on and grabs the black leather reins. As they rock back and forth, Evan clinches the handles as if he fears for his life. Then Evan releases his grip to wave to his best cowgirl, Grandma. All along, the horse's eyes are wide open as he's enjoying Evan's ride. Now it's time for Evan to turn in for the night. The horse is sad to see his favorite cowboy leave, but he knows they have many more trails to rock.

—Michele Stimpson

A Quiet Place

As I make the turn into the small park and leave the rush hour traffic behind, I find the contrast striking. A different world is nestled here in the midst of the city—a place of quietness and beauty. My eyes rest upon the various hues of green and brown bordered by the clear blue sky and water—a portrait of perfection. The sound of children laughing mingles with the chirping birds as I make my way past the playground. As the children climb like little monkeys on the steel equipment, the squirrels play in nature's playgrounds, jumping from limb to limb, tree to tree, seemingly defying gravity. Motorboats sound in the distance as the adults choose the water for their play area. A tiny, gray kitten peeks curiously around a tree to check out the activity. I make my way to the place of the "dancing trees." Here, on a hill overlooking the water, is a gorgeous collection of live oak trees, their branches mingling and intertwined. As though on stage, they stand waiting as the gentle breeze signals the beginning of their choreographed routine for me, their captive audience. The pale green Spanish moss drapes from their darkened limbs like a delicate lace shawl swirling in the breeze. The sun filters through their hair like strands of gold. Butterflies flutter between them, joining in nature's dance. What a beautiful scene—man, animal, and nature all in one accord!

—Joyce Mauge

FOCUS ON PEER REVIEW

After you write your experimental draft, you will be ready to participate in peer review. As you work with your peer reviewer, answer the following questions:

1. Does the topic sentence of your paragraph focus on a particular subject for observation?

2. Does the topic sentence state why the observation is memorable?

3. Is the topic sentence interesting to your reader? Why or why not?

4. Does the writer include enough supporting details in the body of the paragraph so that the reader can share the observation?

5. Does the writer include any information that is not directly related to the focus of the paragraph?

6. Does the concluding sentence reinforce the focus of the observation?

7. List the transitional expressions the writer uses.

8. List four or five sensory details that the writer uses.

9. List five or six specific nouns that the writer uses.

10. Which verb tense does the writer use? Is the verb tense consistent throughout the essay?

11. Are there any choppy sentences that could be combined?

12. Note any misspelled words or punctuation problems.

13. What I like best about this paragraph is _____.

14. The writer could improve this paragraph by _____.

Please let me What is going on.

Use the student samples and the advice of your peer reviewer to revise your observation paragraph before submitting it to your instructor. Keep in mind the techniques discussed in this chapter. Using sensory details and specific nouns, editing for consistency in verb tense, combining sentences for variety, and punctuating compound adjectives for hyphens will show the reader that you are willing to work hard to keep your reader's attention.

The power of observation is your window to the world. The ability to observe what is around you, to shape those observations in words, and to share these observations with others will not only enhance your intellectual growth but will also prepare you for future challenges in the academic and professional worlds.

Writers as Spiders

The World Wide Web features many colorful graphics. These graphics have made possible several virtual art museums. You can practice your observation skills at these sites.

Web Exercise

If you are looking for a topic for your observation paragraph, consider a visit to one of these museums. For a list of several museum sites, see

http://www.biostat.washington.edu/fun/art.html

One of the most fascinating of these sites is

http://mistral.culture.fr/louvre/louvrea.htm

Before you set out on your tour of this site, be sure to choose English (or some other language) for your guide. As you tour the various collections of the Louvre, choose one of the objects of art as the focus of your paragraph. Then click on the work of art to enlarge it on your screen. Consider the following questions:

1. What type of art is presented in this graphic?

2. Who is the artist?

3. When was the work of art created?

4. What is the subject of this work of art?

5. What is the overall shape of the work? What other shapes are present?

6. What colors are predominant? What other colors are used?

7. What do you find interesting about the work? What overall impression does this work of art convey?

Additional Help

For additional help writing observation paragraphs, consult

http://web.uvic.ca/hrd/OLCourse/Unit_3/descrip1.htm

For a sample of descriptive writing, see

http://www.lbcc.cc.or.vs/der-studies/assignments/describe.html

On-line writing labs feature helpful handouts and exercises on verb use. For subject–verb agreement (including an exercise), visit

http://myst.hunter.cuny.edu/~rwcenter/writing/on-line/sva.html

For verb tense, try

http://www.cc.emony.edu/ENGLISH/WC/verbconsist.html
http://owl.english.purdue.edu/Files/72.html

If you want additional information and exercises, use a search engine to access other sites.

CHAPTER 6

Focus on Comparison/Contrast

FOCUS ON PURPOSE

The ability to compare and/or contrast people, ideas, and things is a critical analytical skill—one you use daily. When you compare, you look for similarities between two or more people, ideas, and things. When you contrast, you examine differences. For instance, when you leave a movie theater after seeing a horror movie with your friends, you will probably compare/contrast the movie with other horror movies you have seen. Or when you read a novel, you can compare/contrast the novel to other novels the author has written. As a consumer you face comparisons/contrasts daily as you shop for groceries, clothing, and other consumer goods.

Being able to compare/contrast is an essential skill for classroom success. To be a successful math student, you must be able to recognize similarities and differences between math problems. If you learn how to work one problem and see another problem that is similar, you will probably be able to work that problem as well. English teachers often call on students to compare/contrast. In a literature class, for example, you may be asked to compare/contrast two poems or two short stories. The skills of comparison/contrast will help you recognize patterns you can apply to your academic work.

In the business world the ability to compare/contrast is equally important. Supervisors must compare/contrast employees when they decide who deserves a promotion. Businesses that wish to relocate must compare/contrast the advantages and disadvantages of various sites. Purchasing agents must compare/contrast various types of business equipment.

Comparing/contrasting techniques help college students, consumers, and businessmen and women alike to make choices critical to their future. This chapter will assist you in developing your ability to compare and/or contrast.

FOCUS ON CHOOSING A TOPIC

Here are some possible topics for your comparison/contrast paragraph:

- Two restaurants
- Two friends
- Two family members
- Two movies
- Two cars
- Two places you have lived
- Two classes
- Two vacation spots
- Two jobs
- Two supervisors
- Two forms of exercise
- Two pets

As you choose a topic for your comparison/contrast paragraph, you must establish a fair basis for comparison—that is, the two subjects that you are comparing/contrasting must be in the same general class. For example, comparing/contrasting a subcompact and a luxury sedan is not fair. Neither is comparing/contrasting a fast-food restaurant to a steak house. Comparing/contrasting two subcompacts, two luxury sedans, two fast-food restaurants, or two steak houses would be more effective.

FOCUS ON ORGANIZING

The Topic Sentence

After you have chosen a topic and established a fair basis for comparison/contrast, it is helpful to think through how you are going to develop the paragraph before you write your topic sentence. Are you going to focus on the similarities (compare) or the differences (contrast)? Although it is possible to write a paragraph that compares *and* contrasts two things, this chapter will limit its discussion to comparing *or* contrasting.

As you write your topic sentence, be sure that you identify clearly the two things you are comparing or contrasting. Otherwise, your topic sentence will be out of focus. You will also want to include the specific feature or features you are comparing or contrasting. For this reason, you may want to brainstorm, cluster, or freewrite before you write your topic sentence.

Here are some examples of unfocused topic sentences:

There are many similarities between my brother and me. **(Comparison)**

My brother and I are different in so many ways. **(Contrast)**

In the above topic sentences, the reader has only a general idea about how the paragraph will progress because the writer has failed to provide any specific sense of direction. The following topic sentences are much clearer:

My brother and I share a love for the outdoors. **(Comparison)**

My brother and I have different spending habits. **(Contrast)**

Because the topic sentence presents a clear focus, the reader is confident of the direction the paragraph will take.

EXERCISE 6.1

Read each of the following topic sentences. If you think the topic sentence is unfocused, then rewrite it to sharpen the focus. If you think the topic sentence is focused clearly, write **OK**.

1. There are many differences between my present and my former jobs.

   _____

   _____

2. My reading teacher and my English teacher are similar in appearance.

   _____

   _____

3. Honeymoon Beach and Fort Beach both offer a variety of recreational activities.

   _____

   _____

4. Two fine Tex-Mex restaurants, Taco House and Casa Manana, have similar decor.

   _____

   _____

5. My two sisters are as different as they can be.

   _____

   _____

The Supporting Details

After you have written a topic sentence identifying the two subjects you are comparing or contrasting, you are ready to add the supporting details in the body of the paragraph. At this point you must choose the characteristics you will use to compare or contrast your two subjects. In order to avoid confusing

My Brother	Me
gardening	gardening
vegetable garden	vegetable garden
flower garden	flower garden
summer activities	summer activities
swimming	swimming
boating	boating
winter activities	winter activities
skiing	skiing
ice skating	ice skating

Figure 6.1 Possible supporting points

the reader and to establish a fair comparison, you must use the same points to compare or contrast your two subjects. Then you will need details to support each of your points and demonstrate to your reader your knowledge of both subjects.

Some students use a chart to list possible supporting points. For instance, Figure 6.1 for a comparison paragraph develops the topic sentence, *My brother and I share a love for the outdoors.*

Using this chart will help you see your points of comparison clearly. Next, two different patterns are available to choose from to arrange the ideas listed in the chart:

- Block pattern
- Point-by-point pattern

Block Pattern for Comparison Paragraphs

The first method is called the *block pattern*. Using this pattern, you discuss all your points about your first subject (hereafter called **X**) and then you compare your second (**Y**), using the same points in the same order. The organizational pattern is shown in Figure 6.2.

Figure 6.3 shows the block pattern completed with more detailed information.

Notice how each point of comparison for **X** is also a point of comparison for **Y**. It is critical that comparisons between two subjects be made using the same points. Otherwise, the comparison between **X** and **Y** will be unbalanced.

Below is a sample comparison paragraph using the block method.

My brother and I share a love for the outdoors. Every spring my brother plants a vegetable garden full of tomatoes, green beans, and corn. Outside his front door is a flower garden with perennials and annuals. His favorite flowers are salvia, hollyhock, and periwinkle. In the summer my brother leaves his garden and heads for the beach.

```
Topic sentence
        X
                first point of comparison
                        details
                second point of comparison
                        details
                third point of comparison
                        details
        Y

                first point of comparison
                        details
                second point of comparison
                        details
                third point of comparison
                        details
Concluding sentence
```

Figure 6.2   Block pattern for comparison paragraph

```
Topic sentence
        X = my brother
                gardening
                        vegetable garden
                        flower garden
                summer activities
                        swimming
                        boating
                winter activities
                        skiing
                        ice skating
        Y = me
                gardening
                        vegetable garden
                        flower garden
                summer activities
                        swimming
                        boating
                winter activities
                        skiing
                        ice skating
Concluding sentence
```

Figure 6.3   Block pattern completed with comparison points

He swims in the ocean for exercise and recreation. Whenever he can, he takes out his sailboat for a cruise. Not even the cold winter weather keeps him from a life of outdoor activity. He takes regular ski trips. When he tires of skiing, he finds a frozen pond for ice skating. Like my brother, I plant vegetable and flower gardens. I love a wide variety of flowering plants including my brother's favorite flowers— salvia, hollyhock, and periwinkle. I, too, love the beach. Swimming is relaxing and takes me away from my everyday stresses. I like to feel the wind in my face as I cruise on a sailboat. In the winter I join my brother whenever I can on his ski trips. I have even tried ice skating though I have fallen many times. I am glad that my brother and I both appreciate the joys of outdoor activity.

Point-by-Point Pattern for Comparison Paragraphs

Some writers prefer a point-by-point arrangement for comparison paragraphs, as illustrated by Figure 6.4. Figure 6.5 illustrates a completed point-by-point comparison.

Following Figure 6.5 is a sample comparison paragraph on the same subject using the point-by-point method.

My brother and I share a love for the outdoors. We both enjoy gardening. Every spring my brother plants a vegetable garden full of tomatoes, green beans, and corn. I plant a vegetable garden each spring as well. We also grow perennials and annuals such as salvia, hollyhocks, and periwinkle. Each of us looks forward to summers filled with outdoor activities. In the summer my brother leaves his garden and heads for the beach. He swims for exercise and recreation. When he can, he takes out his sailboat for a cruise. I, too, love the beach. Swimming is relaxing and takes me away from my everyday stresses. I like to feel the wind in my face as I cruise on a sailboat.

Topic sentence
    first point of comparison
        X (details)
        Y (details)
    second point of comparison
        X (details)
        Y (details)
    third point of comparison
        X (details)
        Y (details)
Concluding sentence

Figure 6.4 Point-by-point pattern for comparison paragraph

Topic sentence
    gardening
        my brother (vegetable, flower)
        me (vegetable, flower)
    summer activities
        my brother (swimming, boating)
        me (swimming, boating)
    winter activities
        my brother (skiing, ice skating)
        me (skiing, ice skating)
Concluding sentence

Figure 6.5   Point-by-point pattern completed with comparison points

Even the cold winter does not keep us indoors. My brother takes regular ski trips, and I join him whenever I can. When he tires of skiing, he finds a frozen pond for ice skating. I have even tried ice skating though I have fallen many times. I am glad that my brother and I both appreciate the joys of outdoor activity.

Block Pattern for Contrast Paragraphs

Figure 6.6 shows how to use the block method for a contrast paragraph. Figure 6.7 shows a block pattern for a paragraph contrasting my spending habits and my brother's. The writer developed this contrast paragraph using the block method shown in Figure 6.7.

My brother and I have different spending habits. My brother is an impulse buyer. When he shops for groceries, he never carries a shopping list or coupons. He just buys whatever looks good to him that day. He loves to buy electronic gadgets such as computerized calendars and telephone directories, but he never compares prices at various stores. When he is in the mood for the latest in electronics, he buys without worrying. He shops for clothes the same way. He does not have any overall wardrobe plan, and he never even looks at the price tag. He figures if he likes the clothes, the price should not matter. On the other hand, I am a classic bargain shopper. Unlike my brother, I never enter a grocery store without a shopping list and my coupon collection. I do not share my brother's interest in electronic gadgets, but even if I did, I would never purchase one without comparing the price from at least three different stores. When I shop for clothes, I know my wardrobe needs and buy accordingly. However, I rarely pay full price; I always head for the sales racks. I cannot understand how we could be raised by the same parents and have such varying spending habits.

Topic sentence
    X
        first point of contrast
           details
        second point of contrast
           details
        third point of contrast
           details
    Y
        first point of contrast
           details
        second point of contrast
           details
        third point of contrast
           details
Concluding sentence

Figure 6.6 Block pattern for contrast paragraphs

Topic sentence
    X = my brother, impulse buyer
        groceries
           no shopping list
           no coupons
        electronics
           latest gadgets
           no price comparison
        clothing
           no wardrobe plan
           price not a problem
    Y = me
        groceries
           shopping list
           coupons
        electronics
           no interest in gadgets
           price comparison
        clothing
           wardrobe plan
           sales only
Concluding sentence

Figure 6.7 Block pattern completed with contrasting points

```
        Topic sentence
              first point of contrast
                    X (details)
                    Y (details)
              second point of contrast
                    X (details)
                    Y (details)
              third point of contrast
                    X (details)
                    Y (details)
        Concluding sentence
```

Figure 6.8   Point-by-point pattern for contrast paragraphs

Point-by-Point Pattern for Contrast Paragraphs

Like comparison paragraphs, contrast paragraphs can be developed using a point-by-point pattern as shown in Figure 6.8.

The author then developed a plan (Figure 6.9) to contrast her spending habits to her brother's.

The following paragraph is developed point-by-point using the plan below in Figure 6.9.

My brother and I have different spending habits. This difference is apparent in the grocery store. When my brother shops for groceries, he never carries a shopping list or coupons. He just buys what looks good to him that day. However, when I enter the grocery stores, my shopping list and coupons are always with me. Our attitude toward buying electronic gadgets differs as well. My brother loves to buy electronic gadgets such as calendars and telephone directories, but he never compares

```
Topic sentence
      grocery shopping
            my brother (no shopping list, no coupons)
            me (shopping list, coupons)
      electronics
            my brother (latest gadgets, no price comparisons)
            me (little interest in gadgets, price comparison)
      clothing
            my brother (no wardrobe plan, price not an issue)
            me (wardrobe plan, sales racks)
```

Figure 6.9   Point-by-point pattern completed with contrasting points

prices at various stores. I, on the other hand, rarely buy electronic gadgets. When I do, I never purchase one without comparing the prices from at least three different stores. We do not approach shopping for clothes the same way either. When my brother shops for clothes, he does not have any overall wardrobe plan, and he never even looks at the price tag. He figures if he likes the clothes, the price should not matter. Unlike my brother, I know my wardrobe needs and buy clothes accordingly. However, I rarely pay full price; I always head for the sales racks. I cannot understand how my brother, the impulse shopper, and I, the bargain hunter, could be raised in the same family and have such varying spending habits.

The decision to use the block method or the point-by-point method is the author's. Sometimes one method fits the main idea of the paragraph better than the other. What is most important is that you develop your paragraph with sufficient supporting details that are clearly related to the topic sentence.

The Concluding Sentence

As in all paragraphs, the concluding sentence of a comparison/contrast paragraph should reinforce the main idea. In the earlier comparison paragraph, the concluding sentence

> I am glad that my brother and I both appreciate the joys of outdoor activity.

reinforces the topic sentence

> My brother and I share a love for the outdoors.

However, in some contrast paragraphs, the concluding sentence often does more than restate the main idea. Instead, the concluding sentence states the writer's preference for **X** or **Y**. For example, the concluding sentence of the contrast paragraph could have been:

> When I get my credit card bill in the mail each month, I am glad that I am a bargain shopper—not an impulse buyer like my brother.

In any case, the concluding sentence should end the paragraph on a strong note.

FOCUS ON TRANSITION

When the reader reads your comparison/contrast paragraph, he or she cannot see your plan for the paragraph. Readers rely on transitional words and phrases to guide them through the paragraph's supporting details. Effective transition is especially critical for comparison/contrast paragraphs because you are discussing two people, ideas, or things, and your reader must be clear about when you are moving from discussing one to discussing the other.

When you write a comparison paragraph, these transitional expressions are helpful: *also, too, in the same way, similarly, likewise, in like manner, like* **X . . . Y.** If you are using the block method, provide a transitional expression when you move from **X** to **Y**:

Like my brother, I plant vegetable and flower gardens.

You can also use a transitional expression when you use the point-by-point method and move from **X** to **Y**:

I, **too,** love the beach.

These transitional expressions are useful when you write a contrast paragraph: *however, nevertheless, on the other hand, in contrast, to the contrary, unlike* **X . . . Y,** *conversely.* Again, when you are using the block pattern, provide a transitional word or phrase when you move from **X** to **Y**:

On the other hand, I am a classic bargain shopper.

Once you finish discussing **X,** you can make references back to **X** as you discuss **Y**:

Unlike my brother, I never enter a grocery store without a shopping list and my coupon collection.

In a point-by-point contrast paragraph, you can also use a transition as you move from **X** to **Y**:

I, **on the other hand,** rarely buy electronic gadgets. . . .

Unlike my brother, I know my wardrobe needs. . . .

Caution: The subordinating conjunction *whereas* has the same meaning as *on the other hand* and is often used for transition in contrast paragraphs. Because *whereas* begins a dependent clause, this clause must be connected to an independent clause, or a fragment will occur.

Correct: My brother loves to buy electronic gadgets whereas I rarely buy them.

Incorrect: My brother loves to buy electronic gadgets. Whereas I rarely buy them.

In both comparison and contrast paragraphs, you can use these transitions when you move from one point of comparison/contrast to the other: *also, then, in addition, moreover, furthermore, additionally.*

Your proficiency in using transitional words and phrases will strengthen your comparison/contrast paragraph's impression on your reader.

In the paragraphs below, write an appropriate transitional expression in the blanks.

Two of the city's renowned Chinese restaurants—China Inn and Peking House—feature similar interior decor. When a customer is seated by China Inn's friendly hostess, his or her eye is drawn immediately to the starched linen tablecloths, bright red cloth napkins, and beautiful flower arrangements that adorn each table. _____, Peking House's customers are treated to lovely table settings. _____, the walls at China Inn offer many lovely watercolors of mountains and flowers. _____, Peking House's paintings are genuine Chinese watercolors. _____, China Inn offers lush, green plants to accent the decor. Peking House _____ uses plants to enhance the dining experience. This city is fortunate to have these two fine Chinese restaurants.

The two candidates running for the United States Senate have sharply contrasting views. Mr. Jones has frequently stated that he will never vote to raise taxes. Ms. Smith, _____, has made no such promise. _____, Mr. Jones has declared that he does not support a woman's right to have an abortion. _____, Ms. Smith has asserted that she does support a woman's right to an abortion. _____, Mr. Jones believes that capital punishment is a deterrent that will reduce the number of murders committed in the United States each year. Ms. Smith, _____, does not support capital punishment. In this Senate campaign the voters cannot complain that they do not know where each candidate stands on the issues.

FOCUS ON DICTION

Special forms of adjectives and adverbs are used in many comparisons. These two forms are called

- Comparative
- Superlative

Before you learn about these forms, here are some brief reminders about adjectives and adverbs.

Adjectives

Adjectives help provide color to sentences. They are used before nouns or following linking verbs. (For a list of linking verbs, see Chapter 2.) Adjectives that appear before nouns answer the questions *what kind of, which,* or *how many:*

beautiful waterfall **(what kind of)**

thirty-three years **(how many)**

those curtains **(which)**

Adjectives that follow linking verbs describe the subject of the sentence.

> The room smelled **musty**. (**musty** room)
>
> The model is **stunning**. (**stunning** model)
>
> The meal looked **good**. (**good** meal)
>
> The noise under the car sounded **bad**. (**bad** noise)

Adverbs

Adverbs energize sentences by providing more information about (modifying) verbs, adjectives, or other adverbs. They answer the questions *when, where,* or *how.*

> The guests will leave **soon**. (**when**, modifies verb **will leave**)
>
> You must complete the task **very** quickly. (**how**, modifies adverb **quickly**)
>
> You must complete the task very **quickly**. (**how**, modifies verb **must complete**)
>
> My competitor is **too** fast for me. (**how**, modifies adjective **fast**)

Use an adverb following an action verb.

> The motor runs **well**.
>
> My sick friend is now doing **well**.

Caution: *Well* is an adverb; *good* is an adjective. While you may hear someone in casual conversation say, "I'm doing *good*," that sentence is incorrect in Standard American English dialect. The sentence should be spoken, "I'm doing *well*."

Also many writers and speakers alike omit the *-ly* from an adverb.

> **Incorrect:** Marion ran quick to the car.
>
> **Correct:** Marion ran **quickly** to the car.
>
> **Incorrect:** Bill plays the piano bad.
>
> **Correct:** Bill plays the piano **badly**.

Comparative Form of Adjectives and Adverbs

The comparative form of adjectives and adverbs is used when a writer compares/contrasts *two* persons, ideas, or things. For most adjectives the comparative form is marked with an *-er* ending.

Adjective	Comparative Form
quick	quicker
smart	smarter
happy	happier

A few adjectives have comparative forms that do not end in *-er*:

Adjective	Comparative Form
good	better
bad	worse

Adjectives of more than three syllables form the comparative by adding the word *more*:

Adjective	Comparative Form
beautiful	more beautiful
independent	more independent
responsible	more responsible

A few adjectives of two syllables form the comparative by adding *more*:

Adjective	Comparative Form
welcome	more welcome
wholesome	more wholesome

Most adverbs form the comparative by adding the word *more*:

Adverb	Comparative Form
quickly	more quickly
slowly	more slowly
wisely	more wisely

A few adverbs, most notably the adverb *well*, do not add the word *more*:

Adverb	Comparative Form
well	better

With both adjectives and adverbs, you can use the word *less* to make negative comparisons:

Adjective	Comparative Form
healthy	less healthy
wealthy	less wealthy
wise	less wise

Adverb	Comparative Form
quickly	less quickly
slowly	less slowly

EXERCISE 6.3   In the paragraph below, write in the blank the comparative form of the given adjective or adverb.

The novel, *One for the Money,* is _____ than the
good
novel, *Two for the Show.* First, the characters in *One for the Money* are

_____ . Mary Penny is like many women who have suf-
realistic
fered from poverty. She is _____ than Joe Vegas, the
cautious
main character of *Two for the Show,* about investing in get-rich-quick
schemes. She is _____ to hold on to her money and
likely
_____ to play the slot machines. Second, the plot moves
likely
_____ in *One for the Money.* The author creates
quickly
_____ suspense by using foreshadowing. Overall, the plot is
great
is _____ than the plot of *Two for the Show.*
predictable
Third, *One for the Money*'s ending is _____ . It is
good
_____ and _____ . *Two for the*
interesting   **satisfying**
Show's ending is pointless and aggravating. In sum, *One for the Money*

is a _____ buy than *Two for the Show.*
good

Superlative Form of Adjectives and Adverbs

You should use the superlative form of adjectives and adverbs when you are comparing/contrasting *three or more* persons, ideas, or things. Most adjectives add *-est* to form the superlative.

Adjective	Superlative
quick	quickest
smart	smartest
happy	happiest

A few adjectives do not use *-est* in the *superlative* form:

Adjective	Superlative
good	best
bad	worst

Adjectives of more than three syllables use *most* in their superlative form:

Adjective	Superlative
beautiful	most beautiful
independent	most independent
responsible	most responsible

Also, some adjectives with two syllables use *most* to form the superlative:

Adjective	Superlative
welcome	most welcome
wholesome	most wholesome

The majority of adverbs form the superlative by using the word *most:*

Adverb	Superlative
quickly	most quickly
slowly	most slowly
wisely	most wisely

One exception is the adverb *well:*

Adverb	Superlative
well	best

Use the word *least* to create negative superlatives for adjectives and adverbs:

Adjective	Superlative
healthy	least healthy
wealthy	least wealthy
wise	least wise

Adverb	Superlative
quickly	least quickly
slowly	least slowly

If you are in doubt about how to form the comparative or superlative form of an adjective or adverb, consult a good dictionary.

In the paragraph below, write in the blank the appropriate comparative or superlative form of the given adjective or adverb.

EXERCISE 6.4

The three siblings—Mark, Jim, and Jane—make their own statements as party guests. Mark is the _____ of the three. He is
                                                friendly
the center of attention at every party he attends because he tells the

_____ jokes. He is the _____ to be the
      good   **likely**
first guest to leave. Jim, on the other hand, is the _____ .
                                                          shy
Of all the party guests, he is the _____ to be wander-
                                          likely
ing in the kitchen by himself. Jim never tells jokes at parties. Compared

to his siblings, he is the _____ joke teller because he
bad
forgets the punch line every time. Jane is _____ than
outgoing
Jim but _____ than Mark. She is, however,
outgoing
_____ to leave the party first. She always has the
likely
_____ social calendar because, though she rarely tells
full
jokes, she has the _____ laugh of any party guest.
hearty
Mark, Jim, and Jane always arrive at parties together but never leave the

same impression.

FOCUS ON GRAMMAR

A *modifier* is a word, phrase, or clause that provides additional information about another word or group of words in the sentence. This additional information changes, or *modifies*, the meaning of the word. For example, in the phrase *fascinating movie*, the adjective *fascinating* modifies *movie* by answering the question, *What kind of* movie? In the famous phrase, *A nation of the people, by the people, and for the people*, the phrases *of the people, by the people* and *for the people* modify *nation* by answering, *What kind of* nation?

Readers expect a modifier to be placed next to the word or words it modifies. If it is not, two types of modifier problems can result: misplaced modifiers and dangling modifiers. Being able to anticipate modifier problems will strengthen your sentences and clarify the message you are communicating to your reader.

Misplaced Modifiers

A modifier is said to be *misplaced* when it is separated in the sentence from the word it modifies. Misplaced modifiers confuse readers, and the writer's message is sometimes lost in the confusion.

Consider these confusing sentences:

The mother quickly took the child to her doctor with chicken pox. (According to the writer, who has chicken pox? The mother? The child? No, the doctor!)

I experienced the loss of my father at the age of six. (Think again.)

To correct a misplaced modifier, move the modifier next to the word it modifies:

The mother quickly took the child with chicken pox to her doctor.

At the age of six I experienced the loss of my father.

A common modifier is a clause that begins with *who, whom, which,* or *that.* This type of clause must be placed next to the word it modifies.

> Hugh gave his suit to a charity that he did not like any more. (If Hugh did not like the charity, why did he give it his old clothing?)

To correct this type of misplaced modifier, move the clause:

> Hugh gave his suit thaxt he did not like any more to a charity.

In the following contrast paragraph circle or highlight the five misplaced modifiers and draw an arrow to their proper places in the sentences.

EXERCISE 6.5

> The camping facilities at Lake Jenoway and Lake Lee are quite different. Lake Jenoway scattered throughout the camping area has bathrooms and shower facilities whereas Lake Lee has no shower facilities and few restrooms. Lake Jenoway's camping area also features water and electricity hookups. However, all camping sites at Lake Lee are remote. Campers do not have access to electricity using tents. They must carry their water jugs to the water fountain which is empty. Lake Jenoway offers many family activities during the week including square dances, folk music concerts, and storytelling contests. Campers at Lake Lee can view the moon and stars who are bored, but no planned activities are provided. Families always crowd Lake Jenoway with small children, so the camping area is often noisy. On the other hand, the only noise in Lake Lee's camping area is the chirping of millions of crickets. Before deciding to camp at Lake Jenoway or Lake Lee, campers should carefully consider their needs.

Dangling Modifiers

Sentences sometimes begin with phrase modifiers. These modifiers often being with a word ending in *-ing* or *-ed.* When a phrase modifier appears at the beginning of a sentence, the word that is being modified (or described) must be the subject of the sentence. If that is not the case, the modifier is *dangling.* In other words, it is "dangling" at the beginning of the sentence without any logical connection to the subject that it must modify.

The following sentence features a dangling modifier:

> Driving down Highway 14, Hungry Bob's Barbecue Restaurant cannot be missed.

The phrase modifier is *driving down Highway 14.* Because the modifier occurs at the beginning of the sentence, the word being described in this phrase must be the subject, but *Hungry Bob's Barbecue Restaurant* is clearly not driving down the highway. Thus, the modifier is dangling. This type of dangling modifier is particularly frustrating to the reader because the writer never says who is driving on the highway. Sometimes students try to correct this type of dangling modifier by moving the modifier to the end of the sentence:

Hungry Bob's Barbecue Restaurant cannot be missed driving down Highway 14.

Moving the modifier to the end of the sentence, however, does not correct the problem. To correct the sentence, the writer must rearrange the sentence and add a new subject:

Driving down Highway 14, the barbecue lover cannot miss Hungry Bob's Barbecue Restaurant.

This sentence also has a dangling modifier:

Seated on the porch, the bear was spotted by the cabin owner.

This sentence is clear only if the bear is seated on the porch. Otherwise, it has a dangling modifier because the subject is not modified by the phrase *seated on the porch.*

This sentence can be corrected one of three ways. The first is to move the modifier to the end of the sentence so that the modifier is placed next to the word to which it refers:

The bear was spotted by the cabin owner seated on the porch.

Another way to correct the sentence is to rearrange the sentence so that *the cabin owner* is the subject.

Seated on the porch, the cabin owner spotted the bear.

A third possibility is to rearrange the sentence and change the dangling modifier to a subordinate clause:

While he was seated on the porch, the cabin owner spotted the bear.

To correct a dangling modifier, try one of these methods:

- Reword the sentence and add a subject
- Move the phrase modifier
- Change the phrase modifier to a subordinate clause

After you have reworded the sentence, check to be sure that the word being modified is placed directly next to the phrase modifier.

EXERCISE 6.6

Circle or highlight the five modifiers in the paragraph below. Then correct them using one of the three methods above.

Vincent Van Gogh's paintings, *The Chair and the Pipe and Gauguin's Chair,* were painted in December 1888, but they differ in composition and color. Looking at *The Chair and the Pipe,* the yellow ladderback chair dominates the canvas. Forming the background for one-half of the canvas, the viewer cannot miss the reddish-orange, irregular floor tiles. The room's walls, which form the remainder of the background, consist of varying shades of blue. Running across the canvas from left to right, the viewer can see diagonal lines. These lines are formed by the grouting between the floor tiles and the dividing line between the walls and the floor. Resting on the chair, the center of this painting is a tobacco pipe. On the other hand, the chair at the center of *Gauguin's Chair* is so sophisticated with curved legs and back. Brightly colored splotches of paint, which make up the bottom half of the painting, create the illusion of a rug. Dominating the top half of the canvas, the viewer cannot miss the bright green wall. In contrast to the curved lines of the chair is a straight line that separates the wall from the floor. Resting on the chair, two books and a candle are slightly to the left of the center of the painting. Both of these chairs, empty of all but a few possessions, convey a deep sense of loneliness.

FOCUS ON PUNCTUATION

The Dash

The dash is a special mark of punctuation you can use to energize your sentences. Dashes are used to emphasize a word or phrase within a sentence and to set off a word or phrase at the end of a sentence.

In the first sentence of Exercise 6.4,

> The three siblings—Mark, Jim, and Jane—make their own statements as party guests

a pair of dashes is used to introduce the names of the siblings. The writer uses dashes to draw the reader's attention to the three names in a more dramatic way than by using commas. In the first sentence of Exercise 6.2, *Two of the city's renowned Chinese restaurants—China Inn and Peking House—feature similar interior decor,* the writer uses dashes for a similar effect.

Writers can also use the dash at the end of a sentence for dramatic effect. The word or phrase that follows the dash can surprise the reader, summarize an idea, or provide a contrast to the rest of the sentence. An example of this use of the dash appears in this chapter's section on the concluding sentence:

> When I get my credit card bill in the mail each month, I am glad that I am a bargain shopper—not an impulse buyer like my brother.

The use of the dash in this sentence dramatically reinforces the differences between the writer and her brother.

The decision whether to use dashes is, of course, yours. Before deciding to use the dash, you should consider the degree to which you wish to emphasize the word or phrase. Also, you should be careful not to overuse dashes in a composition because their dramatic effect would then be lost.

Caution: Writers often confuse the dash with a hyphen, which is used to divide words into syllables or separate compound words (see Chapter 4). In handwriting, a dash is longer than a hyphen. In a typed manuscript a dash is formed by typing two hyphens with no space before or after.

Student Sample

Contrast Paragraph—Point-by-Point Pattern

Two State Parks

Those who take the time to visit Florida's Myakka River State Park and Hillsborough River State Park will note differences in size and topography. Myakka, covering approximately 30,000 acres, is by far the larger of the two parks. In fact, it is Florida's largest state park. In contrast, Hillsborough, which covers 3000 acres, can boast of its distinction as the oldest state park. In direct relation to the size of each park is the distance of hiking trails each offers. Myakka has over 39 miles of hiking trails while Hillsborough offers a modest six miles. While hiking in each park, the visitor will likely note a difference in the terrain. Myakka River State Park features many sinkholes, gulleys, small ponds, and even a large lake. This type of terrain is known as "karst." Hillsborough River, however, lies on very flat, low marshlands. The featured rivers of each park also differ. The Myakka River is a slow-moving, meandering river. On the other hand, the Hillsborough River offers several actual whitewater rapids—indeed a rarity in Florida. Despite their differences, both of these parks offer rewards for those who appreciate a glimpse of Florida's natural wonders.

—Bill Cronin

Student Sample

Contrast Paragraph—Block Pattern

Tent Camping versus Motor Home Camping

Everyone should enjoy camping, but the experience is much different for the traditional tent campers than for the sophisticated, high-tech motor home inhabitants. Traditional campers enjoy the experience to its fullest. Sleeping on raw earth, cooking over an open fire, and being exposed to the unforgiving elements with just a tent for protection are all part of the experience. Tenting is also inexpensive.

➡

Most tents cost between $30.00 and $300.00. Furthermore, campsites, which usually cost about $6.00 a night, are free if camping off hiking trails, and the equipment can be stored in the closet or garage, so storage is also free. Even though tenting is inexpensive, it is not easy; traditional camping is what some would call work. Tenters must pitch a tent, gather firewood, and protect the food from the weather, bugs, and animals. Unlike tent campers, motor home campers enjoy camping with all the comforts of home: beds, bathrooms, kitchens, televisions, and VCRs. However, motor homes can be costly. If $35,000 to $500,000 for a motor home, about $25 a night for a campsite, fees for storage, and maintenance and fuel expenses are affordable, then maybe finding a campsite it will fit in, pushing a button to lower the awning, and turning off the key to camp is the way to go. Motor home camping is certainly less work. Although the camping experience may be much different for each individual, camping is an activity anyone can enjoy.

— Michael Nunes

FOCUS ON PEER REVIEW

When you have completed your experimental draft, you are ready for peer review. Use your readers' responses to the following questions as you compose your revised and edited drafts.

1. Does the topic sentence of your paragraph clearly identify the two people, ideas, or things (**X** and **Y**) that will be compared or contrasted?

2. Do **X** and **Y** belong to the same general class so that they can be fairly compared or contrasted?

3. Does the writer use the block pattern or point-by-point pattern to compare or contrast **X** and **Y**? Is this pattern developed logically through the paragraph?

4. Does the writer use transitions to help the reader move through the paragraph? List four transitions that the writer uses. If you note any spots in the paragraph where a transitional expression would be useful, make a suggestion.

5. Are there a sufficient number of supporting details in the body of the paragraph? If not, what details might be added?

6. Does the writer indicate a preference for **X** over **Y** or **Y** over **X**? Based on the evidence that the writer has presented, do you agree with the writer's preference?

7. Are adjectives and adverbs used correctly? If not, what changes should the writer make?

8. Are there any misplaced or dangling modifiers? If so, where do they occur?

9. Does the writer use any dashes? If so, is the use of the dash effective? If not, is there any sentence where the dash could be used for dramatic effect?

10. Are there any fragments, run-ons, or comma splices? If so, where?

11. Are there any grammatical errors? If so, where?

12. Place a check mark at the end of any line where a spelling or punctuation error occurs.

13. What are the strengths of this paragraph?

14. What weaknesses need to be addressed in the revised and edited drafts?

Learning to compose effective comparison/contrast paragraphs will help prepare you for the classroom and the workplace. The analytical thinking skills needed for this assignment will also help you "bridge over" from the paragraph to the essay.

Writers as Spiders

On-line tips are available to those writers who want to improve their comparison/contrast paragraphs. Two sites that provide an overview of comparison/contrast paragraphs and offer assistance with organization (including transition) are

> http://webserver.maclab.comp.uvic.ca/writersguide/Pages/ParDevCC.html
>
> http://204.244.141.13/write_den/tips/paragrap/compare.htm

Web Exercise 1

Revisit one of the art museum sites listed in Chapter 5. Then choose two works by the same artist. Using your observation skills, answer the following questions:

1. What do these two works have in common? Consider the colors, shapes, and focus of each work.

2. How do these works differ? Look again at the colors, shapes, and focus.

3. What is the overall impression that each work of art makes on the viewer? (Think about how you would describe each art work to someone who has never seen it.)

4. Why might a single artist have created both of these works?

After you have answered these questions, compose an outline (see Appendix A). Then write a comparison or contrast paragraph. Be sure to identify both works of art in the topic sentence and limit the focus of your paragraph.

Web Exercise 2

Use the search engines to research two of your favorite vacation spots (or places you would like to visit). In order for your comparison or contrast to be fair, make sure these vacation destinations are in the same general category (two snow skiing resorts, two beaches, two towns of the same approximate population). Consider the following questions:

1. What makes each of these spots desirable from a vacationer's point of view?

2. What accommodations does each of these vacation areas offer?

3. What activities are available for tourists?

4. What do these areas have in common?

5. How do these areas differ?

After answering these questions, choose a focus for your comparison/contrast paragraph. Use the information you have gathered to write a topic outline, and develop this outline into a comparison/contrast paragraph.

Additional Help

For more information about modifiers, see

http://english.byu.edu/writing.ctr/handouts/modifier.htm

http://aix1.uottawa.ca/academic/arts/writcent/hypergrammar/
msplmod.html

You can review the comparative and superlative forms of adjectives and adverbs at

http://aix1.uottawa.ca/academic/arts/writcent/hypergrammar/
compsupl.html

Focus on the Essay

FOCUS ON PURPOSE

Having practiced writing paragraphs for a variety of purposes, you are ready to compose an essay—a multiparagraph composition on a focused subject. The essay is a late sixteenth century invention by a French writer, Michel deMontaigne, whose book *Essais* appeared in 1588. Montaigne used the term *essai* to refer to his prose compositions based on his personal observations of the world around him.

Today inquiring minds recognize the essay as a time-honored way to express an author's opinion, inform an audience, and/or entertain a reader. Essays appear regularly on newspaper editorial pages, in magazines and books, on National Public Radio, and on televised news programs. In the classroom students use essays to respond to test questions, argue a position, present research, analyze literature, and/or share their personal experiences. In the workplace lawyers use the essay form to prepare briefs and judges to render decisions while other professionals write essays to share discoveries and review the work of their colleagues.

An essay, which can vary in length from a few paragraphs to book length, offers the writer several advantages over a single paragraph composition. The focus of an essay is less restrictive than the topic of a paragraph. Thus the essayist, unlike the writer of a single paragraph, has room to focus on several aspects of a particular topic and develop each aspect with supporting details and evidence.

Essays, like paragraphs, are written for a variety of purposes. This textbook, however, limits its discussion of the essay to four types common to the academic setting:

- Development by example
- Comparison/contrast
- Problem-solving
- Persuasion

Because you are already familiar with development by example and comparison/contrast paragraphs, this chapter features development-by-example and comparison/contrast essays to help you bridge over from writing paragraphs to composing essays. Chapter 8 will introduce the problem-solving essay and Chapter 9 the persuasion essay.

FOCUS ON CHOOSING A TOPIC

Some student essays are written on topics assigned by the instructor. In other situations the writer must choose a topic that will address an assignment. In either case, it is important that the student writer focus on a subject that can be discussed within the prescribed length requirements. Academic essays can vary from approximately 350 words to a doctoral dissertation of 100 pages or more.

This chapter will discuss development-by-example and comparison/contrast essays of at least 500 words. In order to demonstrate the connection between the paragraph and the essay, the topics for the development-by-example essay will be the same topics presented at the beginning of Chapter 3, and the topics for the comparison/contrast essay the same as those presented in Chapter 6.

FOCUS ON THE DEVELOPMENT-BY-EXAMPLE ESSAY

Generating Ideas

Once you have chosen a topic from Chapter 3 for your development-by-example essay, you need to think of two or three points to develop your topic. If you like, you can choose for your essay the same general topic you used to develop your paragraph in Chapter 3. You can also use the focus of your paragraph in Chapter 3 as one of the supporting points for your essay. Then you will need to generate one or two additional supporting ideas before you write your essay.

To help you gather your ideas before you begin to compose, try using one or more of these techniques discussed in Chapter 2:

- Brainstorming
- Listing
- Freewriting
- Clustering

At the end of Chapter 3 is a sample development-by-example paragraph by Kathryn Figueroa on the topic, "College Skills for Future Success." Kathryn decided that she had enough ideas to support an essay on the same topic. She also decided to use the main idea of her development-by-example paragraph—math skills—as one of the supporting ideas for her essay. She then developed the following cluster:

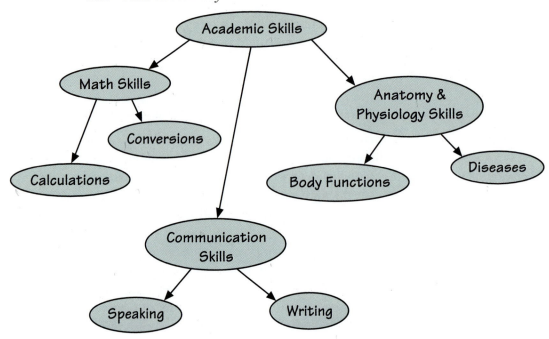

Note that Kathryn's cluster includes not only the main idea and the supporting details of her paragraph from Chapter 3 but also two other major ideas that will develop her topic.

Working individually or in small groups, use one or more of the techniques above to gather ideas on the following topics from Chapter 3. Then, using the first example as a model, list three points you could use to develop an essay on each of the given topics. If your topic from Chapter 3 is not included below, use your topic for Exercise 5.

1. Topic: Challenges Facing College Students Who Work

   First supporting idea: <u>Managing study time</u>

   Second supporting idea: <u>Resolving work conflicts</u>

   Third supporting idea: <u>Fulfilling family responsibilities</u>

2. Topic: Benefits of Regular Exercise

   First supporting idea: _____

   Second supporting idea: _____

   Third supporting idea: _____

3. Topic: Qualities of a True Friend

   First supporting idea: _____

Second supporting idea: _____

Third supporting idea: _____

4. Topic: Problems Facing Today's Adolescents

First supporting idea: _____

Second supporting idea: _____

Third supporting idea: _____

5. Topic: _____ (fill in with your topic from Chapter 3)

First supporting idea: _____

Second supporting idea: _____

Third supporting idea: _____

After you have chosen the topic for your essay and decided upon two or three points to support it, you are ready to write the main idea of your essay.

Thesis Statement

Just as the paragraph has a topic sentence that expresses its central point, an essay also has a main idea called a *thesis* (sometimes referred to as a *thesis statement* or *thesis sentence*). This relationship can be illustrated as follows:

$$\frac{\text{topic sentence}}{\text{paragraph}} = \frac{\text{thesis}}{\text{essay}}$$

A thesis, like a topic sentence, can be stated or implied. However, in most student essays, the thesis is stated. The word *thesis* is a shortened form of *hypothesis*, which is appropriate since in many essays the thesis presents the author's opinion about a subject. In the thesis—a single sentence—the writer should

- Announce the focus of the essay to the reader
- Present the central idea of the essay
- Establish the limits of the essay

A strong thesis, an essential building block for an effective essay, focuses on a subject the writer can discuss knowledgeably. Furthermore, it delivers to the reader the writer's promise of the essay's contents. Once the thesis is written, the writer must fulfill this promise by using supporting points directly related to the thesis.

Some thesis statements provide a road map for the reader by announcing the essay's focus and then presenting two or more supporting points that the writer will discuss in the body of the essay. In this type of thesis, called a *list thesis*, the writer lists the supporting points in the order in which they appear in the essay. The list thesis has several advantages for the writer and the reader. In order to write a list thesis, the writer must decide which supporting ideas to use and how to arrange these ideas. In other words, using a list thesis helps a writer organize the essay. For this reason, beginning college essayists often prefer a list thesis. The reader also benefits from the writer's use of a list thesis because the direction the essay will take is clear.

Two examples of list thesis statements follow:

focused subject   **list of supporting points**

An ideal job offers employees excellent dental, medical, and life insurance coverage.

focused subject   **list of supporting points**

Some advantages of owning a small car include low fuel expenses and reasonable maintenance costs.

Some writers, however, do not wish to "give away" the exact direction of the essay in the thesis. These writers prefer a thesis that presents the central idea without listing the supporting points. This type of thesis is called an *umbrella thesis*. The umbrella thesis also offers benefits for both writer and reader. The umbrella thesis provides the writer with a "cover" under which the author can discuss ideas without specifying the exact order in which the ideas will appear. By using an umbrella thesis, the writer will keep the reader's interest high because the reader must wait until the body of the essay to find out the specific direction the essay will take.

Here are two examples of umbrella thesis statements:

focused subject   **umbrella**

An ideal job offers employees excellent insurance coverage.

focused subject   **umbrella**

Small cars offer their owners distinct economical advantages.

You should word your thesis statements as directly and forcefully as possible. Keep in mind that as you move through the steps in the writing process, your essay will evolve, and you may discover that some ideas that you thought were workable are not and that some ideas you thought were unusable are worthy of inclusion. As your essay takes shape, so will your thesis statement, since it must reflect all the ideas presented in the body of the essay. Consequently, the thesis that appears in the experimental draft of your essay is not likely to be worded the same as the thesis that appears in your final draft. It is helpful if you think of your thesis as a sentence subject to change rather than a sentence carved in rock.

The thesis is arguably the most important sentence in the essay, so take the time to polish its wording. It is not necessary for you to write "I believe," "I think" "in my opinion," or "personally" as part of your thesis because your reader will recognize that a thesis statement reflects your views. Also, try to avoid thesis statements that begin with "There are" or "In this essay I want to discuss." Many readers find these types of thesis statements dull. Try reading your thesis aloud to yourself or to someone else so you can listen for its effect.

Your thesis will generally appear twice in the drafts of your essay:

- In the introductory paragraph
- In the concluding paragraph

These special paragraphs are discussed later in this chapter.

Write a list thesis for each of the topics in Exercise 7.1.

EXERCISE 7.2

1. Topic: <u>Challenges Facing College Students Who Work</u>

    Thesis: <u>The challenges that face working college students include managing study time, resolving work conflicts, and fulfilling family responsibilities.</u>

2. Topic: Benefits of Regular Exercise

    Thesis: _____

    _____

3. Topic: Qualities of a True Friend

    Thesis: _____

    _____

4. Topic: Problems Facing Today's Adolescents

    Thesis: _____

    _____

5. Topic: _____ (fill in your topic)

    Thesis: _____

    _____

Special Paragraphs

An essay, whether written by college students or professional writers, generally has a three-part structure:

- Introduction
- Body
- Conclusion

Readers expect this division into beginning, middle, and end to help them move smoothly through the essay.

While the introductions and conclusions of essays by professional writers may consist of several paragraphs, in a student essay the introduction is usually a single introductory paragraph and the conclusion a single concluding paragraph. These paragraphs are called *special paragraphs* because they do not follow the structure of the topic sentence paragraphs you studied in Chapters 2 through 6. Introductory and concluding paragraphs are shorter than topic sentence paragraphs. The introductory paragraph for a short essay is generally three to six sentences in length, and the concluding paragraph two to four sentences. This text limits its discussion of introductions and conclusions to the introductory paragraph and the concluding paragraph.

Introductory Paragraph

The introductory paragraph gives your reader the first impression of your essay. If you want your reader to continue past the introductory paragraph, you must convince the reader to set aside other concerns to read your essay. After all, you have something worthwhile to say. Therefore, the opening sentences are among the most important of the entire essay. Effective introductory paragraphs should

- Engage the reader's interest
- Provide a bridge to the thesis
- Present the thesis to the reader

You can use a number of different techniques to attract the attention of the reader in the opening sentences. Once you have the reader's attention, you will probably need a "bridge sentence" to connect your opening sentences to the thesis, which, in most student essays, appears as the last sentence of the introductory paragraph. While it is possible for an essay to have an implied thesis or a thesis that appears somewhere other than in the introduction, most readers of student essays will expect the thesis at the end of the introductory paragraph.

Suppose you are writing a development-by-example essay about the different types of students who attend college. Your thesis is

Two types of students who attend college are the eighteen-year-old who just graduated from high school and the returning student who seeks a new career.

Here are some possible ways to begin your essay and engage your reader's interest.

Use a Personal or Fictional Anecdote

As I walked into my first college class, I wondered who would be sitting to my right or left. I remember fearing that everyone would stare at me because I was an "older" student. I soon realized that while many teens were in the class, I was not the only student who had waited a number of years before seeking a college education. Two types of college students are the eighteen-year-old who just graduated from high school and the returning student who seeks a new career.

An anecdote, which relates a brief incident, is an effective way to begin an introductory paragraph because it lends human interest to the essay. An anecdote invites your reader to go where your essay leads. One difficulty of using an anecdote is providing transition between the anecdote and the thesis. If you do not provide transition, the movement from the anecdote to the thesis is likely to be abrupt. In the example above, the bridge sentence

I soon realized that while many teens were in the class, I was not the only student who had waited a number of years before seeking a college education.

prepares the reader for the thesis.

An anecdote can also be fictional, as in the following example:

Jill's hands shook as she took her seat in the front row. She had not been in a classroom for twenty years. If her desire to be a nurse were not so strong, she would be somewhere else. Hoping to see someone else her age, she looked to her left and right. To her surprise, she saw not only many teens but also older men and women who looked just as scared as she. Two types of college students are the eighteen-year-old who just graduated from high school and the returning student who seeks a new career.

The anecdote above is fictional. The writer uses the student, Jill, to represent the returning student who, like the eighteen-year-old, is probably experiencing some anxiety on the first day of class. In this case the bridge sentence

To her surprise, she saw not only many teens but also older men and women who looked just as scared as she

links the anecdote to the thesis.

Cite a Quotation

World War I ace, Eddie Rickenbacker, once said: "Courage is doing what you're afraid to do. There can be no courage unless you're scared." If fear is necessary for courage, then many students entering the college classroom for the first time are courageous. These students, no matter what their ages, are often fearful about the demands of college life, but they have taken the first step to overcome their anxieties by walking through the classroom door. Two types of college students are the eighteen-year-old who just graduated from high school and the returning student who seeks a new career.

If you use a quotation to begin your essay, be sure to include the source. Also you must show your reader the connection between the quotation and the subject of your paper. Otherwise, the quotation will seem "tacked on" to the rest of the introduction. Again a bridge sentence can make this connection clear:

If fear is necessary for courage, then many students entering the college classroom for the first time are courageous.

Raise a Question

Do you remember what it was like the first day of your first college class? Can you remember feeling as if every student in the class were staring at you as you made your way to your desk? Were you surprised to find in your class so many different types of students— students of various ages and backgrounds? Many of today's college classrooms feature an intergenerational student population. Two types of college students are the eighteen-year-old who just graduated from high school and the returning student who seeks a new career.

Try using one or more questions to begin your essay. Be sure, though, that you have clearly tied the questions to the topic you have been assigned or have chosen. Writers who use question openers must also provide a bridge to the thesis, or, like the quotation opener, the questions will seem tacked on.

Many question openers use the second person pronoun *you*. Although the use of the second person is not generally found in formal essays, many readers will accept its limited use in opening questions.

Provide Relevant Statistics

According to a recent college admissions booklet, the average age of a student at Hope Junior College is 28.3 years. This statistic shows that many students in Hope Junior College's classrooms are over the age of 30. These mature students have discovered that they need to upgrade their job skills or learn new ones if they are to compete in an increasingly technological society, so they find themselves in classrooms sitting next to students in their late teens and twenties. Two types of college students are the eighteen-year-old who just graduated from high school and the returning student who seeks a new career.

A statistic, particularly one that may be surprising, is often an effective way to open an essay. When you use a statistic, you should provide the source just as you do with a quotation.

Give Background Information about the Topic

The job market, both nationally and internationally, is becoming increasingly competitive and technologically advanced as the twenty-first century approaches. Many workers are finding themselves educationally underprepared for the challenges of their jobs and are seeking to retool themselves to meet these challenges. These experienced workers are returning to the college classroom for retraining and joining those young people preparing to enter the job market for the first time. Two types of college students are the eighteen-year-old who just graduated from high school and the returning student who seeks a new career.

In order to decide what type of background information you should provide, consider your reader. What kinds of information would help the reader understand your essay? What background does the reader need to understand the importance of your subject? By providing background information, you are convincing the reader that the topic of your essay is worth consideration. In the introduction above, the writer and the reader are both workers or potential workers in the job market. Both the writer and the reader share a desire for economic well-being. The writer appeals to this common interest in the opening sentences.

Create an Analogy

College students walking into a classroom for the first time are like aliens leaving a spaceship and stepping forth in an unknown world. Neither the college students nor the aliens know what lies ahead. College students, no matter what their ages, are often fearful about the demands of college life, but they have taken the first step to overcome their anxieties by walking through the classroom door. Two types of college students are the eighteen-year-old who just graduated from high school and the returning student who seeks a new career.

An analogy is a comparison of two unlike things. One type of analogy is a simile, a comparison that incorporates the use of the word *like* or *as*. In the opening sentence above the writer draws a comparison between beginning college students and aliens—both walking into the unknown. Many readers enjoy analogies because they create suspense. An active reader will think, *How* are college students and aliens alike? Curiosity then will lead the reader into the rest of the essay.

Challenge a Common Perception

Many people, when they think of a freshman classroom, envision row after row of eighteen-year-olds eager to begin their college experiences. These people would be surprised to discover that the average age of a freshman at most colleges and universities is well above eighteen. Men and women are coming back to the classroom after an absence of many years. Some want to learn a new skill; others want to pursue a particular interest such as history. Two types of college students are the eighteen-year-old who just graduated from high school and the returning student who seeks a new career.

This type of introductory paragraph entices the reader to learn something new by challenging the reader's preconceived ideas. Even readers who do not share these preconceptions will be curious about how the writer will address those ideas. If you want to try this type of opener, think about what beliefs your readers might hold and what ideas you might use to counter these beliefs.

Not all of the above techniques will work for every essay topic. Also many introductory paragraphs use a combination of techniques. With practice you will learn to vary your introductory paragraphs according to your subject.

Because your introductory paragraph is so important, you will probably go through a number of drafts before you are satisfied with it. You should think of the introductory paragraph as liquid and subject to change. When you have composed an introduction with which you are satisfied, read the introduction aloud. Will your reader want to continue reading your essay?

Although the introductory paragraph appears first in your essay, you do not have to write it first. Many writers, including this one, often find it helpful to compose the body of the essay before the introduction. That way the author can tailor the introduction to fit the ideas in the body of the paper. If you write your introductory paragraph first, be sure to reread it after you have composed the body of the essay. Check to be sure that the introductory paragraph sets forth all the major ideas that you discuss in the body paragraphs.

EXERCISE 7.3

Use the thesis statement you developed for your topic in Exercise 7.1. Then compose three possible introductory paragraphs for your thesis. Use a different technique to begin each introductory paragraph. Then in small groups read your introductory paragraphs to the other group members. Consider the following questions: Which of the three do your group members like best? Why? Which introductory paragraphs need improvement? Which of the three do you think is best? Why?

Concluding Paragraph

Just as your essay has a clear beginning, it should have a clear ending. Otherwise, the essay will seem incomplete, and you will leave your reader bewildered. An effective concluding paragraph is essential because it is your last chance to communicate your message to your reader. Readers are more likely to remember what they read at the end of an essay rather than what they read in the opening sentences, so you need to make the most of these ending sentences. Specifically, a concluding paragraph should redeliver the thesis statement and remind the reader of the significance of the subject.

Before you write your concluding paragraph, reread the draft of your essay. Pay close attention to your introductory paragraph, including your thesis. Then compose a sentence that restates the thesis and reinforces the essay's supporting points. Use this sentence to begin your concluding paragraph. Be sure not to repeat the exact wording of the thesis from the introductory to the concluding paragraphs. If you use a list thesis in the introductory paragraph, try using an umbrella thesis in the concluding paragraph, and vice versa. The key is to vary the wording of the thesis each time it appears.

Once you have redelivered the thesis statement, you have just a few sentences in which to create a lasting impression for your reader. One way to make the most of these sentences is to return to the technique you used in the opening sentences. In the concluding paragraph, you can use any of the following techniques.

Complete the Anecdote

Both the recent high school graduate and the returning student play important roles in the college classroom. Now that I am completing my first college course, I value the opportunity I have had to make friends of all ages in my classes. I have learned from them, and I hope they have learned from me.

In this concluding paragraph the reader learns the ending of the story. Following is the end of Jill's story:

Both the recent high school graduate and the returning student play important roles in the college classroom. Now Jill's hands shake as she reaches for her diploma. When she returns to her seat, she again looks to her left and right. This time she sees happy faces, not fearful ones.

Refer to the Opening Quotation

Both the recent high school graduate and the returning student have important contributions to make in any college classroom. With motivation and perseverance, they, like Eddie Rickenbacker, can overcome their fears and achieve their dreams.

Predict an Outcome

Both the recent high school graduate and the returning student have important contributions to make in any college class. Eventually, however, returning students will outnumber eighteen-year-olds in many classrooms. As the economy becomes more diverse and increasingly international, more workers will return to the classroom for retraining, and the average age of a college student will continue to climb.

Create a Final Analogy

Both the recent high school graduate and the returning student have important contributions to make in any college classroom. With motivation and perseverance, they will no longer feel like aliens on unfamiliar ground, but like explorers marching forward to chart undiscovered planets.

Just as your opening sentences will vary depending on the topic of your essay, your concluding sentences will also vary depending on the essay's purpose. As with introductory paragraphs, your concluding paragraphs will improve with practice.

EXERCISE 7.4

In Exercise 7.3 you wrote three possible introductory paragraphs to introduce your thesis statement. Using the same thesis, write three concluding paragraphs. In small groups read your concluding paragraphs. Which concluding paragraph do the group members like best? Why? Which concluding paragraph do the group members like least? Why? Which concluding paragraph do you think is strongest? Why?

Body Paragraphs

The body paragraphs form the heart of the essay because they deliver to the reader the ideas that support the thesis. Each body paragraph is a topic sentence paragraph like the ones you have studied in this text. If you have learned to write effective paragraphs by focusing your topic sentences and providing specific, relevant supporting details to develop your main idea, then you are ready to compose the body of an essay.

Each body paragraph focuses on a single idea that develops the thesis. Look back at your responses to Example 5 in Exercise 7.1. If you developed your topic into an essay, each body paragraph would focus on one of your supporting ideas. For example, suppose you were writing an essay with the following list thesis:

The challenges that working college students face include managing study time, resolving work conflicts, and fulfilling family responsibilities.

Each of your body paragraphs would develop *one* of the supporting ideas included in the thesis. The body of this essay would have three body paragraphs. The topic sentence of the first body paragraph would focus on *managing study time*, the second on *resolving work conflicts*, and the third on *fulfilling family responsibilities*. You would then develop each body paragraph with supporting examples.

If you used an umbrella thesis for your essay, such as

> Working college students face many challenges as they attempt to balance their responsibilities inside the classroom with their obligations to their employers and their families.

then you would announce each supporting idea in the topic sentence of each of the body paragraphs. The topic sentence of the first body paragraph might be

> College students who work often have difficulty finding time to study.

The second body paragraph might begin

> One of the most difficult situations these students face is resolving conflicts between work and school.

The topic sentence of the final body paragraph might be

> Finally, working college students must find time to fulfill their family responsibilities.

Like the ideas in the body of a paragraph, the ideas in the body of an essay must be organized for your reader. The most common arrangement is by order of importance. Using this organizational pattern, you organize your supporting ideas from least important to most important. That way, you end the body of your essay on your strongest note.

Transition

As you arrange your ideas for your reader, use transitional expressions to improve the flow of the essay. In addition to including transitional words and phrases within your body paragraphs, consider using these expressions as you move from your first body paragraph to your second and from your second body paragraph to your third. You can also use a transitional expression to mark the beginning of the concluding paragraph.

The same transitional words and phrases that you used in your development-by-example paragraph will also be helpful in your development-by-example essay. For a list of these expressions, see Chapter 3. For a more complete list of transitional words and phrases, see Chapter 2.

Kathryn Figueroa is the author of the cluster that appears at the beginning of this chapter and one of the student samples at the end of Chapter 3. She decided to use her cluster to build an essay on the topic "College Skills for Future Success." To do so, she began with her development-by-example paragraph focusing on math skills and then added one paragraph on communication skills and another on human anatomy/physiology skills. After she completed her body paragraphs, she added introductory and concluding paragraphs to complete the essay. The final draft of Kathryn's essay appears below. Transitional expressions appear in bold print.

Student Sample

Development-by-Example Essay

College Skills for Future Success

When I was eight years old, I began to read a series of books called *Cherry Ames: The Nurse*. The series featured Cherry Ames from her beginnings as a nursing assistant through her nursing career. Ever since I read those books, all I have ever wanted is to be a registered nurse. I have partially completed that goal by becoming a practical nurse. **Now** I plan to learn academic skills in college that will enable me to be a registered nurse and further my career.

Developing math skills in college will help prepare me for a career as a registered nurse. As a licensed practical nurse, I have to calculate almost every day, whether it be a simple math problem or a complicated formula. Prior to my completing elementary algebra and a math topics course, whenever I needed to figure out dosages, the process took me a long time. I had to break down each part of the problem and then bring all these parts together to reach the correct answer. After completing my math courses, I was able to incorporate what I had learned on my job, thereby saving myself a lot of time. **In addition,** most medications in pill form are usually prepackaged, but the nurse must measure liquids. Most conversions such as how many milliliters make an ounce are simple. **However,** when dealing with continuous flows such as intravenous infusions and artificial feedings, the nurse needs to calculate the rate of flow. **For example,** if the doctor orders 1000 milliliters to infuse over 12 hours, the nurse needs to calculate how many drops will equal a milliliter, how many milliliters per minute, and then how many milliliters per hour. Being able to obtain correct answers with an easier method is beneficial for both the nurse and the patients. My successful completion of college math classes has made these skills possible for me.

➤

A nurse must **not only** possess excellent math skills **but also** strong communication skills. Each day I am required to speak with doctors, patients, family members, therapists, and other nurses. I have to present myself in a professional manner by speaking articulately. **Furthermore,** everything I do or say regarding a patient must be documented on a chart. Everyone who treats the patient reads this documentation. One major point all of my instructors and supervisors have stressed is "If it's not written, it's not done." Patient continuity of care, treatment plans, insurance reimbursements, and the outcome of lawsuits rely heavily on nurses' notes. Every piece of information must be documented comprehensively and concisely. At times I have wondered whether all the information I have written is understandable. When I complete my communications classes, I want to know not only how to speak effectively but also how to write clearly, accurately, and completely.

Finally, being a nurse requires comprehensive knowledge of anatomy and physiology. College anatomy classes will inform me about the different body organs as well as their locations and functions. Each part of the human body has a different function; **however,** these parts are often interdependent. If one part is not functioning properly, it will affect another. Physiology classes will teach me the functions of the parts of the body as well as what sometimes causes these parts to malfunction. In anatomy and physiology classes I will learn to recognize symptoms of certain diseases and disorders. For a nurse, recognizing a patient's symptoms can mean saving a life. Usually the first health care professional to evaluate a patient is the nurse, who then relays information about the patient to the doctor. Anatomy and physiology skills are the most important skills I will learn in college.

Mastery of these skills—math, communications, and anatomy and physiology—is essential if I am to achieve my goal to become a registered nurse. I am no longer a child, yet my childhood dreams are still with me.

—Kathryn Figueroa

To complete your development-by-example essay, follow these steps.

1. Choose a topic from Chapter 3 (or a similar topic).
2. Brainstorm, cluster, or freewrite your chosen topic.
3. Select two or three ideas that will support your topic.

4. Write a list or umbrella thesis statement.

5. Write an introductory paragraph.

6. Write a body paragraph to develop each supporting idea.

7. Write a concluding paragraph.

8. Submit your draft for peer review.

9. Revise/edit your draft.

10. Prepare your final draft to submit to your reader.

Note: You can complete steps 5, 6, and 7 in any order.

FOCUS ON THE COMPARISON/CONTRAST ESSAY

In the last chapter you learned to write a comparison or contrast paragraph. In this chapter you will learn to compose

- A comparison essay
- A contrast essay
- A comparison/contrast essay

A comparison essay focuses on the similarities between two people, ideas, or things while a contrast essay focuses on the differences. In a comparison/contrast essay you will examine the similarities *and* the differences.

Generating Ideas

Choose a topic from those listed at the beginning of Chapter 6. Decide whether you want to compare, contrast, or compare *and* contrast. If you choose to compare or contrast, you will need two or three points you can develop in your essay. If you want to compare and contrast, you will need two or three similarities and two or three differences. Use the idea-gathering techniques discussed earlier in this chapter—brainstorming, listing, freewriting, and clustering—to generate your supporting points.

EXERCISE 7.5

Working individually or in small groups, list supporting ideas for the following topics. Use your chosen topic for question 4.

1. Topic: Contrast two restaurants.

   First point of contrast: _____

   Second point of contrast: _____

   Third point of contrast: _____

2. Topic: Compare two movies.

First point of comparison: _____

Second point of comparison: _____

Third point of comparison: _____

3. Topic: Compare and contrast two forms of exercise.

Similarities:

First point of comparison: _____

Second point of comparison: _____

Third point of comparison: _____

Differences:

First point of contrast: _____

Second point of contrast: _____

Third point of contrast: _____

4. Topic: _____

First supporting point: _____

Second supporting point: _____

Third supporting point: _____

Thesis Statement

As in a development-by-example essay, the thesis statement for a comparison, contrast, or comparison/contrast essay can be a *list thesis* or an *umbrella thesis*. Below are some examples of list thesis statements.

focused subject **list of similarities**

Comparison essay: My husband and his sister share mannerisms, appearances, and personalities.

focused subject

Contrast essay: Corporate funeral homes and family-owned funeral

list of differences

homes differ in their staffs, community involvement, and business practices.

focused subject

Comparison/contrast essay: Although my two daughters' height,

list of similarities

weight, and hair color are similar, their eating habits, academic interests,

list of differences

and extracurricular activities vary.

These thesis statements can be written as umbrella thesis statements.

focused subject

Comparison essay: My husband and his sister share many personality

umbrella
characteristics.

focused subject

Contrast essay: Corporate funeral homes and family-owned funeral

umbrella
homes operate their businesses differently.

focused subject

Comparison/contrast essay: Although my daughters' physical

umbrella
appearances are similar, their interests greatly vary.

All of the principles regarding the thesis statement of a development-by-example essay are true of comparison and/or contrast essays:

- Polish the wording of your thesis
- Revise your thesis as necessary
- Check your thesis by reading it aloud
- Place the thesis in your introductory and concluding paragraphs
- Vary the wording of the thesis each time it appears

EXERCISE 7.6

Write an umbrella or list thesis statement for each of the topics below.

1. Topic: Contrast two restaurants.

   Thesis: _____

   _____

2. Topic: Compare two movies.

   Thesis: _____

   _____

3. Topic: Compare and contrast two forms of exercise.

   Thesis: _____

   _____

4. Topic: _____ (use your chosen topic from Exercise 7.5)

   Thesis: _____

   _____

Special Paragraphs

Like all essays, comparison, contrast, and comparison/contrast essays have clear beginnings and endings. The techniques for writing these special paragraphs are the same as those introduced earlier in this chapter.

Introductory Paragraphs

Introductory paragraphs of comparison, contrast, and comparison/contrast essays should accomplish the following purposes:

- Attract the reader's attention
- Identify the two people, ideas, or things being compared and/or contrasted
- Communicate the thesis to the reader

When Lisa Jones decided to write a comparison essay about the similarities between her husband and his half-sister, she introduced them in her introductory paragraph:

> Recently, my husband, Marshall, discovered that he had a half-sister named Jodi. Jodi, who had been a family secret for over thirty years, was born and raised in Ohio. After Jodi was introduced to the family, she decided to move with her three children to our hometown so she could get to know her father and half-siblings. Although my husband and his sister have only known each other for two years, they share mannerisms, appearances, and personalities.

Another student, Debra Klingensmith, decided to open her essay by defining two different types of funeral homes before presenting her umbrella thesis:

> A corporate funeral home is owned by a large state or nationwide company. Most large communities have at least one corporate funeral home. On the other hand, family-owned funeral homes are privately owned. Many small communities rely heavily on these locally operated businesses. Although corporate funeral homes and family-owned funeral homes both provide the same services for the community, they operate their businesses differently.

Bill Cronin, who authored one of the student samples in Chapter 6, wanted to expand his ideas from a contrast paragraph to a comparison/contrast essay. To open his essay, he wrote the following introductory paragraph, which combines two of the techniques discussed earlier in this chapter: raising a question and providing background information about the two state parks he is comparing/contrasting.

Have you ever wondered what Florida was like before condominiums, shopping centers, and mobile home parks, when native Americans lived and hunted in its forests? If you have, why not visit Florida's state parks and see what you have missed? Two state parks are located within a short driving distance of the Tampa Bay area. Myakka River State Park is located east of Sarasota, and Hillsborough River State park is located northeast of Tampa. While Myakka River and Hillsborough River State Parks have much in common, they differ in size and topography.

Concluding Paragraphs

Concluding paragraphs for comparison, contrast, or comparison/contrast essays should restate the thesis and reinforce the importance of the topic.

Lisa decided to end her essay by emphasizing the importance of genetics:

After observing Marshall and Jodi for the past two years, their similarities are remarkable. My husband is more like his half-sister than his full siblings. The influence of genetics is unmistakable and amazing.

Debra, however, decided to indicate her preference for one of the subjects she was contrasting:

Families in their times of need should consider the differences between a corporate and a family-owned funeral home. Those who want personalized service should choose a small, family-owned funeral home that prides itself on quality service and a caring, comforting atmosphere.

Bill decided to conclude his comparison/contrast essay by answering the questions he had raised in the opening sentences:

Myakka River and Hillsborough River State Parks both offer their visitors reasonable fees, excellent recreational facilities, and an abundance of wildlife, yet their size and terrain vary. Next time you wonder about Florida's past, visit one of these state parks, lace up some hiking boots, and see what Florida was like 150 years ago. If you are quiet and let your imagination wander, you may even catch a glimpse of an Indian brave.

Body Paragraphs

In Chapter 6 you learned two patterns of arrangement for comparison/contrast paragraphs: the block pattern and the point-by-point pattern. You can use these same patterns to arrange the body paragraphs of comparison, contrast, and comparison/contrast essays.

Body Paragraph 1 = Topic sentence (focus on **X**)
    first point of comparison or contrast
        details
    second point of comparison or contrast
        details
    third point of comparison or contrast
        details
Body Paragraph 2 = Topic sentence (focus on **Y**)
    first point of comparison or contrast
        details
    second point of comparison or contrast
        details
    third point of comparison or contrast
        details

Figure 7.1   Block pattern for comparison/contrast essays

If you are writing a comparison or contrast essay, you can use the block pattern. Your first body paragraph will focus on **X** and your second on **Y,** as shown in Figure 7.1.

Each point of comparison for **X** is also a point of comparison or contrast for **Y.** The details, of course, vary according to the characteristics of each subject.

To arrange a comparison or contrast essay using the point-by-point method, use the pattern shown in Figure 7.2

Body Paragraph 1 = Topic sentence (first point of comparison or
                contrast)
   X
        supporting details
   Y
        supporting details
Body Paragraph 2 = Topic sentence (second point of comparison or
                contrast)
   X
        supporting details
   Y
        supporting details
Body Paragraph 3 = Topic sentence (third point of comparison or
                contrast)
   X
        supporting details
   Y
        supporting details

Figure 7.2   Point-by-point pattern for comparison/contrast essays

Body Paragraph 1 = Similarities
first point of comparison
X (details)
Y (details)
second point of comparison
X (details)
Y (details)
third point of comparison
X (details)
Y (details)
Body Paragraph 2 = Differences
first point of contrast
X (details)
Y (details)
second point of contrast
X (details)
Y (details)
third point of contrast
X (details)
Y (details)

Figure 7.3   Organization of body of comparison and contrast essay

If you are writing a comparison and contrast essay, there are many ways to organize the body of your essay. The most common arrangement is shown in Figure 7.3.

Transition

Regardless of which organizational pattern you use to compose your comparison, contrast, or comparison/contrast essay, you will need to provide transitional expressions to help your readers move smoothly through the body of your essay. Use the "Focus on Transition" section in Chapter 6 as a guide. For additional transitional words and phrases, see Chapter 2.

EXERCISE 7.7

The following essays illustrate a comparison (point-by-point pattern), a contrast (block pattern), and a comparison/contrast essay (point-by-point). In the first sample essay, transitional expressions appear in bold print. In the sample contrast and comparison/contrast essays, circle (or highlight) transitional expressions.

Student Samples

Comparison Essay

Marshall and Jodi: Nature versus Nurture

Recently, my husband, Marshall, discovered that he had a half-sister named Jodi. Jodi, who had been a family secret for over thirty years, was born and raised in Ohio. After Jodi was introduced to the family, she decided to move with her three children to our hometown so she could get to know her father and half-siblings. Although my husband and his sister have only known each other for two years, they share mannerisms and personalities.

Many of Marshall's mannerisms are the same as Jodi's. **For example,** when Marshall speaks, he gains attention by using his hands and body to help express himself. Marshall **also** has certain facial expressions that I catch at a certain moment. Another of Marshall's mannerisms is his confidence and control in his movements. When Marshall enters a room, he has a certain boldness about him and exudes confidence. Jodi shows these same traits. **For instance,** when Jodi speaks or wants to emphasize something, she, **like Marshall,** uses her hands and body to explain herself. Jodi **also** has a devilish grin as if she is up to some mischief—the same expression I see on Marshall's face. **In the same way as Marshall,** Jodi moves with a confident and carefree attitude. When they enter a room, everyone knows it. They would make great politicians or evangelists because they would have no problem gaining millions of followers.

The most obvious comparison between Marshall and Jodi is their personalities. Marshall is known for his wit. He can be so funny at times that he is great entertainment. He is also known for his pranks. Everyone in the Jones family knows to be aware. **For example,** he will call his two sisters and mother on the phone and disguise his voice as an irritating or irrational person. **Furthermore,** he has an outgoing, energetic disposition. He seems to know somebody everywhere he goes. One time on a cruise to the Bahamas, he ran into an old friend. I am convinced he could go halfway around the world and see someone he knows. Jodi can be just as witty as Marshall. She **also** pulls pranks on family and friends. One time at a barbecue Jodi left an old, gross-looking can of baked beans on the counter for me to find. She knows how important cleanliness is to me. When I gasped, "What are these for?" she said, "To bake tonight for dinner." Jodi is also just as

➡

outgoing as her half-brother. In the past two years I have noticed that she has more friends and knows more people than I do, and I was born and raised in Florida. When Marshall and Jodi are together, there is never a dull moment.

After observing Marshall and Jodi for the past two years, I have discovered their remarkable similarities. My husband is more like his half-sister than his full siblings. The influence of genetics is unmistakable and amazing.

—Lisa Jones

Contrast Essay

Corporate Funeral Homes versus Family-Owned Funeral Homes

A corporate funeral home is owned by a large state or nationwide company. Most large communities have at least one corporate funeral home. On the other hand, family-owned funeral homes are privately owned. Many small communities rely heavily on these locally operated businesses. Although corporate funeral homes and family-owned funeral homes both provide services for the community, they operate their businesses differently.

Many corporate funeral homes feature large staffs, little community involvement, and distinct business practices. They usually have a large number of employees with embalmers, directors, counselors, finance managers, grounds crew, office workers, and even door greeters. Furthermore, they employ young professionals who are paid standard salary wages for entrance-level jobs. Many corporate funeral homes are members of local consumer organizations such as the local Chamber of Commerce or civic association. However, their community involvement may be limited because their employees often commute from areas outside the local community. They buy their supplies and equipment from company distribution warehouses or companies that offer large discounts for high-volume buying rather than from local businesses. Even the floral arrangements they offer are usually catalog orders that are shipped the next day. When families come in, they are received by the greeter who takes them to the receptionist. The receptionist then takes them to the counselor who makes up the file with all their information. A director finalizes the funeral arrangements, and a finance officer fills out insurance forms and makes payment arrangements. Each case is assigned a number because of the volume of the business. All in all, this level of activity can seem quite confusing for a grieving family.

On the other hand, a family-owned funeral home has a small staff, a high level of community involvement, and personalized business practices. The owner, funeral director, and embalmer are always the same individual. There are usually only three or four employees, and these are often family members. Because of smaller staffs, wages are generally higher in contrast to those at a corporate funeral home. Community involvement is high because the family lives in the community and is involved in local business organizations. Family-owned funeral homes generally buy their supplies and equipment locally. Floral arrangements are bought from a local florist and gas from the corner gas station. Their business practices are relaxed unlike those of a typical corporate funeral home. When family members enter a family-owned funeral home, they deal with one person, the director, throughout the process from the first call to the ending service. No identification numbers are needed. This type of service can be a great comfort for a grieving family.

Families in their times of need should consider the differences between a corporate and a family-owned funeral home. Those who want personalized service should choose a small, family-owned funeral home that prides itself on quality service and a caring, comforting atmosphere.

—Debra Klingensmith

Comparison/Contrast Essay

Two State Parks

Have you ever wondered what Florida was like before condominiums, shopping centers, and mobile home parks, when native Americans lived and hunted in its forests? If you have, why not visit Florida's state parks and see what you have missed? Two state parks are located within a short driving distance of the Tampa Bay area. Myakka River State Park is located east of Sarasota, and Hillsborough River State Park is located northeast of Tampa. While Myakka River and Hillsborough River State Parks have much in common, they differ in size and topography.

Both parks are affordable, convenient, and intriguing. Daily admission fees at both parks are $3.25 per vehicle (up to six persons included). Exploring these parks by canoe is convenient for park visitors. Both parks, located along rivers, have excellent canoe launch facilities and also offer canoe rentals on site. In addition, food and drink concessions are available at both parks. Hiking is another great way to enjoy both parks. The quiet hiker may get a chance to view some of the wildlife that inhabits both parks. At either park, the lucky visitor can see deer, alligators, otters, or even a glimpse of a rare bald eagle.

Visitors will note differences in size and topography. Myakka, covering approximately 30,000 acres, is by far the larger of the two parks. In fact, it is Florida's largest state park. In contrast, Hillsborough, which covers 3000 acres, can boast of its distinction as the oldest state park. In direct relation to the size of each park is the distance of hiking trails each offers. Myakka has over 39 miles of hiking trails while Hillsborough offers a modest six miles. While hiking in each park, the visitor will likely note a difference in the terrain. Myakka River State Park features many sinkholes, gullies, small ponds, and even a large lake. This type of terrain is known as "karst." Hillsborough River, however, lies on very flat, low marshlands. The featured rivers of each park also differ. The Myakka River is a slow-moving, meandering river. On the other hand, the Hillsborough River offers several actual whitewater rapids—indeed a rarity in Florida. Despite their differences, both of these parks offer rewards for those who appreciate a glimpse of Florida's natural wonders.

Myakka River and Hillsborough River State Parks both offer their visitors reasonable fees, excellent recreational facilities, and an abundance of wildlife, yet their size and terrain vary. Next time you wonder about Florida's past, visit one of these state parks, lace up some hiking boots, and see what Florida was like 150 years ago. If you are quiet and let your imagination wander, you may even catch a glimpse of an Indian brave.

—Bill Cronin

To compose your comparison, contrast, or comparison/contrast essay, follow these steps:

1. Choose a topic from Chapter 6 (or a similar topic).

2. Identify the two subjects you will compare and/or contrast.

3. Generate ideas by brainstorming, clustering, listing, or freewriting.

4. Compose a list or umbrella thesis statement.

5. Write an introductory paragraph.

6. Decide on a block or point-by-point pattern for your body paragraphs.

7. Develop your body paragraphs using the pattern chosen in step 6.

8. Write a concluding paragraph.

9. Submit your experimental draft for peer review.

10. Compose your revised and edited drafts.

11. Complete your final draft to submit to your reader.

FOCUS ON GRAMMAR

Writers of essays make extensive use of *pronouns*. Using pronouns is a short-cut for writers because pronouns substitute for nouns that appear in the same sentence or in a previous sentence. These nouns are called *antecedents*.

Without pronouns writers would have to repeat the same word or phrase many times. For instance, in the first body paragraph of her contrast essay, Debra uses the pronouns *they* and *their* to replace the antecedent *corporate funeral homes*:

> Many **corporate funeral homes** feature large staffs, little community involvement, and distinct business practices. **They** usually have a large number of employees. . . . **They** employ young professionals. . . . **Their** community involvement may be limited. . . . **They** buy supplies and equipment from company distribution warehouses. . . . Even the floral arrangements **they** offer are usually catalog orders. . . .

Without pronouns the sentences would read this way:

> Many **corporate funeral homes** feature large staffs, little community involvement, and distinct business practices. **Corporate funeral homes** usually have a large number of employees. . . . Usually **corporate funeral homes** employ young professionals. . . . **Corporate funeral homes'** community involvement may be limited. . . . **Corporate funeral homes** buy supplies and equipment from company distribution warehouses. . . . Even the floral arrangements **corporate funeral homes** offer are usually catalog orders. . . .

Like Debra, you would have difficulty communicating without the help of pronouns. The most common type of pronoun is the personal pronoun. Personal pronouns are classified as *first person*, *second person*, and *third person*. They are also classified as *singular* or *plural*. Third person singular pronouns

TABLE 7.1	Personal pronouns	
	Singular	*Plural*
First person I, me, my, mine, myself		**First person** we, us, our, ours, ourselves
Second person you, your, yours, yourself		**Second person** you, your, yours, yourselves
Third person he, him, his, himself (male) she, her, hers, herself (female) it, its, itself (neuter)		**Third person** they, them, their, theirs, themselves

also have gender; they are either *male* (he, him, his, himself) *female* (she, her, hers, herself), or *neuter* (it, its, itself).

Pronoun–Antecedent Agreement

Most essays are written using first person and/or third person pronouns. Because of the extensive use of pronouns in essays, readers must be sure which pronouns substitute for which antecedents. Otherwise, confusion can result.

Writers make this relationship clear by practicing a grammatical principle called *pronoun–antecedent agreement*. This principle states that pronouns must agree with their antecedents in number, gender, and person. The "Focus on Diction" section of this chapter discusses the concepts of person and gender. This section limits its focus to agreement in number.

In order for your pronouns to agree with their pronouns in number:

- Use a third person singular pronoun to refer to a singular antecedent.
- Use a third person plural pronoun to refer to a plural antecedent.

Many antecedents are easily identified as singular or plural, and the choice of pronoun is obvious. In some cases, however, the number of the antecedent is difficult to determine.

Case 1: When a pronoun is separated from its antecedent by one or more prepositional phrases, the antecedent is usually not found within the prepositional phrase(s).

   antecedent   pronoun   pronoun

Lily (along with **her** sisters) forgot **her** ticket.

                 antecedent

The **construction company** (as well as additional contractors)

               pronoun

is working hard to complete **its** project.

In the first sentence the personal pronoun *her* substitutes for *Lily*, the antecedent. Note that more than one pronoun in a sentence can have the same antecedent. In the second sentence the antecedent *construction company* is singular, so the writer must use the singular pronoun *its*.

Case 2*:* When the conjunction *and* joins two or more antecedents, the antecedents are plural, and the pronoun must also be plural.

antecedent　　　antecedent　　　pronoun
Lily and her **sisters** forgot **their** tickets.

Both *Lily* and *sisters* are antecedents for the plural pronoun *their*.

　　　　antecedent　　　　　　　antecedent
The **construction company** and **additional contractors** are

pronoun
working hard to complete **their** project.

Because of the presence of the conjunction *and*, the antecedents and the pronoun are plural.

Case 3*:* When two or more antecedents are joined together by *or, nor, either . . . or,* or *neither . . . nor,* the antecedent closest to the pronoun determines if the pronoun is singular or plural.

antecedent　　　　　pronoun
Dan nor his **friends** have finalized **their** plans for this weekend.

antecedent　　　　　pronoun
Neither his friends nor **Dan** has finalized **his** plans for this weekend.

antecedent　　　　　pronoun
Lily or her **sisters** will have to buy **their** tickets at the door.

antecedent　　　　　pronoun
Either her sisters or **Lily** will have to buy **her** ticket at the door.

Because the use of *or, nor, either . . . or,* or *neither . . . nor* presents special problems with pronoun–antecedent agreement and awkward constructions, many writers reword their sentences to avoid these problems.

Dan nor his friends have finalized plans for this weekend.

Neither his friends nor Dan has finalized plans for this weekend.

Lily or her sisters will have to buy tickets at the door.

Either her sisters or Lily will have to buy a ticket at the door.

Case 4*:* When the antecedent is a collective noun that represents a group of people acting as a whole, the pronoun is singular. When the antecedent is a collective noun but the members within the group are acting individually, the pronoun is plural. Collective nouns include *class, committee, company, crew, family, group, jury,* and *team.*

antecedent   pronoun
The **jury** presented **its** verdict to the court.

antecedent   pronoun
The **team** played **its** final game of the season.

antecedent   pronoun
The **jury** voted according to **their** individual consciences.

antecedent   pronoun
The **team** retired to **their** lockers after the loss.

In the first two sentences the members of the group are acting as one; therefore, the pronoun is singular. In the last two sentences the members of the group are taking individual actions, so the pronoun is plural.

Case 5: When the antecedent is an indefinite pronoun, the pronoun is singular or plural according to which indefinite pronoun is used. These indefinite pronouns take singular personal pronouns:

any**one**	any**body**	
every**one**	every**body**	either (of)
some**one**	some**body**	neither (of)
no **one**	no**body**	each (of)

Did anyone leave **his or her** books in the room?

Everyone left **his or her** books in the room.

Someone left **his or her** books in the room.

No one left **his or her** books in the room.

Everybody left **his or her** books in the room.

Nobody left **his or her** books in the room.

Either of the students left **his or her** books in the room.

Neither of the students left **his or her** books in the room.

Each of the students left **his or her** books in the room.

Singular indefinite pronouns present special challenges to the writer. First, because these pronouns are indefinite, it is not clear whether the person being referred to is male or female. Should the writer use *his, her,* or *his or her?*

Another difficulty is that many speakers often do not observe this rule. They instead say, "Everyone left their books in the room." Because most of us hear language spoken this way, it is difficult to recognize that the use of the singular pronoun is correct in the Standard American English dialect.

One way to edit your sentences to eliminate the difficulties of singular indefinite pronouns is to substitute the indefinite pronouns *none, some,* or *all:*

None of the students left **their** books in the room.

Some of the students left **their** books in the room.

All of the students left **their** books in the room.

In the paragraphs below circle each pronoun (use the pronoun chart as a guide). Then draw an arrow back to each antecedent. If the pronoun does not agree with the antecedent, cross through the pronoun and correct it. When the pronoun is corrected, the verb may also need to be changed.

EXERCISE 7.8

Too many people consider the environment someone else's problem. However, everyone has made their contribution to the problem. The Environmental Protection Agency as well as other government organizations may use their influence to combat pollution, but the government alone cannot solve the environmental problem. Each citizen must take upon themselves the responsibility for improving the environment. No one should feel they are free of blame for the destruction of the ecology. For example, a family that goes on a picnic and leaves their garbage scattered over the ground is to blame. A person who carelessly throws their trash out of the car window is at fault. A boater who tosses their beer caps or soda bottles into the water must assume their share of the guilt.

Members of a college ecology group spent their summer working to improve the environment. Neither the club sponsor nor the members knew when he became affiliated with the group the amount of time that would be involved. However, each of the members worked diligently in the areas they were most interested in. For instance, some members planned a butterfly garden. Other students devoted themselves to studying the various ecological problems of the area. Still another group drew up a comprehensive recycling program. After much study the club brought their suggestions to the administration. Both the members of the administration and the club members acknowledged that they must work together in the community to preserve the environment.

Follow the directions for Exercise 7.8.

EXERCISE 7.9

Not every college student knows what they want to pursue as a major. Many students can remember that growing up they wanted to be teachers or doctors or police officers. However, a person's childhood fantasies don't always become their choices later. A boy who once dreamed of fighting fires when he was younger may decide that the life of adventure is not for him after all. Or a girl who wanted to be a doctor may decide that they are not willing to spend so much time in training. As an adult, they may decide to pursue a job in the business field. Often, freshmen and sophomores will delay making their career choices. However, a student with enough hours to graduate may still be unsure what they want to do once they get that diploma.

Often a student makes a career choice as a freshman and discovers that when they are a sophomore or junior they want to change their major. Either the strong influence of a teacher or excitement over subject matter may have its influence on a student's change of heart. Very often either a group of students or an individual student will want to pattern themselves after an important person in their lives. Each student must decide for themselves on what grounds they will make their choices. Deciding on a major is not easy, but college students should not put off this decision for too long.

FOCUS ON DICTION

Shift in Person

Pronouns must also agree with their antecedents in person. For example, if the antecedent is a first person pronoun, then all the pronouns that refer to this antecedent must also be first person:

antecedent   pronoun   pronoun
I forgot to get **my** homework assignment during **my** algebra class.

The same principle applies to second person and third person.

antecedent   pronoun   pronoun
You must be sure to tell **your** friends about **your** situation.

antecedent   pronoun   pronoun
He believes in **himself** and the morality of **his** actions.

This principle is easy to see at the sentence level, but in paragraphs and essays students sometimes shift from one person to another. Particularly confusing to readers are unexpected shifts from first person to second person.

An early draft of Lisa's comparison essay illustrates shift in person. Look carefully for the sudden shift from first to second person pronouns.

Many of Marshall's mannerisms are the same as Jodi's. For example, when Marshall speaks, he gains attention by using his hands and body to help express himself. Marshall also has certain facial expressions that I catch at a certain moment. Another of Marshall's mannerisms is his confidence and control in his movements. When Marshall enters a room, he has a certain boldness about him and exudes confidence. Jodi shows these same traits. For instance, when Jodi speaks or wants to emphasize something, she, like Marshall, uses her hands and body to explain herself. Jodi also has a devilish grin as if she is up to some mischief—the same expression you see on Marshall's face. Like Marshall, Jodi moves with a confident and carefree attitude. When they enter a room, you notice immediately. They would make great politicians or evangelists because they would have no problem gaining millions of followers.

When Lisa edited her draft, she eliminated the pronoun shift.

Jodi also has a devilish grin as if she is up to some mischief—the same expression **I** see on Marshall's face. . . . When they enter a room, **everyone** notices immediately.

With the exclusion of business letters and technical manuals, the use of second person pronouns is rare in formal writing. One difficulty with the use of second person is determining who is being addressed—*you* (a single reader) or *you* (all possible readers)? In some foreign languages, such as German and Spanish, a different word is used for *you* (second person singular) and *you* (second person plural). However, in English a reader of an essay cannot tell the difference between *you* singular and *you* plural. Therefore, the pronoun *you* is generally reserved for informal writing.

EXERCISE 7.10

On a separate sheet of paper, rewrite the following paragraphs. Change all second person pronouns to first person pronouns. Check your answers by rereading the second and third body paragraphs of Kathryn Figueroa's essay, which appears earlier in this chapter.

A nurse must not only possess excellent math skills but also strong communication skills. Each day you are required to speak with doctors, patients, family members, therapists, and other nurses. You have to present yourself in a professional manner by speaking articulately. Furthermore, everything you do or say regarding a patient must be documented on a chart. Everyone who treats the patient reads this documentation. One major point all of your instructors and supervisors will stress is "If it's not written, it's not done." Patient continuity of care, treatment plans, insurance reimbursements, and the outcome of lawsuits rely heavily on nurses' notes. Every piece of information must be documented comprehensively and concisely. At times you will wonder whether all the information you have written is understandable. When you complete your communications classes, you will want to know not only how to speak effectively but also how to write clearly, accurately, and completely.

Finally, being a nurse requires not only math and communication skills but also comprehensive knowledge of anatomy and physiology. College anatomy classes will inform you about the different body organs as well as their locations and functions. Each part of the human body has a different function; however, these parts are often interdependent. If one part is not functioning properly, it will affect another. Physiology classes will teach you the functions of the parts of the body as well as what sometimes causes these parts to malfunction. In anatomy and physiology classes you will learn to recognize symptoms of certain diseases and disorders. For a nurse, recognizing a patient's symptoms can mean saving a life. Usually the first health care professional to evaluate a patient is the nurse, who then relays information about the patient to the doctor. Anatomy and physiology skills are the most important skills you will learn in college.

Gender Bias

Not only do pronouns agree with their antecedents in number and person but also in gender. Gender agreement is only an issue when you are using third person singular pronouns and third person singular antecedent. You practice gender agreement when you

- Use a third person singular masculine pronoun to refer to a singular masculine antecedent.

  Hugh enjoys playing with **his** son, George.

- Use a third person singular feminine pronoun to refer to a singular feminine antecedent.

  Teri is pleased with **her** new job at the university.

- Use a third person singular neuter pronoun to refer to a singular antecedent that is neither masculine nor feminine.

  The jury rendered **its** verdict.

In most cases the gender of the antecedent is clear, and so is the choice of the pronoun. However, in some cases the gender of the antecedent is not clear. Traditionally, the response has been to use masculine pronouns in such cases. Consider these sentences taken from a teacher's manual:

The **teacher** must accompany **his** students on any field trip.

He must drive the school van **himself.**

The difficulty with using masculine pronouns when the antecedent's gender is unclear is that for many readers these pronouns specifically refer to men only and thus exclude women. This concept is known as *gender bias*. Do these sentences mean that only male teachers must accompany students on field trips?

Following are some suggestions you can use to avoid gender bias:

- Use first person or second person pronouns when possible. If the manual had been written in second person, these sentences would have been written:

You must accompany **your** students on any field trip.
You must drive the school van **yourself.**

- Use plural antecedents.

    Teachers must accompany **their** students on field trips.
    They must drive the school van **themselves.**

- Omit pronouns when possible.
    Teachers must accompany students on field trips and drive the school van.
- Substitute *he or she, his or her, him or her,* or *himself or herself.*

    The teacher must accompany **his or her** students on any field trip.
    He or she must drive the school van **himself or herself.**

Caution: Use this solution sparingly. These substitutions can become awkward with repeated use.

- Substitute: *chairperson, salesperson, humankind,* and *police officer.* Avoid nouns such as *chairman, salesman, mankind,* and *policeman.*

Beginning with the second sentence of each paragraph, change all pronouns and their antecedents from singular to plural. In some sentences you will also need to change the verb from singular to plural.

EXERCISE 7.11

One type of student who decides to attend college is the recent high school graduate. The high school graduate often goes to college because of his parents' and friends' expectations. If he is in the classroom for his parents and friends and not for himself, he will probably lack an interest in his course work. He will often be bored in class and will not listen to the teacher's instructions or complete his homework on time. In addition, he may not have a clear career goal and will be undecided about his major because he is not motivated to make a career choice. This student often ends up with a weak grade point average and may even withdraw from college. This lack of motivation is fortunately not typical of every eighteen-year-old first-year college student. A new high school graduate often has a specific career goal. Therefore, he will take interest in his course work, ask questions, in class, listen carefully to the instructor, and complete his homework in a timely manner. He will declare a major as soon as possible. Because he has a clear goal, he will do well in school. Another type of student attending college is the returning student. Sometimes a returning student enters the college classroom because of a divorce. She may have depended on her spouse's income, but now finds she needs employment. Because she needs a vocational skill, she decides to return to college. Also she may want the intellectual stimulation of a college classroom. She may want to pursue an interest in a particular subject. Another reason a student returns to the classroom is she wants to change her career. Therefore, she needs additional job training. A returning student is usually highly motivated. She is enthusiastic about her course work, takes careful notes, and is punctual in completing her assignments. As a result, she will do well academically.

FOCUS ON PEER REVIEW

After you have written experimental drafts for your development-by-example and comparison, contrast, or comparison/contrast essays, participate in peer review using the following guide questions. Then use your peer reviewer's comments to revise and edit your essays before submitting them to your instructor.

Guide Questions for Development-by-Example Essay

1. Does the introductory paragraph attract the reader's interest? Why? If not, why?

2. What is the thesis of the essay? Does the writer use a list thesis or an umbrella thesis? Does the thesis appear in the introductory paragraph?

3. What two or three supporting ideas does the writer use to develop the thesis?

4. What is the topic sentence of each of the body paragraphs? Does each topic sentence focus one of the supporting ideas?

5. Is the topic sentence of each body paragraph developed with sufficient examples? If not, what additional details could be used to support the topic sentence?

6. Are there any sentences in the body paragraphs that do not support the topic sentence? Specifically, which sentences should be omitted?

7. Are the body paragraphs logically arranged? If not, how could the body paragraphs be rearranged to improve the flow of the essay?

8. Is the thesis of the essay reinforced in the concluding paragraph? What technique does the writer use to close the essay?

9. Are there any fragments, run-ons, or comma splices? If so, where?

10. Are any words misspelled? Where?

11. Do punctuation errors occur? Where?

➡

12. Are there subject–verb agreement or pronoun–antecedent agreement errors? Be ready to point out these errors to the writer.

13. Are shifts in person present in the essay? If so, how could the writer correct this problem?

14. Is gender bias present in the essay? Why? How could sentences be revised to eliminate this bias?

15. This essay's strengths are _____ .

16. This essay's weaknesses are _____ .

Guide Questions for Comparison, Contrast, or Comparison/Contrast Essay

1. Does the introductory paragraph draw the reader's attention? Tell why or why not.

2. Does the introductory paragraph identify the two things that will be compared, contrasted, or compared and contrasted? What is **X**? What is **Y**?

3. Does the writer use a list or umbrella thesis?

4. Is this a comparison, contrast, or comparison/contrast essay?

5. What are the points that the writer is using to compare, contrast, or compare and contrast?

6. What pattern does the author use to organize the body paragraphs—block or point-by-point?

7. Is the comparison and/or contrast balanced? Does the writer discuss the same points about **X** and **Y**?

8. Does the writer use transitions to help the reader move through the essay? List four transitions that the writer uses. If you note any spot in the essay where a transition would be useful, make a suggestion. Also be sure that the writer is not repeating the same transitions too often.

9. Does the writer provide a summary of the major points in the concluding paragraph? Does the writer indicate a preference for **X** or **Y**? Is there sufficient evidence to support that preference?

10. Point out any fragments, run-ons, or comma splices.

11. Make a list of spelling errors.

12. Are there subject–verb agreement or pronoun–antecedent agreement errors? How can the writer correct these errors?

13. What strengths does the writer bring to this essay?

14. What areas need improvement?

You have now bridged over from the paragraph to the essay—an important step in achieving academic success. With the essay you, like many writers before you, can share your discoveries with your readers and, by doing so, learn more about yourself and the world around you.

Writers as Spiders

The World Wide Web offers many resources for writers of essays. For an overview of a wide variety of topics related to essay writing, see

http://webserver.maclab.comp.uvic.ca/writersguide/pages/ MasterTOC.html

This site features hints for writing introductory and concluding paragraphs as well as examples of these special paragraphs:

http://www.csuohio.edu/writingcenter/html/introcnc.html

Writing a strong thesis statement is critical to effective essay writing. For more information about thesis statements, consult

http://leo.stcloud.msus.edu/acadwrite/thesistatement.html

Web Exercise

Review the elements of the comparison/contrast essay at

http://leo.stcloud.msus.edu/acadwrite/comparcontrast.html

Then using a search engine, research information about two of the planets in the solar system (one of these can be your own planet, Earth.) Consider these questions:

1. What is the size of each of these planets?
2. What is the make-up of the atmosphere?
3. How long does it take each planet to complete a turn on its axis?
4. How long does it take each planet to orbit the sun?
5. Does the planet have moons? If so, how many?
6. What are other distinguishing characteristics of each planet?

Use the information you gather to form an outline and then write an essay comparing and/or contrasting these two planets.

You may want to download graphics to accompany your paper. Click on the image you wish to download, and save the image to your disk or hard drive. Then you can insert the images into your text document.

Additional Help

For additional exercises on pronoun agreement, visit

http://www.esc.edu/HTMLpages/Writer/pandg/npmen.htm

You can consult the National Council of Teachers of English guidelines regarding gender bias at

http://owl.english.purdue.edu/Files/26.html

CHAPTER

Focus on the
Problem-Solving Essay

FOCUS ON PURPOSE

The ability to use critical reasoning to solve problems is what separates humankind from lower forms of life. From the discovery of the wheel to the landing on the moon, humankind has engaged in creative problem solving. Without this ability, humankind would be left in chaos. Think what your everyday life would be like if you were not able to solve problems.

In the college classroom your teachers will require that you demonstrate your ability to solve problems. All of your math courses will require problem-solving skills, and in general, the higher the level of the course you are taking, the more challenging the problems you will solve. Your science classes will develop your critical thinking skills as you use scientific methods to investigate hypotheses and examine possible solutions to problems. In addition, your liberal arts courses will demand that you demonstrate your reasoning ability not only on objective examinations but also through written assignments and essay questions.

Your future success as a worker and as a citizen depends upon your development of problem-solving skills. As a worker you will face such decisions as where to work, when to change jobs, when to relocate to another city, and when to seek a raise or a promotion. Furthermore, participating in a democratic society gives you the freedom to address the problems you face in your community, including whether to raise taxes, how to improve the schools, whether to build new roads, and which candidates to elect for public office. Whether you are solving problems in the role of student, worker, or citizen, the decisions you make will greatly affect the course of your life.

This chapter will provide you the opportunity to develop your problem-solving skills by writing an essay that identifies a problem and proposes solutions. Your problem-solving essay will not only inform your readers about a problem but also will persuade them that this problem needs to be addressed.

FOCUS ON CHOOSING A TOPIC

Your problem-solving essay begins with a problem that concerns you. If you feel strongly that a problem needs attention, your concern will affect your reader as well.

As you choose your topic, keep in mind that the final draft of your essay will be approximately 500 words. Therefore, your essay should not focus on problems such as world hunger or homelessness, which are too complex to be discussed adequately in a short essay. Instead, focus your essay on a problem that impacts you directly. Use the following questions to help you focus your topic:

1. What is a problem facing your community? Does your community need new sidewalks, improved roads, more parks, new traffic lights, or better schools?

2. What is an environmental problem your community needs to address? Does your community need to conserve water, preserve natural areas, improve recycling programs, or restrict growth?

3. Have you recently had difficulty with a consumer product or with a business? Have you had problems with your car repair shop, local department store, or bank?

4. What is a current decision you must make? Are you considering moving to another city, changing your major, or taking another job?

5. What is a personal challenge you are facing? Are you trying to improve your time management, quit smoking, lose weight, or start an exercise program? (*Caution:* Remember your reader is not likely to be a professional counselor or a pastor!)

6. What is a problem you face at work? Are there employee policies that need improvement or procedures that require revision? Are there employees who need to improve their efficiency or supervisors who need to communicate more clearly?

FOCUS ON GENERATING IDEAS

After you have decided on a topic and before you begin your first draft, you need to investigate the problem. As you investigate the problem, you will generate ideas that will be useful to you as you develop the body paragraphs of your essay. Brainstorming, clustering, listing, and freewriting are all valuable ways to begin your investigation. Another effective investigative method is using reporters' questions:

- **What?**
- **Who?**
- **When?**
- **Where?**

- **Why?**
- **How?**
- **What** is the problem?
- **Who** is involved in the problem?
- **When** did the problem occur?
- **Where** did the problem occur?
- **Where** is the problem still occurring?
- **Why** does the problem continue?
- **Why** should the reader be concerned about the problem?
- **How** can the problem be solved?

A young reporter, Katherine Preble, wrote an editorial, "Chasing Suspects Costs Innocent Lives." In her editorial she addresses the following reporters' questions:

- **What** is the problem? *Deaths from high-speed police chases.*
- **Who** is involved in the problem? *Suspects, police pursuits, innocent victims, victims' families*
- **When** did the problem occur? *October 18, 1993, when her mother died*
- **Where** did the problem occur? *In front of the hospital where her mother worked*
- **Where** is the problem still occurring? *Throughout the country*
- **Why** does the problem continue? *Failure to adopt stringent rules regarding police chases*
- **Why** should the reader be concerned about the problem? *Anyone a potential victim*
- **How** can the problem be solved? *Adopt strict police pursuit policies, eliminate high-speed chases*

The answers to these questions helped her plan her editorial, which appears later in this chapter. Using these questions will also help you plan your problem-solving essay.

EXERCISE 8.1   In a small group, focus on a needed improvement at the college or university you attend. Are classes too large, parking lots too small, course offerings limited, food services inadequate? Once you have decided on a focus, use reporters' questions to investigate the problem. Then share your group's responses with the class.

FOCUSING ON ORGANIZING

After you have chosen a topic for your essay and gathered your ideas, you are ready to organize your essay. At this point you need to decide whether to

- Focus on the problem (**problem essay**)
- Focus on the problem and a possible solution (**problem/solution essay**)
- Focus on several possible solutions (**solution essay**)

Your decision will affect how you organize your essay. If your problem is complex, you may want to focus your entire essay on the problem and develop the body of the essay by providing the reader with relevant examples and other supporting details. If so, you do not have to suggest a solution. Instead, you develop a *problem essay*.

Another possibility is to focus not only on the problem but also on a single possible solution. This pattern of development—the *problem/solution essay*—works well for any problem that seems to have a single feasible solution. Using this pattern, the writer can spend approximately half of the essay discussing the problem and the other half proposing a solution.

A third possibility is to focus on several possible solutions. The *solution essay* works well when the problem is not difficult to state, but a single solution is not clear. In the body of a solution essay the writer works through several solutions and weighs each according to its advantages and disadvantages.

Thesis Statement

Whether you write a problem essay, a problem/solution essay, or a solution essay, your thesis statement should

- Identify the problem to your reader
- Convey to your reader the importance of solving the problem

A student, Stacey Powell, decided to focus her problem essay on a personal challenge she faced: her decision to enter nursing school. Stacey chose to write a problem essay to explore the ramifications of this decision on her personal life. The thesis statement of her essay conveys the urgency of the decision she faces.

> Now that I am ready to advance my career, I must decide which route to take to pursue my dream.

As you will note in her essay later in this chapter, she does not arrive at a solution to her problem. As the essay ends, she is still struggling with this problem.

In her editorial, a problem-solution essay, Katherine Preble uses a powerful thesis statement to end her introduction.

> A minor traffic violation ended the life of an innocent woman who had done nothing but give life to people through her work as a nurse.

In this sentence the reader is struck by the irony of the *minor traffic violation* and the death of *an innocent woman*, the writer's mother. The reader wants to read further about this problem that strongly warrants a solution.

In Chapter 7, you learned about umbrella and list thesis statements. If you write a solution essay, you may want to use a list thesis statement that states one or more solutions to the problem. For example, Bill Cronin wrote a solution essay to address the endangerment of a resident of Florida waters—the manatee. In his thesis he lists steps that government must take if the manatee is to survive.

If boaters can be persuaded to use safer boating equipment and the government to establish safe manatee areas, enforce boating regulations, and educate boaters, the manatee may survive.

Tamara Doseck faced a problem common to many Americans—a need to improve her physical health. In her thesis she sets forth the solution to her problem.

If I am to improve my health, I must develop a plan which includes both regular exercise and good eating habits.

A forceful thesis statement will provide a strong foundation for the remainder of your essay. Your reader will sense the urgency of the problem you are exploring and be eager to continue your essay.

EXERCISE 8.2

Read the responses to the reporters' questions below. Then using the responses, write two possible thesis statements—one for a problem essay and one for a solution essay—on the subject of battered women. (***Note:*** You do not have to incorporate all the responses in your thesis.) In small groups discuss your thesis statements with your classmates. Which is the strongest thesis statement for a problem essay? Which is the most forceful thesis for a solution essay? Why?

- **What** is the problem? *Battered women, number one cause for injuries of women between the ages of 15 and 44.*
- **Who** is involved in the problem? *Approximately 4 million women battered each year and the men who batter them.*
- **When** did the problem occur? *Every day. In 1992 over 1400 women were killed by husbands or boyfriends.*
- **Where** did the problem occur? *In homes throughout America.*
- **Where** is the problem still occurring? *With women of all ages, socio-economic classes, and races.*
- **Why** does the problem continue? *Those who batter feel loss of control and extreme rage, threats not always taken seriously.*
- **Why** should the reader be concerned about the problem? *Violence is not an acceptable way to address problems between husband and wife or between lovers. Innocent children are often witnesses.*
- **How** can the problem be solved? *Recognize warning signs, call 911, get restraining order, prosecute, call shelter hotline, seek refuge in a shelter.*

Thesis statement for problem essay: _____

_____

Thesis statement for solution essay: _____

_____

Use your group's response in Exercise 8.1 to write a thesis statement for a problem essay and a thesis statement for a solution essay.

EXERCISE 8.3

Thesis statement for problem essay: _____

_____

Thesis statement for solution essay: _____

_____

FOCUS ON THE PROBLEM ESSAY

Introductory Paragraph

The introductory paragraph of a problem essay has the same purpose as the introductory paragraph of any other essay, namely to announce the topic to the reader and to present the thesis statement.

In Chapter 7, you learned several different techniques you can use in the opening sentences of your essay. These same techniques apply to the introductory paragraph of the problem essay. For example, if you were writing about the problem of battered women, you could use a dramatic anecdote to begin your essay.

> She lies on the bed waiting for her husband's anger to subside. But she knows it will not. She watches him approach with his fist held high behind his back. Before she can move, his fist makes contact with her cheek. Stunned, she prays he will stop. She is just one of the approximately four million women battered each year in homes throughout America. Battering women, a form of domestic violence that cuts across socioeconomic, racial, and age boundaries, is unacceptable behavior in a civilized society.

This introduction is effective for a number of reasons. First, the woman is unnamed. Although the writer could have easily provided a name for her, leaving the woman nameless reinforces the idea that many women are in this same position. Second, the writer provides a bridge to the thesis statement.

> She is just one of the approximately four million women battered each year in homes throughout America.

Both the anecdote and the bridge serve to engage the interest of the reader and prepare the reader for the thesis and the body paragraphs that follow.

Another opening device that works well with problem essays is the use of relevant statistics.

> According to a recent newspaper article, battering by husbands or boyfriends is the number one cause of injury for women between the ages of 15 and 44. Last year almost four million women were battered by the men in their lives, and in 1992 fourteen hundred women died as a result of their injuries. This problem deserves national attention. Battering women, a form of domestic violence that cuts across socioeconomic, racial, and age boundaries, is unacceptable behavior in a civilized society.

These shocking statistics should convince readers to set aside any preoccupation to read your essay.

Other writers use the introductory paragraph to provide background information about the problem. This type of introduction often includes a brief history of the problem. For example, Stacey Powell uses her introduction to explain briefly the career choice she is facing.

> After graduating from high school, I did what I had planned to do ever since I was twelve years old. I joined the Navy with hopes of entering the nursing field as a Navy nurse. That plan ended abruptly when after only three weeks in boot camp, I was on crutches due to a knee problem. Currently I am working as an emergency medical technician. Now that I am ready to advance my career, I must decide which route to take to pursue my dream to become a nurse.

After reading her introductory paragraph, the reader not only senses the frustration that Stacey has felt in pursuing her childhood dream but is also curious about her future plans.

Body Paragraphs

In the body paragraphs of your problem essay you will deliver the evidence necessary to convince your reader that the problem must be addressed. You can use what you have observed and/or what you have read to demonstrate the existence of the problem. You can also use your answers to the reporters' questions to generate ideas for your body paragraphs.

In an essay on domestic violence with the following thesis—

> Battering women, a form of domestic violence that cuts across socioeconomic, racial, and age boundaries, is unacceptable behavior in a civilized society.

—the topic sentence of the first paragraph should focus the reader's attention on the fact that battered women come from all socioeconomic classes. Then the paragraph would develop with examples of such women. The topic sentence of the second paragraph might be

Not only can battered women be found in all socioeconomic classes but also in all racial groups.

The writer could also develop this paragraph with examples. Finally, the last paragraph would focus the reader's attention on battered women of all ages.

In Stacey Powell's problem essay, she uses the body paragraphs to explore why she is in her current position as well as the choice she must make: whether to attend a two-year registered nurse program or a one-year licensed practical nurse program. She then thinks through how each program would affect her relationship with her husband and their future plans.

It is important that you use enough details in the body paragraphs to convince your reader that you are knowledgeable about the problem and that the reader should share your concern about its existence. As in all paragraphs that you write, check to be sure that each detail is clearly related to the focus in the topic sentence and in the thesis.

Concluding Paragraph

A concluding paragraph of a problem essay, like the concluding paragraph of any essay, picks up where the introductory paragraph ends. Therefore, you should reread your introductory paragraph before writing your concluding paragraph.

If you began your introductory paragraph with an anecdote, you might want to finish the anecdote in the concluding paragraph. If you do so, you might want to hint at a solution to the problem. However, since you are writing an essay that focuses on the problem, do not develop this solution to any great extent. For example, the essay on domestic violence might end as follows:

> It does not matter to what socioeconomic, racial, or age group this battered woman belongs. She must communicate to her abuser that his behavior is not acceptable. As he leaves the room, she calls 911, packs her suitcase, and waits for the police.

This concluding paragraph ends on an uncertain note. Yet that uncertainty is deliberate on the part of the writer because this problem has no single solution.

An essay that begins with startling statistics can end with a future prediction:

> Unless society turns its attention to the problem of battered women and works toward strict punishment of the perpetrators, the number of women battered and killed by the men in their lives will continue to grow. How many women will be killed next year or the next?

This concluding paragraph ends with a forceful question to reinforce the urgency of addressing this problem.

Stacey's essay also ends on a note of uncertainty. As you will notice in Stacey's essay below, she does not reach a solution to her problem but instead shares with the reader her struggle to make a decision.

Student Sample

Problem Essay

Career Decisions

After graduating from high school, I did what I had planned to do ever since I was twelve years old. I joined the Navy with hopes of entering the nursing field as a Navy nurse. That plan ended abruptly when after only three weeks in boot camp, I was on crutches due to a knee problem. Currently I am working as an emergency medical technician. Now that I am ready to advance my career, I must decide which route to take to pursue my dream to become a nurse.

After my knee injury at boot camp, I had to make another career choice. So at eighteen years old I decided to become a paramedic. My initial plan was to bridge over from being a paramedic to becoming a registered nurse. However, by the time I finished EMT school, I was facing my second knee surgery, so I never became a paramedic. I am currently working as a CAT scan EMT in the department of radiology. After working in the radiology department for almost five years, I still have not forgotten my dream to become a nurse.

To fulfill my dream I must first go through nursing school. One program I can choose is a two-year registered nurse program. For two years I would have to go to school full-time during the day. This schedule would affect my current position at the hospital. Also, I married in February 1993. Even though my husband and I both have good jobs, we cannot afford for me not to work full-time. Our monthly bills will not go away while I am in school. Furthermore, this degree may take longer than two years for me to finish. However, I would finish the program as an R.N.

My other choice is to enroll in a one-year licensed practical nursing program. This program is offered in the evening, a schedule that would allow me to still keep my job. After finishing I would then be able to get a job at a higher salary and begin another year of classes to bridge over to the registered nursing program. In the long run, this one-year program would take more time to finish than the two-year registered nurse program. Also my husband and I would like to have a baby within the next few years, so I would like to be qualified for a stable medical position within two years.

I love helping sick people, so I know the medical field is the best choice for me. I just cannot decide in which direction I should go.

—Stacey Powell

FOCUS ON THE PROBLEM/SOLUTION ESSAY

Introductory Paragraph

The introductory paragraph of the problem/solution essay has the same purpose as that of the problem essay. Opening techniques such as using an anecdote or providing background information work just as well for the problem/solution essay as they do for the problem essay. Other techniques introduced in Chapter 7, such as citing a quotation, raising a question, creating an analogy, or challenging a common perception, are also effective.

In Katherine Preble's problem/solution editorial, she answers the reporters' questions of **who, what,** and **when** in her introductory paragraph:

> High-speed police chases may never cross most people's minds. They never entered mine until one changed my life on October 18, 1993, when my mother, Mary Creamer, was killed in a senseless and avoidable accident after a county sheriff's deputy started an 80 mph pursuit over an expired tag. A minor traffic violation ended the life of an innocent woman who had done nothing but give life to people through her work as a nurse.

In journalism this technique is called a *lead* because the opening sentences provide information crucial for the reader's comprehension of the subject. The assumption is that the newspaper reader wants this critical information as soon as possible. The term *lead* is appropriate for introductory paragraphs as well since their purpose is to *lead* the reader into the essay.

Body Paragraphs

In a problem/solution essay approximately half of the body (in a 500-word essay one or two paragraphs) is devoted to investigating the problem and the remainder to exploring a possible solution. While the purpose of the first half of the essay is **to inform** the reader about the problem, the purpose of the second half is **to persuade** the reader that a solution is possible.

As you offer evidence of the problem's existence in the first half of the essay, remember to refer back to your answers to the reporters' question to help generate ideas for your body paragraphs. In addition to the reporters' questions, ask yourself:

- What are the causes of this problem?
- What are the effects of this problem?

The answers to these questions will also help you think through the information you need to provide your reader in your body paragraphs.

In the second half of the essay you need to answer a new set of questions as you explore a potential solution:

- Why might this solution be workable?
- What are the advantages (strengths) of this solution?
- What are the disadvantages (weaknesses) of this solution?

Because most problems lack perfect solutions, it is important to anticipate possible drawbacks as well as explore the solution's strengths.

You need to provide transition between the problem and the solution sections of the essay. In her editorial, which appears below, Ms. Preble ends the problem section with a moving sentence in which she shares with the reader the effects of her mother's death:

It was as if someone had punched me out, and I had awakened inside someone else's life.

Then she begins the solution section by arguing that since this problem could affect anyone, it must be addressed.

This penetrating loss could have touched anyone with the pursuit policies currently in place in parts of the county.

Concluding Paragraph

The concluding paragraph should remind the reader of both the problem and the solution and thus reinforce the essay's thesis. A logical way to conclude your problem/solution essay is to communicate your hopes that the situation will improve in the future.

In her concluding paragraph, Katherine Preble not only reminds the reader of her personal pain but also of her wish that no one else will have to go through what she did.

Nothing will bring back my mom. However, we can prevent the same tragedy from happening to other innocent citizens and their families by establishing laws that will protect all of our citizens.

Sample Editorial

Problem/Solution Essay

Chasing Suspects Costs Innocent Lives

High-speed police chases may never cross most people's minds. They never entered mine until one changed my life on October 18, 1993, when my mother, Mary Creamer, was killed in a senseless and avoidable

➡

accident after a county sheriff's deputy started an 80 mph pursuit over an expired tag. A minor traffic violation ended the life of an innocent woman who had done nothing but give life to people through her work as a nurse.

The chase had just been called off when a 19-year-old man ran through a red light and broadsided my mom's car, which was pulling into the parking lot of the hospital where she worked. It didn't matter there was no longer a chase; the man was still trying to get away. He was sentenced to 17 years in prison for manslaughter by culpable negligence, leaving the scene of an accident involving death, and possession of marijuana.

My mother died less than three hours after she was taken by helicopter to a trauma unit. When I arrived, it was too late to even say goodbye to the woman who had raised me alone since my father died of cancer 14 years ago. It didn't seem possible that she could be taken away so easily. She was much more than a mom; she was my best friend. And for the first time in my life—at age 24—I felt completely alone. It was as if someone had punched me out, and I had awakened inside someone else's life.

This penetrating loss could have touched anyone with the pursuit policies currently in place in parts of the county. Officials in the county's largest cities have recently made a positive step by tightening their pursuit policies. Police in these cities may chase only motorists suspected of committing violent crimes such as rape, murder, or kidnapping. But these policies wouldn't have saved my mother. She was fatally injured in another municipality that will soon decide whether to adopt new rules.

How could they not opt for a change in policy? Officials should not only be adopting these more stringent rules but thinking of ways to eliminate high-speed pursuits completely. We have the technology in this day, with the use of helicopters and radios. We should not be putting innocent citizens in danger. The state of Michigan has a no-pursuit policy. Others, such as New Jersey, California, and Minnesota, have very strict limitations. These laws are possible for our state.

This county should get rid of its antiquated methods of catching criminals by unifying its policy on high-speed pursuits instead of giving law enforcement the discretion that creates a danger to the public. This would be a tiny step toward protecting the community. Even more needs to be done by Florida lawmakers.

Nothing will bring back my mom. However, we can prevent the same tragedy from happening to other innocent citizens and their families by establishing laws that will protect all of our citizens.

—Katherine Preble

FOCUS ON THE SOLUTION ESSAY

Introductory Paragraph

Because the focus of a solution essay is examining possible solutions, the introductory paragraph must present the problem to be solved. Again, think through the answers to the reporters' questions. What does your reader need to know about the problem before you begin discussing solutions?

Perhaps you want to dramatize the problem through the use of an anecdote. The following introductory paragraph begins with the same anecdote the writer used for the problem essay. Note, however, how the bridge sentence sets up the thesis for a solution essay.

> She lies on the bed waiting for her husband's anger to subside. But she knows it will not. She watches him approach with his fist held high behind his back. Before she can move, his fist makes contact with her cheek. Stunned, she prays he will stop. This woman, one of approximately four million women battered each year, needs to know that help is available. Battered women can call 911, get a restraining order, and seek refuge in a shelter.

This introductory paragraph ends with a thesis statement that lists three possible ways that battered women can seek help.

Tamara Doseck does not need a lengthy introduction for her solution essay.

> For the past two years I have tried unsuccessfully to exercise faithfully and eat wisely. I have always failed because I have never sat down and made out a complete plan for good health. If I am to improve my health, I must develop a plan that includes both regular exercise and good eating habits.

Tamara's problem is briefly stated but not easily solved.

In his essay Bill Cronin introduces the manatee and his natural enemy to lead his reader to the thesis.

> The manatee, a mammal that resides primarily in Florida's waters, is in danger of becoming extinct. The manatee's only natural enemy is man! Collisions with powerboats are the primary cause in the majority of manatee deaths. If boaters can be persuaded to use safer boating equipment and the government to establish safe manatee areas, enforce boating regulations and educate boaters, the manatee may survive.

Body Paragraphs

In each body paragraph of a solution essay you will examine a possible solution to the problem. You will then develop the body paragraphs by exploring the strengths and weaknesses of each solution.

For example, the first body paragraph of a solution essay with the thesis

Battered women can call 911, get a restraining order, and seek refuge in a shelter.

might read:

A woman who has been battered should call 911 during or immediately following the incident. By taking this step, the victim will know that the police are aware of her situation. She should then follow through by filling out a police report and following through with prosecution of her abuser. These steps will let her abuser know that his behavior violates the law. Even though many women know what steps they should take, they are reluctant to do so. They may be afraid that the abuse will worsen before the police arrive. They may fear that their abuser will convince the police that nothing is the matter, and then the abuse will continue. If the abuser is the main financial support for the family, then the woman may not want to prosecute her abuser because the family will lose income if he is incarcerated.

In this paragraph the writer discusses both the advantages and disadvantages of filing a police report. To support the thesis the second body paragraph would discuss the advantages and disadvantages of getting a restraining order, and the third body paragraph the advantages and disadvantages of seeking refuge in a shelter.

It does not matter whether you begin your body paragraphs by discussing the strengths or weaknesses of your solution. In her solution essay Tamara chooses to start her first body paragraph by acknowledging a major drawback to any exercise plan she might develop—the amount of time she will need for a good workout. Then she discusses how cardiovascular activities and strength training exercises will benefit her overall health. On the other hand, Bill Cronin first sets forth in each body paragraph what he feels must be done to protect the manatee and then mentions possible objections. Whether you decide to discuss strengths and then weaknesses or vice versa, keep the order consistent in each body paragraph.

Concluding Paragraph

The concluding paragraph of your solution essay should briefly restate the problem and evaluate the solutions you have proposed in the body of the essay.

If appropriate, you should identify which of the solutions appears most workable. In other situations, you can argue that any approach to the problem must involve a number of different solutions.

An essay exploring ways that women in abusive relationships might seek help could conclude:

> Any woman who is being battered must seek help. She must recognize that she is the victim, not the perpetrator. Even though calling 911, getting a restraining order, and entering a shelter all involve risk-taking on her part, she should pursue each of these actions when violence occurs. Not one of these actions is as dangerous to her well-being as staying in an abusive relationship.

As you will see in the essay below, Tamara concludes that any plan to improve her health must include exercise and a good nutrition plan. The ultimate success of the plan, however, is dependent upon her willingness to work hard to achieve her goal.

In his concluding paragraph, Bill Cronin realizes that humankind has the chance to save the manatee from extinction.

Student Samples

Solution Essay

Wanted: A Game Plan for Good Health

For the past two years I have tried unsuccessfully to exercise faithfully and eat wisely. I have always failed because I have never sat down and made out a complete plan for good health. If I am to improve my health, I must develop a plan that includes a regular exercise and good eating habits.

One way to improve my overall health is physical exercise. However, before I develop an exercise plan, I must consider a major drawback—a lack of time. Between work and school, I have a hard time finding twenty to thirty minutes three times a week for exercise. I know that I must block out at least that much time if my exercise plan is to work. After I make the commitment of time, I must prepare myself for regular exercise by getting a trainer, reading an exercise book, or watching an exercise video. Many exercises can cause injuries if not properly performed. Reviewing proper form will enable me to get the most out of my workouts. My workout plan must include both cardiovascular and strength-training exercises. My goal is to participate in outdoor cardiovascular activities three days a week: Mondays, Wednesdays, and Fridays. Cardiovascular activities such as

➡

running, jogging, roller blading, biking, tennis, and swimming will strengthen my heart and blood vessels. On other days my goal is to go to the gym for strength training using either free weights or machines to build and strengthen my muscles. For example, on Tuesdays I will do upper body exercises to develop my biceps, triceps, back, chest, and shoulders. On Thursdays I will exercise my lower body including calves, quads, and buttocks.

Not only must I plan for regular exercise, but also for healthy eating. A healthy diet plan means watching my calories, fat intake, and caffeine consumption. It is important to try not to exceed 1500 calories in one day. However, it is more important to count fat grams than calories because it is much easier for me to burn calories than fat. The cardiovascular and strength training exercises that I perform during the week will enable me to burn calories efficiently. Therefore, the most important part of my nutritional plan must be watching my fat intake. Monitoring fat grams will be difficult because some labels are misleading. I must read every label carefully and not exceed the serving size. I want to keep my fat intake under 30 grams per day. Limiting my caffeine will also help me achieve my goal of good health. Caffeine gives me a "sugar high." Then in a few hours I start to feel sluggish and need more caffeine to get through the day. This cycle will be difficult for me to break particularly at work because of the convenience of coffee and soda machines. I must plan to replace sodas and coffee with water or fruit juices.

Now that I have thought through my plan, I am ready to work to achieve my goal. My chances of success are great if I make regular exercise and good eating habits a way of life.

— Tamara Doseck

A Call for Action

The manatee, a mammal that resides primarily in Florida's waters, is in danger of becoming extinct. The manatee's only natural enemy is man! Collisions with powerboats are the primary cause in the majority of manatee deaths. If boaters can be persuaded to use safer boating equipment and the government to establish safe manatee areas, enforce boating regulations and educate boaters, the manatee may survive.

Presently, powerboat equipment exists that is safer for the manatee than the traditional propeller drive. For example, boaters may equip their boats with jet propulsion units as opposed to propeller drives. These jet units do not have a rotating propeller to maim and scar the manatee as it swims and breathes at the surface. Also available, but rarely used, are propeller guards that help the manatee avoid contact with propellers. Admittedly, boaters are reluctant to use this available equipment because it is expensive and may diminish the performance and fuel efficiency of their craft.

Although regulations presently exist to protect the manatee, they need to be expanded greatly. In areas that are currently "manatee zones," the government should ban all powerboat traffic. Powerboat operation should be allowed at "idle speed" only in areas that are known manatee habitats but which are less densely populated than "manatee zones." Boaters may feel that such stringent regulations would infringe on their rights. However, the manatee's right to survive is at stake.

Furthermore, present and future regulations to aid the manatee will be useless if the marine patrol does not have the power to enforce them. The state legislature must designate funds for additional manpower and equipment to patrol our waters. Enforcing these laws will generate revenue in the form of fines and promote manatee awareness. Unfortunately, the financial burden of this enforcement will fall on the taxpayers. New taxes are never an easy "sell." However, humans must ensure the survival of the manatee.

In addition, powerboat operators must be educated in the safe operation of their craft. Presently, anyone may legally operate a powerboat in Florida's waters. There are no age, training, or licensing requirements. The time has come to require a formal license to operate a powerboat. Before being issued a license, the applicant would have to complete a course in boating safety. The course would include a segment on manatee preservation. With the implementation of this training program, all boaters would learn how to spot areas where manatees congregate, spot manatees in the water, and operate their vessels in a way that does not endanger the manatee. A program of this magnitude would be very expensive to implement. Simply put, boaters would have to bear the expense in the form of licensing fees.

As a result of powerboat collisions, the manatee population has dwindled to less than 2000. Humankind has the ability to save the manatee from extinction. If the manatee is to survive, boaters must use the safest equipment available and agree to obey strict regulations designed to protect the manatee. Most importantly, boaters must learn to operate their vessels in a manner that does not endanger the few remaining manatees. Man and manatee can coexist only if we are willing to sacrifice.

— Bill Cronin

FOCUS ON TRANSITION

Use traditional expressions and repeated key words to help your reader through your essay. Transition is especially important when you move

- From one aspect of the problem to another
- From the statement of the problem to the proposal of the solution
- From one proposed solution to another

In the essay above, Bill Cronin uses transitional words and phrases effectively. Circle or highlight each transitional expression Bill uses to begin sentences. Be prepared to explain how each transitional expression prepares the reader for what is to follow.

EXERCISE 8.4

FOCUS ON GRAMMAR

Pronoun Case

In Chapter 7 you learned to classify pronouns according to *person* (first, second, or third) and *number* (singular or plural). You can also classify pronouns according to *case*. The term *case* in grammar refers to how the pronoun functions in the sentence. The three cases of pronouns are: subjective, objective, and possessive.

Subjective Case. **Subjective case** (sometimes referred to as nominative case) **pronouns** are *I, you, he, she, it, we, they, who,* and *whoever.* These pronouns function

- **As subjects**

No one is likely to say,

> **Me** need a ride to school.

You can usually follow this rule easily in your speaking and writing because you can "hear" the correct response:

> **I** need a ride to school.

Some difficulty, however, may occur when the pronoun used as a subject is preceded by the words *you and* or by a noun followed by *and*:

> **Incorrect: You and me** need to go to the bank immediately.

> **Incorrect: Joan and me** were late for class.

To check for the correct pronoun, read the sentences above and omit the words *You and* and *Joan and:*

> **I** need to go to the bank immediately.

> **I** was late for class.

Then edit the sentences.

> **Correct: You and I** need to go to the bank immediately.

> **Correct: Joan and I** were late for class.

- **Following linking verbs** (*am, is, are, was, were, will be, shall be*, etc.) For a complete list of linking verbs, see Chapter 2. In everyday casual conversation someone may call you on the phone and ask, "Hey, is that you?" and informally you may reply, "Yeah, it's me." However, in formal communications if someone asks, "Is that you?", your response should be,

> Yes, it is **I.**

If someone asks, "Is this the president of the company?", your response should be

> Yes, this is **he.**
> > *or*
> Yes, this is **she.**

Whenever you are speaking or writing for a general audience, you should obey this grammatical principle.

- **In comparisons using** *than* **or** *as.* In many comparisons using the words *than* or *as,* subjective case pronouns are necessary. For example, if you are comparing yourself to your sister who is taller, you should speak or write,

> My sister is taller than **I.**

The subjective pronoun *I* is used because it serves as a subject for the understood verb *am.* Also note that the understood verb follows the pronoun:

> My sister is as tall as **I (am).**

If you compare yourself to your sister who is the same height, you should speak or write,

> My sister is as tall as **I (am).**

Objective Case. **Objective case pronouns** are *me, you, it, him, her, us, them, whom,* and *whomever.* These pronouns serve

- **Following action verbs.** This rule is generally easy to apply because the correct pronoun sounds right:

  Mother took **me** along to the store.

  Sue gave **them** an assignment for the next class period.

- **As objects of the preposition.** As you learned in Chapter 2, prepositions are followed by objects. These objects can be nouns or objective case pronouns.

  Beth sent the present to **me.**

  My supervisor suggested that I work with **her.**

Sometimes speakers and writers have a difficult time choosing the correct pronoun when the preposition is followed by a compound object consisting of the pronoun *you* followed by the conjunction *and.* Many speakers and writers think that the words *you and* should automatically be followed by the pronoun *I.* That is true when the words *you and I* form the subject of the sentence:

  You and I received the assignment from the instructor.

However, in the sentence

  The instructor gave the group assignment to you and me.

the pronoun *me* is correct because the phrase *you and me* forms the object of the preposition *to.* (For a complete list of prepositions, see Chapter 2.) To check your answer omit the words *you and* from the sentence.

  The instructor gave the group assignment to **(you and) me.**

This same principle applies not just to phrases beginning with *you and* but also beginning with other nouns.

  The instructor gave the group assignment to John and **me.**

  The gift is for my sister and **me.**

It also applies to sentences using the preposition *between:*

> This secret is just between you and **me.**

- **In comparisons using** *than* **or** *as.* In some comparisons an objective case pronoun follows *than* or *as.*

> Regular exercise can help you as much as **me.**
> The overcrowded store disturbs Laura more than **him.**

In these sentences the words that are understood come before the pronoun.

> Regular exercise can help you as much as **(it can help) me.**
> The overcrowded store disturbs Laura more than **(it disturbs) him.**

Possessive Case Pronouns. Possessive case pronouns are *my, your, yours, its, his, her, hers, our, ours, their, theirs,* and *whose.* These pronouns are used

- **To show possession.** This rule is not difficult for speakers or writers because the pronoun choice "sounds right" to the ear. However, sometimes the pronoun is misspelled. Note how the possessive case pronouns listed above do not have apostrophes. No apostrophes are needed on pronouns. Yet many writers confuse the possessive pronoun *its* with the contraction *it's* meaning *it is.*

> **Correct:** The bird ate **its** dinner.
> **Correct: It's** time to leave for class. (Check by substituting *it is* for *it's:* **It is** time for class.)

The possessive pronoun *theirs* is also confused with the contraction *there's* *(there is).*

> **Correct:** The textbooks are **theirs.**
> **Correct: There's** the book we need for class. (**There is** the book we need for class.)

- **Before** *-ing* **words used as nouns.** This rule, which is not always practiced in informal speaking or writing, calls for a possessive case pronoun before a noun ending in *-ing.*

> **His** coming to class late bothered the instructor.
> I do not think I should be penalized for **my** failing to pay the bill on time.

Who, Whom, and Whose

As noted above, *who* and *whoever* are subjective case pronouns, *whom* and *whomever* are objective case pronouns, and *whose* is a possessive case pronoun. While the case of the possessive pronoun *whose* is easy to determine, deciding when to use *who* and *whom* can be troublesome. The following suggestions can make this choice less difficult:

- **Remember that *who* and *whoever* are subjective pronouns and will serve as subjects for verbs.**

  Who is on the phone? (*Who* is the subject for the verb *is*.)

  She is the one **who** will make the decision. (*Who* is the subject for the verb *will make*.)

  I wonder **who** will be elected president in the next election. (*Who* serves as the subject for the verb *will be elected*.)

  Whoever enters the room will be the committee's next chairperson. (*Whoever* is the subject of the verb *enters*.)

- **Check your choice of the pronoun *who* or *whoever* by substituting *he* or *she* for *who*.** If the pronoun *he* or *she* is used correctly, *who* or *whoever* is the correct pronoun.

  He is on the phone.

  She will make the decision.

  She will be elected president in the next election.

  He enters the room.

- **Remember that *whom* and *whomever* are objective case pronouns so the verbs that follow will already have subjects.**

  The letter was addressed To **Whom** It May Concern. (The verb *may concern* already has a subject—the pronoun *it*. Therefore, the correct pronoun is *whom*.)

  It is not clear for **whom** the letter was written. (The verb *was written* has a subject *the letter*, so the pronoun choice is *whom*.)

  With **whom** are you going? (*You* is the subject of the verb *are going*.)

  You may go with **whomever** you please. (The subject of the verb *please* is *you*.)

- **To check your pronoun choice,** create a new sentence that begins with the subject and verb now following the pronoun *whom* or *whomever.* Then substitute *him* or *her* for *whom* or *whomever.* If the pronoun *him* or *her* is used correctly, *whom* or *whomever* is the correct pronoun.

It may concern **her.**

The letter was written for **him.**

You are going with **him.**

You please **her.**

EXERCISE 8.5

In the following exercise mark through the incorrect pronouns and replace with the correct pronoun choice.

A woman whom is experiencing domestic violence should seek refuge in a shelter for battered women. Her and her children should leave their residence as soon as possible after the abuse occurs. At the shelter her and her children will be safe and can receive counseling. In counseling she will realize that it is not her but her abuser who is the perpetrator of the violence. Also she will find that other women are experiencing the same type of abuse as her. The counseling will likely benefit her children as much as she. Entering a shelter is difficult, however. She must leave all but a few possessions behind at her home. The children who she may be traveling with may experience anxiety. She may resist counseling because she feels her problems can be worked out between she and the man in her life with no outside help. Furthermore, her community may not have a shelter for her children and she. Despite it's drawbacks, a shelter can offer battered women a lifeline. Every abused woman should consider taking this important step.

FOCUS ON PEER REVIEW

For your problem-solving essay to be effective, you must communicate clearly to your reader. The following peer review questions will help you determine whether your reader has received your message.

1. What is the the focus of the essay—the problem, solution(s), or the problem and a solution?

2. What is the problem the writing is addressing?

3. What technique does the writer use to open the essay?

4. Does the writer answer the questions *what, who, when,* and *where* in the introductory paragraph?

5. Why should you as a reader care about this problem? What type of reader do you think would most be interested in this essay?

6. List two examples or facts that the writer uses to demonstrate the problem. Does the writer seem knowledgeable about the problem?

7. If the essay focuses on solution(s) or problem/solution, what is the most workable solution the writer offers? Does the writer examine both the advantages and disadvantages of the solution? Do you agree or disagree that this solution is workable? Why or why not?

8. Does the concluding paragraph effectively sum up the essay? If not, what loose ends remain?

9. List three transitional expressions the writer uses to help the reader move through the essay.

10. Are any fragments, run-ons, or comma splices present in the essay? If so, where? Make a suggestion how the writer might correct one of these errors.

11. List any spelling errors you find.

12. Are there punctuation errors? Place a check mark at the end of any line where a punctuation error occurs.

13. Circle any subject–verb agreement or pronoun–antecedent agreement errors you notice.

14. Are any pronoun case errors present in the essay? If so, list them.

15. What are the strengths of the essay?

16. What can the writer do to improve the essay?

Every day you face problems in the classroom, at home, and in the workplace. Failure to address those problem can be costly personally and professionally. Learning to think through your problems and the solutions needed to address them is critical to your future success.

Writers as Spiders

The World Wide Web was originally designed as a research tool for the military and educational organizations. Today the Web is an invaluable source of information about a wide variety of societal problems.

Web Exercise

Use a search engine to research one of the following problems (or choose your own topic):

- Teen pregnancy
- Domestic violence
- Political campaign reform
- Global warming
- Welfare reform
- Prison reform
- Sexual harassment in the workplace
- Violence in schools

Read several web pages related to your problem. Then, in your own words, answer the following questions:

1. What did you learn about the history of this problem? How long has this problem existed?
2. What are the factors contributing to this problem? Which of these factors do you think is most important?
3. Has this problem worsened or improved in recent years? What are some statistics that support your response?
4. How urgent is this problem? What are the implications for society if this problem is not addressed?
5. Why does this problem continue? Why should you be concerned about the problem?
6. Do the web pages offer any suggestions for solving this problem? Which suggestion do you think is most workable? Why?

You may decide to use in your problem-solving essay some of the information you have gathered. You do not have to give credit to the web site if you use historical and scientific facts, because scholars consider these facts common knowledge. However, if you incorporate into your essay any opinions or statistics (statistics are not considered scientific facts), you must give credit to the web site where you located the information—even if you use your own words.

You can acknowledge the source informally by using an introductory phrase such as *According to . . .* or *As stated in . . .* and then including a Works Cited (bibliography) at the end of your paper. Another possibility is to acknowledge the source formally with parenthetical citations and a Works Cited page. Whether you acknowledge the source informally or formally, you should use the Modern Language Association (MLA) format for documenting World Wide Web sites. For more information about MLA format, see

http://leo.stcloud.msus.edu/research/mla.html#Computer

Additional Help

For additional information about writing a problem-solving essay, consult

http://www.temple.edu/writingctr/cw06001.htm

For a review of pronoun case, try

http://www.english.uiuc.edu/cws/wworkshop/case.htm

Focus on the Persuasive Essay

FOCUS ON PURPOSE

The ability to persuade others to accept a particular point of view (and to understand when others are trying to persuade you) is a critical skill for everyday living. From advertising in the mass media to the editorial page of the local newspaper, those who want to influence the decisions in your life bombard you daily. Some of these avenues of persuasion are blatantly obvious while others are deceptively subtle. Whatever the form of persuasion, it is important that you recognize the intent of the author of the message and apply your critical thinking skills before you make a decision whether to accept the author's plea.

In the college classroom your teachers will ask that you demonstrate your skills of persuasion. Your speech instructor, for example, may ask you to take a stand on a particular issue and support this stand with evidence. In addition, many college research papers are not only informative, but also persuasive because they require information from outside resources arranged to support a specific point of view. Some instructors may even require that your essays examine the opposing viewpoints. These instructors recognize that the ability to look carefully at two or more viewpoints on a single issue and evaluate the evidence is essential for successful academic work. While in the outside world you can often make a statement of opinion and not be called upon to back up your assertion with evidence, in the academic world your readers will expect you to defend your position with information from reputable sources.

Your success in the workplace and in your community also depends on the development of your persuasive skills. Whenever you apply for a job, you are not just providing information such as your address, former employment, and salary history. You are also trying to persuade someone to interview you and hire you for the position. Once you receive the job, you can use your persuasive ability to ask your boss for a raise, apply for a promotion, or seek increased job responsibilities. Furthermore, every time you exercise your right to vote, you are essentially stating your agreement with a particular candidate's stand on the issues. When you serve on a jury, you must listen to both the prosecution and the defense, weigh the evidence, and make a decision. Whether you are persuading someone to accept your point of view or acting upon someone else's influence, the stands you take will often have long-lasting consequences.

This chapter will help you develop your skills of persuasion by composing an essay that takes a stand on an issue and also examines opposing viewpoints. Your persuasive essay will not only provide evidence to support your position, but will also attempt to persuade your readers to agree with your position and act accordingly.

FOCUS ON CHOOSING A TOPIC

You should begin your persuasive essay (sometimes called an *argumentation essay*) with an issue that is important to you. When you feel strongly about an issue, your chances of persuading your reader are enhanced because your reader can sense your interest and concern.

When you select your topic, remember that you should be able to discuss this topic thoroughly in a single essay. Unless you carefully limit your topic, do not attempt to write about such multi-faceted social issues as abortion, welfare, or capital punishment—issues too complex for a short academic essay. Try to select an issue that affects you and your reader directly.

The following is a list of possible persuasive topics. For other possibilities, ask your instructor.

1. Persuade a student to learn to compose essays on a computer (as opposed to handwriting them).

2. Argue whether college students should be required to take a year of foreign language courses.

3. Persuade your reader to conserve an important environmental resource.

4. Argue for or against a curfew for teenagers in your community.

5. Persuade the citizens of your community to accept a tax hike to fund a needed project.

6. Argue for or against donating organs for transplants.

7. Argue whether college classes should have mandatory attendance policies.

8. Argue for or against lowering the minimum drinking age to 18.

9. Argue for or against stricter penalties for drunk drivers in your state.

10. Argue for or against raising the minimum driving age to 18.

11. Persuade your readers to sign a living will.

12. Convince your readers to recycle.

13. Argue for or against couples living together before marriage.

14. Argue for or against owning a gun.

15. Convince your readers to volunteer in a shelter for the homeless or for some other community service.

16. Persuade your reader to donate money to a specific worthy cause.

17. Which college football (or basketball, etc.) team is the best in the nation? Convince your reader.

18. Argue whether animal experimentation should be used for commercial research.

19. Argue whether Congress should continue to fund space exploration.

20. Who should be the next President of the United States? Convince your reader.

FOCUS ON GENERATING IDEAS

All the strategies for generating ideas discussed in this textbook will be helpful as you plan your persuasive essay. Try the following methods:

Brainstorm with a Partner or in a Small Group

Share your issue and your position with your partner or group. Then discuss the reasons why you have adopted this point of view. Ask your partner or group to play devil's advocate by discussing as many opposing viewpoints as possible. Take notes (or ask someone in the group to take them) for later use in developing your body paragraphs.

Develop a Cluster for Each Major Reason to Support Your Point of View

Be sure to include in your cluster two or more reasons that support your stand on the issue. When you have completed your cluster, form another cluster using reasons your opposition might give to counter your position. Taking this step will help you not only visualize the support for your point of view but also anticipate your opposition's viewpoints.

Make a Chart and List the Major Arguments You Will Use to Support Your Position

Create another chart (preferably alongside your previous one) and list the major points of your opposition. When you are filling out the charts, do not worry about the order in which the arguments appear. The goal is to have a list to work from as you gather supporting evidence. You can arrange your ideas in a logical order at a later date. However, if you notice an argument on your opposing list that counters one of your supporting arguments, you may want to draw a line between the two for later reference.

Do One or More Freewritings About the Issue

When you freewrite, you may be surprised to find that you feel so strongly about your position or that you have so much to say. If you are unsure which issue to choose as a topic for your essay, try freewriting about several topics to see which issue generates the most ideas. A friend calls this process "stirring the stew to see what comes to the top."

Use the Reporters' Questions

What is the issue?

Who is likely to care about this issue?

Who is likely to agree with your position?

Who is likely to disagree?

When did the issue arise?

Why should your reader take action on this issue?

What action should the reader take?

The answers to these questions will help you focus your topic and clarify your position.

Carefully Consider Your Reader

Understanding your reader is critical for a persuasive essay because you are attempting to convince your reader to agree with your position and take action. Therefore, you need to know as much about your reader as possible. To help focus your attention on your reader, use the questions from the "Focus on the Reader" section in Chapter 1. The more you know about your reader, the more likely you will be able to persuade your reader to accept your point of view.

EXERCISE 9.1

In a small group choose one of the issues listed in the "Focus on Choosing a Topic" section of this chapter. Write a position on this issue for the purpose of group discussion. Then brainstorm arguments both supporting and opposing the position. Make a chart of supporting arguments and a chart of opposing viewpoints. Be prepared to share these charts with the rest of the class.

FOCUS ON ORGANIZING

Once you have selected an issue, decided on a position, and brainstormed supporting and opposing arguments, you can begin to organize your essay. Although it is possible to write an effective persuasive essay that does not consider opposing viewpoints, this chapter assumes that you wish to acknowledge the opposition in your essay.

Thesis Statement

As in all the essays discussed in this book, your persuasive essay needs a clear, forceful thesis statement. Your thesis statement should

- Summarize opposing viewpoints
- Set forth your position on the issue

One way to compose your thesis statement is to use an introductory subordinate clause to summarize the opposing arguments followed by an independent clause in which you assert your position.

Although _____ summary of opposing viewpoints _____ ,

_____ your position on the issue _____ .

Even though _____ summary of opposing viewpoints _____ ,

_____ your position on the issue _____ .

Despite the fact that _____ summary of opposing viewpoints _____ ,

_____ your position on the issue _____ .

Two students, Mary Ann Saravanos and Laura Brower, wrote persuasive essays arguing that the drinking age should remain twenty-one. Both of their thesis statements acknowledge the opposition while setting forth the writer's stand:

Although many young people would argue that those who are old enough to vote, fight, and die for their country are old enough to drink responsibly, the drinking age should remain twenty-one.

—*Mary Ann Saravanos*

Despite the fact that some people argue that a person who can marry, vote, and fight wars should also have the right to drink, the drinking age should remain twenty-one.

—*Laura Brower*

Both thesis statements assert the writers' position—*The drinking age should remain twenty-one*—but do not list the reasons supporting the writers' position. In other words, each thesis statement is an umbrella thesis. It is also possible to write a list thesis that announces the supporting reasons. Mary Ann's thesis, for instance, could have been

> Although many young people would argue that those who are old enough to vote, fight, and die for their country are old enough to drive responsibly, the drinking age should remain twenty-one because of the dangers of alcohol-related accidents and the lack of alcohol education programs.

The difficulty with list thesis statements for persuasive essays is that they can easily become lengthy and wordy. Also a list thesis statement is not necessary if you clarify your supporting arguments in the topic sentence of your body paragraphs.

Whether you compose a list thesis or an umbrella thesis, a strong thesis statement will lay the groundwork for the rest of your essay. Your reader will sense your commitment to your position and anticipate the evidence you will use in your body paragraphs to support your stand.

Suppose you want to write a persuasive essay on the topic *Should You Own a Gun?* You have considered the following arguments:

EXERCISE 9.2

For Gun Ownership	**Against Gun Ownership**
—protection of property	—increased chance of accidental death
—protection of self	—increased chance of suicide
—protection of others	—increased chance of homicide

Write a thesis statement for each of the following:

Umbrella thesis in favor of gun ownership: _____

_____

Umbrella thesis against gun ownership: _____

_____

List thesis in support of gun ownership: _____

_____

_____

List thesis opposing gun ownership: _____

_____

_____

Introductory Paragraph

The introductory paragraph of a persuasive essay serves the same purpose as the introductory paragraph of a problem-solving essay. The introduction should

- Attract the reader's interest
- Convince the reader of the importance of the issue
- Provide any necessary background information on the topic
- Provide a bridge from the opening sentences to the thesis
- Present the thesis statement

Mary Ann Saravanos introduces her essay by directing the reader's attention to the misery that is often a consequence of alcohol use among teens.

Many young people would like to see the current drinking age of twenty-one lowered to eighteen. Yet the facts to date make a clear statement as to the need to maintain and enforce the twenty-one-year-old drinking age restriction. The adverse effects of alcohol-influenced automobile crashes, crimes, and illnesses on teens equal a sizable sum of human misery. Although many young people would argue that those who are old enough to vote, fight, and die for their country are old enough to drink responsibly, the drinking age should remain twenty-one.

Laura Brower emphasizes the messages some parents send their teens about alcohol use.

Any time teenagers consume alcohol, they are breaking the law. Yet many parents let their children take a sip or two at home under their supervision. What many parents do not realize is that they are giving their children mixed messages about drinking. These same children when they become teenagers may think that it is all right to drink alcohol even though such consumption is clearly against the law. These teens do not realize that alcohol-related problems are eating away at America's youth. Despite the fact that some people argue that a person who can marry, vote, and fight wars should also have the right to drink alcohol, the drinking age should remain twenty-one.

A dramatic way to begin an introductory paragraph for a persuasive essay is to use an anecdote. If you were composing an essay arguing in support of gun ownership, you might begin:

Joan is home alone. Suddenly she hears a noise at the door as if someone is trying to come inside. She reaches for the handgun she bought last month and aims it at the door. The robber barely reaches the threshold before, reeling from the gunshot wound to his leg, he falls to the floor. Joan calls 911 and waits for the police to arrive. Joan is just one of many women who bought handguns last year. Although some argue that the presence of a gun in the home increases the chances of accidental deaths, suicides, and homicides, owning a gun is a necessary step for security of property and self-defense.

If you were arguing against gun ownership, your introductory paragraph might be:

Joan is home alone. Suddenly she hears a noise at the door as if someone is trying to come inside. She reaches for the handgun she bought last month and aims it at the door. Her elderly next-door neighbor barely reaches the threshold before, reeling from the gunshot wound to his leg, he falls to the floor. After calling for emergency assistance, Joan sits crying softly with her head in her hands. Joan is just one of many women who bought handguns last year. Although some argue that owning a gun is a necessary step for the security of property and self-defense, the presence of a gun in the home increases the chances of accidental deaths, suicides, and homicides.

Whether you use an anecdote to begin your essay or some other technique such as citing a quotation, raising a question, creating an analogy, or providing relevant statistics, remember that your introductory paragraph makes your first impression on your reader. Your reader will appreciate the care you take to create a positive first impression.

Body Paragraphs

In your body paragraphs you must provide sufficient evidence to convince the reader to agree with your position on the issue. Effective persuasion essays include various types of evidence including

- Statements of fact
- Statements of opinion
- Statistics
- First-hand experience and observations

A fact is different from an opinion. A factual statement, unlike an opinion, can be verified in several sources. Historical incidents and scientific findings are examples of facts. For example, the statement, *President John F. Kennedy was assassinated on November 22, 1963,* is a fact. This date will not change, no matter which source you consult. Statements of fact will be useful to you in your persuasive essay because you can use them to provide background information and to convince your reader that you are knowledgeable about your subject.

Your reader cannot disagree with a fact. However, any statement of opinion you make is open to debate. When you state an opinion about an issue, you will need to support it with further facts and opinions if you are to persuade your reader to agree with your point of view. The statement, *President John F. Kennedy was the best president of the twentieth century*, is an opinion. A reader may or may not agree with this statement.

Writers use opinions as well as facts to establish their credibility with their readers. If your reader is to adopt your point of view, you must argue convincingly and logically in support of your opinions. A competent reader is able to distinguish facts from opinions and will evaluate your opinions according to his or her experiences.

Many writers rely on statistics to influence the reader's point of view. A careful reader will realize that statistics are generally not statements of fact because statistics may vary from one source to another. Your readers will expect you to provide the source of any statistics you use in your essay. You can provide the source informally by using an introductory phrase such as *According to . . .* or *In a recent survey . . .* or formally through the use of a documentation style such as the Modern Language Association (MLA) format. Check with your instructor about documentation requirements.

First-hand experiences and observations are also acceptable support for your thesis, providing, of course, that these experiences and observations are relevant to the issue. Using first-hand experience is an effective way to appeal to the emotions of your reader. For example, if you are arguing in support of gun ownership and you have been a victim of a robbery, your experience will lend credibility to your argument. Or if you have lost a relative or a friend to a suicide as a result of a gunshot wound, your observations can help your reader understand your opposition to gun ownership. Readers generally accept first-hand experiences on face value and are unlikely to question your credibility.

EXERCISE 9.3

Write the letter **F** in the blank to the left of any sentence that presents a statement of fact. Write the letter **O** in the blank to the left of any sentence that states an opinion.

_____ **1.** Congress ratified the Twenty-Sixth Amendment to the Constitution in 1971.

_____ **2.** The Twenty-Sixth Amendment grants eighteen-year-olds the right to vote.

_____ **3.** The majority of eighteen- to twenty-one-year olds are able to make responsible decisions about alcohol consumption.

_____ **4.** Raising the drinking age will continue to reduce dramatically the fatalities among teen drivers in this country.

_____ **5.** Drunk driving is a contributing factor in many motor vehicle accidents involving teen drivers.

———— **6.** Raising the drinking age to twenty-one is the most effective way to reduce alcohol abuse among teenagers.

———— **7.** Eighteen-year-old waiters can serve alcohol but cannot legally consume it.

———— **8.** Eighteen-year-old males are eligible for the armed services draft.

Once you have thought through which facts, opinions, statistics, experiences, and observations to use to support your position, you are ready to organize your body paragraphs. Although there are many ways to present supporting and opposing arguments in the body paragraphs of a persuasive essay, this chapter will discuss two common methods: the block pattern and the point/counterpoint pattern.

Block Pattern for Persuasive Essays

When you use the block pattern, you list the major opposing viewpoints in your first body paragraph. The goal is to let the reader know that you understand the arguments of your opposition although you disagree with them. The goal is not to provide supporting evidence for these opposing arguments. In general, you should list these arguments from the one you consider the least important to the one you consider the strongest.

Mary Ann Saravanos uses the block pattern in her persuasive essay. Her first body paragraph appears below.

> Those who support a drinking age of eighteen argue that eighteen-year-olds are legal adults. They are old enough to fight for their country and sacrifice their lives on the battlefield. They are responsible enough to vote their political convictions. Furthermore, eighteen-year-olds can purchase cigarettes. They can even serve alcohol as bartender and waiters. Finally, some would argue that many eighteen-year-olds already have access to alcohol through fake identification cards.

By listing these opposing viewpoints, she is convincing her reader of her knowledge of the issue—including the arguments of those who disagree with her.

In an essay supporting gun ownership the opposing viewpoints paragraph might be:

> Gun opponents believe the presence of a gun increases the chances of injury and death in the home. They argue that the seriousness of domestic disputes escalates quickly when one of the parties brandishes a weapon. They assert that someone contemplating suicide may be more likely to make the attempt if a gun is readily available. Finally, they cite cases of children accidentally shooting, and sometimes killing, other children in the home. These opponents see a direct relationship between injuries and deaths in the home and the presence of a gun.

An author opposing gun ownership might compose the following opposing viewpoints paragraph:

> Gun proponents quickly point to the increase in violent crime in this country. They are especially concerned about the recent rise in home invasions. They argue that in many cases a gun owner can stop a robbery from occurring without even discharging the weapon. Just the presence of a weapon will deter many burglars. They also cite the increased number of random acts of violence. Gun owners who are properly trained to use their guns have a powerful weapon of self-defense. Those in favor of gun ownership frequently say, "Guns don't kill people. People kill people."

The block pattern offers several benefits to you. First, you can group the opposing viewpoints in one location in the essay. Once you have presented the reader with the opposing arguments, you can focus on your position and your supporting evidence. You do not have to address the opposing arguments individually. Second, many persuasive topics do not lend themselves to a point-counterpoint arrangement. For instance, suppose you want to persuade your reader to use fewer products that damage the ozone layer. The opposition arguments may not be clear at first. After all, who is going to oppose improving the ozone layer? Yet the ozone layer is still being depleted. Your opponents are a lack of knowledge about the environment and a reluctance to change personal habits. For this type of topic the block pattern is helpful. You can acknowledge your opposition and then move forward with your evidence.

Point/Counterpoint Pattern for Persuasive Essays

A second method of organizing the body paragraphs of a persuasive essay is the *point/counterpoint method*. This pattern allows the writer to engage in a

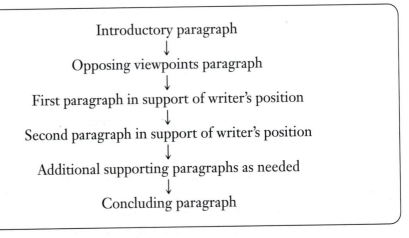

Introductory paragraph
↓
Opposing viewpoints paragraph
↓
First paragraph in support of writer's position
↓
Second paragraph in support of writer's position
↓
Additional supporting paragraphs as needed
↓
Concluding paragraph

Figure 9.1   The block pattern of organization for persuasive essays

back-and-forth exchange between an opposing point of view (point) and a supporting argument (counterpoint). When you use this pattern, you begin each body paragraph with an opposing viewpoint. Then you immediately refute, or counter, this viewpoint with your evidence.

> Those opposed to a drinking age of twenty-one cite the fact that the drinking age was once eighteen.

Then she refutes the argument by asserting that lowering the drinking age resulted in alcohol use beginning at an early age.

> However, when the drinking age was eighteen, alcohol use moved down from the eighteen-year-olds to their younger friends.

Her second paragraph begins with an acknowledgment of an opposing argument.

> It is true that the abuse of alcohol can be a problem at any given age.

However, she soon returns the reader's focus to the issue of teen drinking.

> Indeed, society needs to stress alcohol education at all ages—but particularly with teens.

If you were writing an essay supporting gun ownership, your first body paragraph might begin:

> Gun opponents argue that the presence of a gun increases the chances of injury and death in the home. However, "guns don't kill people. People kill people."

Your second paragraph might start this way:

> Those opposing gun ownership cite cases of injuries and deaths from accidental shootings. However, gun owners who are properly trained to use their guns have powerful weapons of self-defense that can save lives.

On the other hand, if you opposed gun ownership, your first paragraph might begin:

> Gun proponents are fond of stating, "Guns don't kill people. People kill people." However, the truth is that the presence of a gun increases the chances of injury and death in the home.

The beginning of your second body paragraph might be:

> Gun proponents argue that gun owners who are properly trained to use their guns have powerful weapons of self-defense. Yet each year too many children maim, and sometimes kill, other children in accidental shootings.

The point/counterpoint method of organizing persuasive essays is beneficial to those writers who want to engage in an open debate. You can begin each paragraph with a polite nod to the opposing argument and then counter immediately with your supporting evidence. This pattern works well for issues with clearly defined opposing viewpoints.

Concluding Paragraph

The concluding paragraph of a persuasive essay should be forceful. These few closing sentences are your last chance to persuade your reader to adopt your position on the issue. Therefore, the concluding paragraph should

- Briefly acknowledge your opposition
- Restate your position
- Reinforce your reasons for your position
- Call for action (if appropriate)
- Make a prediction (if appropriate)

In the concluding paragraph of her essay, Mary Ann Saravanos issues a wake-up call for society to work to reduce the number of alcohol-related teen deaths and keep the drinking age at twenty-one.

While it is true that eighteen-year-olds are legal adults, as a society we must do everything possible to reduce the number of teen deaths attributed to alcohol. If everyone considered the consequences of alcohol

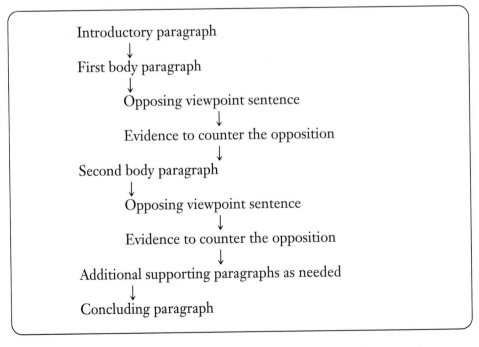

Figure 9.2 The point/counterpoint pattern of organization for persuasive essays

consumption, perhaps there would be no need for an age restriction. However, as long as alcohol-related automobile crashes continue to take young lives, the drinking age should remain twenty-one.

Laura Brower reminds her readers of the importance of the years between eighteen and twenty-one and calls for parents and educators to work together to address the problem of teen drinking:

> The legal age of adulthood in this country will likely remain eighteen. Yet many teens will still need three extra years to give them an increased chance of surviving the dangers of alcohol. Parental awareness and alcohol education must address the alcohol problem where it begins— with our youth. Raising the drinking age to twenty-one not only makes it illegal for an adolescent to drink, but also reinforces the right to use alcohol intelligently.

If you use an anecdote to begin your introductory paragraph, you may want to complete this anecdote in the concluding paragraph. Look back at the section in this chapter on the introductory paragraphs and reread the sample introductory paragraph in support of gun ownership. A concluding paragraph for this essay might be:

> Even though gun opponents argue vehemently that the mere presence of a gun increases the chances of accidental injuries and deaths, many property owners insist that they need guns to secure their property and defend themselves. If Joan had not bought her handgun, she would likely have been the one bleeding on the floor—not the intruder.

Now reread the sample introductory paragraph for an essay arguing against gun ownership. The concluding paragraph for this essay might be:

> Even though some property owners insist that they need guns to secure their property and defend themselves, the mere presence of a gun increases the chances of accidental injuries and deaths. If Joan had not bought that handgun last month, she might have been exchanging a few words with her neighbor over her fence instead of watching him bleeding on her floor.

When you finish composing your concluding paragraph, read it aloud. Have you made your case to your reader as clearly and as forcefully as possible?

FOCUS ON TRANSITION

You will need to use effective transition in your essay to help your reader move from one argument to another. If you are using the block pattern, you will need to provide transition between the opposing viewpoints paragraph and the first paragraph in support of your position.

One way to provide this transition is through the use of a transitional word or expression. In the sample block pattern essay below, Mary Ann Saravanos uses the transitional word *but* to direct the reader's attention away from the opposing viewpoints to the problem of teenage drinking and driving.

But does the young adult of eighteen have the experience of a twenty-one-year-old behind the wheel of an automobile—especially when he or she has been drinking?

If you use the point/counterpoint pattern, you will need strong transition between the opposing argument opening each of your body paragraphs and the evidence in support of your position. In Laura's essay she uses a transitional expression as a bridge between the opposing viewpoint and her own.

Those opposed to a drinking age of twenty-one cite the fact that the drinking age was once eighteen. **However,** when the drinking age was eighteen, alcohol use moved down from the eighteen-year-olds to their younger friends.

You will also need transitional expressions to help the reader follow the logic of your arguments. When you draw conclusions based on your evidence, these transitional expressions are helpful:

therefore	accordingly
as a result	hence
thus	consequently
indeed	

---

1. Choose an issue that is important to you.

2. Take a stand on this issue.

3. Think through your supporting reasons and your opposition's viewpoints by brainstorming, clustering, listing, freewriting, or using reporters' questions.

4. Compose a list or umbrella thesis statement that summarizes your opposition's viewpoints and presents your stand on the issue.

5. Write an introductory paragraph.

6. Decide on a block or point/counterpoint pattern for your body paragraphs.

7. Compose your body paragraphs using the pattern in step 6.

8. Write a concluding paragraph.

9. Submit your experimental draft for peer review.

10. Compose your revised and edited drafts.

11. Complete your final draft for submission to your reader.

Figure 9.3   Steps for composing a persuasive essay

When you use effective transition, you keep the reader's focus on the power of your arguments and enhance your chances of persuading the reader to accept your point of view.

Student Sample

Block Pattern for Persuasive Essay

Keep the Drinking Age at Twenty-One

Many young people would like to see the current drinking age of twenty-one lowered to eighteen. Yet the facts to date make a clear statement as to the need to maintain and enforce the twenty-one-year-old drinking age restriction. The adverse effects of alcohol-initiated automobile crashes, crimes, and illnesses equal a sizable sum of human misery. Although many young people would argue that those who are old enough to vote, fight, and die for their country are old enough to drink responsibly, the drinking age should remain twenty-one.

Those who support a drinking age of eighteen argue that eighteen-year-olds are legal adults. They are old enough to fight for their country and sacrifice their lives on the battlefield. They are responsible enough to vote their political convictions. Furthermore, eighteen-year-olds can purchase cigarettes. They can even serve alcohol as bartenders and waiters. Finally, some argue that many eighteen-year-olds already have access to alcohol through fake identification cards.

But does the young adult of eighteen have the experience of a twenty-one-year-old behind the wheel of an automobile—especially when he or she has been drinking? Each year teens are involved in fatal crashes in which alcohol is a contributing factor. The three-year-period from eighteen to twenty-one allows for personal growth and perhaps better decision making about drinking while driving. Twenty-one-year-olds are closer to making a lifetime career decision and may not want to jeopardize their records with a black mark for a driving-under-the-influence arrest.

Students need to be made aware of the dangers of alcohol and drunk driving. Therefore, education about alcohol abuse should be a priority in our grade schools, middle schools, and high schools. In addition, the media need to promote public education regarding drinking and driving. Young adults must educate themselves about the destructive effects of alcohol on their physical and emotional well-being.

➡

While it is true that eighteen-year-olds are legal adults, we as a society must do everything possible to reduce the number of teen deaths attributed to alcohol. If everyone considered the consequences of alcohol consumption, perhaps there would be no need for an age restriction. However, as long as alcohol-related automobile crashes continue to take young lives, the drinking age should remain at twenty-one.

—Mary Ann Saravanos

Student Sample

Point/Counterpoint Pattern for Persuasive Essay

Alcohol and America's Youth

Any time teenagers consume alcohol, they are breaking the law. Yet many parents let their children take a sip or two at home under their supervision. What many parents do not realize is that they are giving their children mixed messages about drinking. These same children when they become teenagers may think that it is all right to drink alcohol even though such consumption is clearly against the law. These teens do not realize that alcohol-related problems are eating away at America's youth. Despite the fact that some people argue that a person who can marry, vote, and fight wars should also have the right to drink alcohol, the drinking age should remain twenty-one.

Those opposed to a drinking age of twenty-one cite the fact that the drinking age was once eighteen. However, when the drinking age was eighteen, alcohol use moved down from the eighteen-year-olds to their younger friends. Many of these same teens then drove automobiles while they were under the influence of alcohol. Alcohol-related accidents involving teen drivers have resulted in much misery for our nation. Raising the legal drinking age to twenty-one makes it more difficult for teenagers to get alcohol and less likely that teens will drive drunk.

It is true that abuse of alcohol can be a problem at any given age. Indeed, society needs to stress alcohol education at all ages—but particularly with teens. Alcohol abuse, including binge drinking, is rampant among today's teenagers. Some teenagers try alcohol because they want to feel accepted or they want to feel older. Peer pressure to try alcohol is enormous—and occurs at an increasingly early age. A recent survey showed that even fourth to sixth graders have tried alcohol. Too many teens are more loyal to their friends' influence to try alcohol than they are to their own well-being.

The legal age of adulthood in this country will likely remain eighteen. Yet many teens will still need three extra years to give them an increased chance of surviving the dangers of alcohol. Parental awareness and alcohol education must address the alcohol problem where it begins—with our youth. Raising the drinking age to twenty-one not only makes it illegal for an adolescent to drink, but also reinforces the right to use alcohol intelligently.

—Laura Brower

FOCUS ON DICTION

Logical Fallacies

In your persuasive essay you must support your opinions with supporting evidence. In order to be effective, this evidence—whether it consists of statements of fact, statements of opinions, statistics, or first-hand experiences and observations—must be clearly relevant to the issue. Relevant evidence uses clear, logical reasoning to provide a bridge between your opinion and the conclusion you wish your reader to draw from it.

Unfortunately, errors in logical reasoning frequently occur in persuasive arguments. These errors are called *logical fallacies.* These *logical fallacies* confuse the reader because they

- Direct the reader's focus away from the argument
- Attack the opposition
- Present faulty evidence

Some of these logical fallacies occur so frequently that they have specific names. Among the most common are

- Ad hominem
- Ad populum
- Bandwagon
- Red herring
- Hasty generalization
- Either/or
- Faulty cause and effect

Ad hominem. The term *ad hominem* is Latin for *to the person.* An *ad hominem* argument directs the reader's focus away from the issue by attacking the opponent. *Ad hominem* attacks are personal and may involve not just the opponent but the opponent's family, community, political convictions, religious beliefs, and so on. Consider the following:

> My neighbor, Jane, who opposes gun ownership, is obviously a Communist.

This *ad hominem* argument is unfair to Jane. Is Jane not able to disagree with someone over the issue of gun ownership without being called a Communist?

> Because William had a driving-under-the-influence conviction, he has no right to support a legal drinking age of eighteen.

What does William's DUI conviction have to do with his right to an opinion on this issue?

Ad hominem attacks are hurtful. Writers who want their readers to consider an issue fairly do not use *ad hominem* arguments.

Ad populum. The term *ad populum* is Latin for *to the people*. The intent of an *ad populum* argument is the same as that of an *ad hominem* argument—to distract the reader from focusing on the issue. Using *ad populum* reasoning, the writer appeals to popular group loyalties not directly related to the issue at hand. For example,

> Those who oppose owning guns have no loyalty to the U.S. Constitution.

Just because someone opposes gun ownership does not mean he or she does not support the U.S. Constitution. Sometimes *ad populum* arguments are extreme.

> A drinking age of eighteen would mean the end of America as we know it—the land of the free and the home of the brave.

The reader of this sentence could easily get caught up in the patriotic fervor and forget that the drinking age in this country has no relationship to patriotism.

Bandwagon. A *bandwagon* argument can be very appealing in that it invites the reader to "get on board" and "join the group." Its intent, however, is to make the reader believe that he or she has no right to an individual opinion—only a right to the opinion "everyone" holds. The method is to create peer pressure by making the reader feel left out if he or she does not agree. The sentence

> Everyone I know is buying a gun for protection.

is a bandwagon argument. Does the writer really expect the reader to believe that everyone in the writer's acquaintance either owns a gun or plans to own one? Unfortunately, bandwagon statements such as the following are all too commonly heard:

Every teenager has a fake identification card and easy access to alcohol.

Can the author of this statement provide sufficient evidence to prove its validity? Of course not.

Red Herring. The origin of this phrase is a hunting term used to describe the practice of dragging a fish across a trail to divert the dogs away from a scent. A *red herring* in a persuasive essay confuses the reader by raising an irrelevant argument and making it sound as if the argument is directly related to the issue when it is not. Here is an example of a red herring.

When the economy is worsening each year, we should not worry about whether we should own guns.

The state of the economy is not related to gun ownership. If the economy were improving each year, would gun ownership not be an issue?

Why should we lower the drinking age when there are so many homeless on our streets?

If there were no homeless on our streets, should the drinking age be lowered then? Careful readers should be alert to red herrings and not let them distract their attention away from the issue.

Hasty Generalization. Writers who use *hasty generalizations* present their readers with faulty evidence by "jumping" to a conclusion so quickly that important information is not considered. For instance, a writer arguing for a drinking age of twenty-one may make the statement that

All twenty-one-year-olds are responsible drivers.

This statement is patently false. Some twenty-one-year-olds are responsible drivers; some are not. Some eighteen-year-olds are responsible drivers; some are not. Some forty-year-olds are responsible drivers; some are not. Since the writer cannot provide evidence that *all twenty-one-year-olds are responsible drivers,* the statement is faulty.

Since I have owned a gun, I have already prevented one break-in from occurring at my home. I can prevent any other robbery from occurring as well.

The author of this statement has been hasty in drawing this conclusion. Next time robbers try to break into this home, the home owner may be away on a trip or the robbers may have bigger guns and be more willing to use them!

Either/Or. The writer of an *either/or* statement presents two extreme alternatives and ignores any other choices. A careful examination of the statement will reveal that this evidence is invalid.

> Either keep the drinking age at twenty-one or watch the numbers of alcohol-related accidents among teens increase.

Is an increase in the numbers of alcohol-related accidents among teens a sure thing if the drinking age is lowered to eighteen? The author of this statement may think so, but where is the evidence? Is it not logical to assume that lowering the drinking age to eighteen might just as well result in a decrease in alcohol-related accidents among teens?

> Either you own a gun, or you will die at a gunman's hands.

Those people who do not own guns die in just as many ways as those people who do. Some readers may consider an *either/or* statement like this one a threat.

Faulty Cause and Effect. When the writer uses a *faulty cause-and-effect statement*, he or she asks the reader to believe that because a statement of cause is true, so is the accompanying statement of effect. This relationship may seem reasonable to the reader at first glance, but upon further examination, the cause presented in the *if* statement and the effect given in the *then* statement are unrelated.

> When the drinking age was raised to twenty-one, the arrests for drunk driving in my town decreased that same year.

Was the decrease in drunk-driving arrests related to other factors other than the raising of the drinking age? Does the writer have the statistics to show that this decrease in DUI arrests did not occur in any previous year? If the number of arrests for drunk driving increases the next year, will the author still claim that raising the drinking age was the cause?

> I own a gun, and I have never been the victim of a crime.

Is owning a gun the cause of this writer's good fortune? If this writer became the victim of a crime, would he or she cite gun ownership as the reason?

As you compose your persuasive essays and read the persuasive essays of others, think carefully about the supporting evidence. As a reader and as a writer, ask yourself these critical questions.

- Is the evidence directly related to the issue?
- Is the evidence presented in an attempt to divert the reader's focus away from the issue?
- Is the evidence an unfair attack on an opponent?
- Is the evidence that is presented faulty?

Use the following initials to indicate the logical fallacy found in each of the sentences below: **AH** = ad hominem, **AP** = ad populum, **BW** = bandwagon, **RH** = red herring, **HG** = hasty generalization, **EO** = either/or, **CE** = faulty cause and effect.

_____ **1.** If children and teens could drink beer freely as they can in Europe, then drunk driving would not be a problem among teens.

_____ **2.** Owning a gun is the "way of the American West."

_____ **3.** Why shouldn't the drinking age be lowered to eighteen? Every high school senior I know has tried alcohol.

_____ **4.** Keeping the drinking age at twenty-one will end all under-age drinking.

_____ **5.** Senator Jones has stated publicly that he owns a gun. Obviously all he cares about is being elected again.

_____ **6.** Either you believe in the Second Amendment of the Constitution, or you don't.

_____ **7.** Why should we be concerned about accidental deaths in the home when children are being murdered on our streets every day?

_____ **8.** Owning a gun always creates more problems than it solves.

_____ **9.** If the drinking age were lowered to eighteen, the high school dropout rate would increase.

_____ **10.** Either purchase a gun or feel unsafe about the security of your home.

Repetition and Rhythm

Repetition of key words and phrases is a common device in persuasive essays and speeches. This repetition

- Reinforces the urgency of the issue and the need for action
- Creates rhythmic sentence structure that makes the key phrases easy for the reader (or listener) to remember

Sample Persuasive Speech

"I Have a Dream"
by Dr. Martin Luther King, Jr.

In his 1963 "I Have a Dream" speech, Martin Luther King, Jr., made brilliant use of repetition and rhythm as he urged blacks and whites to work together to achieve civil rights for all. Following are the opening paragraphs of this great speech:

> . . . Five score years ago, a great American, in whose symbolic shadow we stand today, signed the Emancipation Proclamation. This momentous decree came as a great beacon light of hope to millions of Negro slaves who had been seared in the flames of withering injustice. It came as a joyous daybreak to end the long night of captivity.
>
> But *one hundred years later,* the Negro still is not free. *One hundred years later,* the life of the Negro is still sadly crippled by the manacles of segregation and the chains of discrimination. *One hundred years later* the Negro lives on a lonely island of poverty in the midst of a vast ocean of material prosperity. *One hundred years later,* the Negro is still languishing in the corners of American society and finds himself an exile in his own land. So we have come here today to dramatize a shameful condition. . . .
>
> We have also come to this hallowed spot to remind America of the fierce urgency of now. . . . *Now is the time* to make real the promises of democracy. *Now is the time* to rise from the dark and desolate valley of segregation to the sunlit path of racial justice. *Now is the time* to lift our nation from the quicksands of racial injustice to the solid rock of brotherhood. *Now is the time* to make justice a reality for all of God's children.

Notice the repeated phrases noted in italics. Early in the speech Dr. King repeats the phrase *one hundred years later* to emphasize that the promises of the Emancipation Proclamation signed in 1863 had still not been realized in 1963.

The repetition of the phrase *Now is the time* reinforces the urgency of the situation of America's blacks in 1963 and the need for change. This phrase is a stark contrast to the phrase *one hundred years later* because it does not emphasize the past but the present.

As you will see, Dr. King continues to use this repetition to lend rhythm to his sentences so that they ring in the ears of his listeners.

 Parallelism

Another rhythmic device is parallelism—the repetition of grammatical structures. Parallelism not only provides sentences with rhythm but also with balance.

One famous example of a parallel structure is from Abraham Lincoln's Gettysburg Address when he speaks of a government *"of the people, by the people,* and *for the people."* Each italicized group of words is a prepositional phrase. These groups of words are parallel because they are in the same grammatical form. You can also create parallel structures with nouns, verbs, other types of phrases, and clauses.

As the "I Have a Dream" speech continues, Dr. King uses parallel structures for rhythm, balance, and dramatic effect.

> . . . And as we walk, *we shall make* the pledge that *we shall* always *march* ahead. We cannot turn back. There are those who are asking the devotees of civil rights, "When will you be satisfied?" *We can never be satisfied as long as the Negro is the victim of the unspeakable horrors of police brutality. We can never be satisfied as long as our bodies, heavy with the fatigue of travel, cannot gain lodging in the motels of the highways and the hotels of the city. We cannot be satisfied as long as the Negro in Mississippi cannot vote and the Negro in New York City believes he has nothing for which to vote.* No, no, we are not satisfied, and we will not be satisfied until *justice rolls down like waters and righteousness like a mighty stream.*
>
> I am not unmindful that some of you have come here out of great trials and tribulations. Some of you have come fresh from narrow jail cells. Some of you have come from areas where *your quest for freedom left you battered by the storms of persecution and staggered by the winds of police brutality.* You have been the veterans of creative suffering. Continue to work with the faith that unearned suffering is redemptive.
>
> *Go back to Mississippi, go back to Alabama, go back to South Carolina, go back to Georgia, go back to Louisiana, go back to the slums and ghettos of our northern cities,* knowing that somehow this situation can and will be changed. Let us not wallow in the valley of despair.

In these powerful paragraphs, Dr. King continues to speak his convictions and engage the attention of his audience through the devices of repetition and parallelism (see italicized sentences). Consider this clause:

> . . . *justice rolls down like waters and righteousness like a mighty stream.*

Here the repetition of the preposition *like* sets up two moving, parallel similes:

justice. . . like waters

righteousness. . . like a mighty stream

In the following excerpt Dr. King uses parallel past tense verbs to create parallelism:

> . . . *your quest for freedom left you battered by the storms of persecution and staggered by the winds of police brutality.*

The repetition of a past tense verb followed by two prepositional phrases creates a balanced, rhythmic sentence.

battered by the storms of persecution

staggered by the winds of police brutality

Knowing that his audience has come from around the nation to rally on the steps of the Lincoln Memorial, Dr. King uses parallel structure to bless his followers as they go home.

> *go back to Mississippi*
>
> *go back to Alabama*
>
> *go back to South Carolina*
>
> *go back to Georgia*
>
> *go back to Louisiana*
>
> *go back to the slums and ghettos of our northern cities*

EXERCISE 9.5

Below is the remainder of Dr. King's "I Have a Dream" speech. Use this speech to answer the questions that follow.

I say to you today, my friends, that even though we face the difficulties of today and tomorrow, I still have a dream. It is a dream deeply rooted in the American dream. I have a dream that one day this nation will rise up and live out the true meaning of its creed: "We hold these truths to be self-evident that all men are created equal."

I have a dream that one day on the red hills of Georgia the sons of former slaves and the sons of former slave owners will be able to sit down together at the table of brotherhood.

I have a dream that one day even the state of Mississippi, a state sweltering with the heat of injustice, sweltering with the heat of oppression, will be transformed into an oasis of freedom and justice. I have a dream that my four little children will one day live in a nation where they will not be judged by the color of their skin but by the content of their character.

I have a dream today.

I have a dream that one day down in Alabama with its vicious racists, with its governor having his lips dripping with the words of interposition and nullification, one day right there in Alabama little black boys and black girls will be able to join hands with little white boys and white girls as sisters and brothers.

I have a dream today.

I have a dream that one day every valley shall be exalted, every hill and mountain shall be made low, the rough places will be made plain, and the crooked places will be made straight, and the glory of the Lord shall be revealed, and all flesh shall see it together.

This is our hope, and this is the faith that I go back to the South with. With this faith we will be able to transform the jangling discords of our nation into a beautiful symphony of brotherhood. With this faith we will be able to work together, to pray together, to struggle together, go to jail together, to stand up for freedom together, knowing that we will be free one day.

This will be the day when all of God's children will be able to sing with new meaning: "My country 'tis of thee, sweet land of liberty, of thee I sing. Land where my fathers died, land of the pilgrim's pride, from every mountainside, let freedom ring."

And if America is to be a great nation, this must become true. So let freedom ring from the prodigious hilltops of New Hampshire. Let freedom ring from the mighty mountains of New York. Let freedom ring from the heightening Alleghenies of Pennsylvania!

Let freedom ring from the snow-capped Rockies of Colorado!

Let freedom ring from the curvaceous slopes of California!

But not only that; let freedom ring from Stone Mountain of Georgia!

Let freedom ring from Lookout Mountain of Tennessee!

Let freedom ring from every hill and mole hill of Mississippi. From every mountainside, let freedom ring.

When this happens, and when we allow freedom to ring, when we let it ring from every village and every hamlet, from every state and every city, we will be able to speed up that day when all of God's children—black men and white men, Jews and Gentiles, Protestants and Catholics—will be able to join hands and sing in the words of the old Negro spiritual, "Free at last, free at last, thank God Almighty, we are free at last."

List five repeated phrases or clauses.

1. _____

2. _____

3. _____

4. _____

5. _____

What do you think is the most memorable phrase of the speech?

Why? _____

_____

List five examples of parallel structures.

1. _____

2. _____

3. _____

4. _____

5. _____

Which parallel structure do you think is most memorable? Why?

As you revise the experimental draft of your persuasive essay, try to use repetition and parallel structures to strengthen your sentences and the impact of your message on your reader.

FOCUS ON PEER REVIEW

After you have composed the experimental draft of your persuasive essay, use the following guide questions for peer review. Then revise and edit your essay carefully before submitting it to your teacher.

Guide Questions for Persuasive Essay

1. Does the introductory paragraph focus the reader's attention on a specific issue?

2. What technique does the writer use to begin the introductory paragraph? Is this technique effective? Why or why not?

3. Does the thesis statement of the essay summarize the opposing viewpoints? Does the thesis present the writer's stand on the issue?

4. What type of reader is most likely to agree with the writer's position? What type of reader is most likely to disagree?

5. Does the writer use the block pattern or the point/counterpoint pattern to organize the body paragraphs?

6. If the writer uses the block pattern, does the opposing viewpoints paragraph include the major arguments of the opposition? Can you think of any additional arguments that should have been included?

7. If the writer uses the point/counterpoint pattern, does each body paragraph begin with an opposing argument?

8. Does the writer include sufficient evidence for each of the arguments supporting his or her position?

9. Which of the supporting arguments do you think is the strongest? Which do you think is the weakest?

➡

10. Are all the arguments valid? In other words, are any of the arguments logical fallacies? If so, why?

11. How does the concluding paragraph reinforce the writer's position on the issue? Does the writer call for the reader to take a specific action? If not, how does the writer end the essay?

12. Does the writer use any parallel structures? If so, list them.

13. Check the essay carefully for run-ons, comma splices, or fragments. If you see any of these errors, let the writer know on which page the error occurs. Suggest how the writer might correct these errors.

14. Make a list of spelling errors.

15. Are any punctuation errors made repeatedly? If so, let the writer know.

16. List any subject–verb agreement, pronoun–antecendent agreement, or pronoun case errors you spot.

17. What are the strengths of this essay?

18. What are the weaknesses of this essay?

Persuasion is all around you. There are those who will try to persuade you fairly and those who will try to persuade you deceptively. As a critical thinker and writer you must remain vigilant if you are to make sound judgments in the classroom and in the workplace.

Writers as Spiders

Because argumentation is such an important form of oral and written communication, many web sites provide strategies for improving persuasive skills. One web site that offers suggestions for organizing a persuasive essay is

http://server/uofdhigh.k12.mi.us/~jmoran/5grphEssay/grphint.htm

Other web sites offer facts, opinions, statistics, and personal observations on a wide variety of controversial, social, economic, and educational topics.

Web Exercise 1

Using a search engine, locate an on-line edition of a newspaper. Then read one of the editorials on the editorial page, and answer the following questions:

1. What is the thesis of the editorial? Is this thesis stated or implied?

2. What facts does the author use to support his or her position? Why do you think the author has chosen to include these facts?

3. What opinions does the author use to support his or her position? Why do you think the author has chosen to include these opinions?

4. Does the author include any opposing arguments? If so, what are they? How does the author address these arguments?

5. Do you detect any logical fallacies? If so, give an example.

6. What type of reader will likely agree with the writer's position? What type of reader will likely disagree?

7. Do you agree with the author's position? Why or why not?

Web Exercise 2

Assume that you are writing an essay on one of the controversial topics listed below (or choose one of the topics provided at the beginning of this chapter):

- Year-round schools
- Genetic engineering
- Boot camps for juvenile offenders
- Home schooling
- Drug testing in the workplace
- Open adoptions

Use one or more search engines to locate related web pages. Then read through several of these pages. After you have completed your reading, answer the reporters' questions listed earlier in this chapter.

After you have finished the reporters' questions, take a stand on this issue and state your position in a single sentence. Then, using the information from the web pages, make a chart and list the arguments that support your position. Also complete a chart listing the arguments that do not support your position. Remember that these arguments can be facts, opinions, or statistics, as well as first-hand observations.

If you choose to use any of the information from the World Wide Web in your essay, you will need to give credit to the web pages as needed (see "Writers as Spiders," Chapter 8).

Additional Help

For another look at logical fallacies, including additional examples, see

http://www.ilstu.edu/~gmklass/ids189/fallac2.txt

For more information about parallelism, visit

http://webserver.maclab.comp.uvic.ca/writersguide/Pages/
SentParallel.html

For examples of both parallelism and rhythmic writing, consult

http://webware.princeton.edu/Writing/parallel.htm

CHAPTER 10

Revising and Editing Strategies

WHY REVISE AND EDIT?

If your writing is to have its maximum desired effect on your reader, you must revise and edit your work carefully. The revising and editing stages of the writing process are a challenge for any writer. Both activities are time-consuming and energy-dependent. Therefore, revising and editing require the writer's discipline and commitment. The pay-off for the writer's revising and editing work comes with the satisfaction of submitting a composition that represents his or her best work.

Many writers fail to spend enough time revising and editing their compositions. These writers think that the process of writing is over when they have typed or copied the last word from an experimental draft. The effects of such thinking can be disastrous, ranging from a failing grade on a paragraph or an essay to a loss of productivity in the workplace.

Some college students make the mistake of thinking that only compositions written for English classes should be edited for grammar and revised for clarity. What these students fail to realize is that all academic writing is written for educated readers (whether these readers are English teachers, history instructors, or math professors), and these readers are accustomed to reading clear, accurate prose and expect such prose from their students. Would you assign a passing grade to a paragraph or essay riddled with spelling, punctuation, and grammatical errors?

The ability to write well is clearly a valuable skill in the workplace. If you were an employer reading through application letters and resumes, would you take seriously a job candidate whose application letter and resume were full of omitted words, misspellings, and punctuation and grammatical errors? If you were watching a sales presentation, and the accompanying sales brochures were filled with unclear sentences and spelling errors, would you buy the product?

What all writers must come to terms with at some point is that *how a writer communicates a message affects how the message is received.* Therefore, writers must revise and edit

- To communicate the message in the best possible way
- To meet the reader's demands for clear, accurate prose

REVISING VERSUS EDITING

This chapter focuses on strategies for *revising* and *editing*. In this chapter the term *revising* means examining the composition for

- Unity of focus
- Ideas that need further support
- Unrelated sentences
- Repeated ideas
- Order of presentation of ideas
- Transition between ideas

The term *editing* refers to locating and correcting the following types of errors:

- Misspelled words
- Omitted punctuation
- Unnecessary punctuation
- Grammatical errors (including comma splices, run-ons, fragments, subject–verb agreement errors, pronoun–antecedent agreement errors, and pronoun case errors)
- Omitted words
- Unnecessary words
- Modifier errors (misplaced modifiers, dangling modifiers)

Both revising and editing require an *objective eye*, sometimes referred to as *critical distance.* If you are to revise and edit your writing effectively, you must learn to see your writing as the reader will see it. But how do you train yourself to read your writing the way your reader will? How do you keep from reading what you think is on your paper instead of what is really there? Think of it this way. When you revise, you use a wide-angle lens, always focusing on your big picture (the message you want to communicate). When you edit, you use the zoom lens on your camera, focusing on each word carefully.

The following strategies will help you develop an *objective eye* as you revise and edit your compositions. Both the revising and editing sections offer strategies any writer can use. Keep in mind that not every method will work with every writer or on every paper. The more experience you have with revising and editing your work, the more you will learn which strategies are best for you.

FOCUS ON REVISING STRATEGIES

The verb *revise* derives from the Latin root *vis* meaning *to see* (as in *vision*) and the prefix *re* meaning *again*. That is what writers do when they revise—they see the composition again in a new light.

Musicologists assert that the composer Mozart rarely revised his musical scores. He heard the music in his head and transcribed the hauntingly beautiful sounds onto paper. His first musical draft was often his last. Unfortunately, few writers have Mozart's ability to "get it right" the first time. True writers—those dedicated to communicating the written word—know that they must dedicate their time and energy to shaping and reshaping the text so that the reader can clearly understand the message.

This section offers general strategies for revising as well as specific strategies for unity, coherence, and computer-generated writing. As you try various revision techniques, keep in mind that writers tend to be individualistic in their choice of revising strategies. Also as writers practice their craft over time, these strategies often change.

General Revising Strategies

If possible, begin your revision work with the comments of your peer reviewers. Many of the guide questions at the end of each chapter have been written to help you through the revising stage. As soon as you receive the reviewer's comments, read through them and determine which of the peer reviewer's suggestions you should consider. Then set aside your writing for a while—ideally, for at least a day.

When you pick up your work again to begin revising, ask yourself: "What is the focus (central point) of my writing?" You need to have your main idea clearly in mind throughout the revising stage. Then ask yourself, "Who is my reader?" Use the questions about the reader in Chapter 1 as your guide. Identifying your reader will help you make your revision decisions. With a clear sense of your focus and your reader, try these strategies as you shape your revised draft.

Strategies for Unity

The term *unity* means that all ideas within the composition support a single central focus (main idea). A composition lacking unity confuses the reader, who must struggle to discover what the writer is trying to communicate. The following are some ways to revise for unity:

Locate the Main Idea of Your Composition. If you are revising a paragraph, use a highlighter to identify the topic sentence. If your topic sentence is implied, write your main idea on a separate sheet of paper for easy reference.

If you are revising an essay, highlight your thesis statement. You may also want to highlight the restatement of the thesis in your concluding paragraph.

Consider the following questions: Is the focus of your composition clear? Is your main idea clearly and directly stated? Rewrite your main idea using different words. Is this rewording better or worse than the original? Keep revising your topic sentence (or thesis statement) until you are satisfied with its clarity and effectiveness.

Locate Your Supporting Details. If you are revising a paragraph, circle or highlight each major support. Then reread your topic sentence and, with your focus in mind, answer these questions: Does each support clearly relate to the topic sentence? Is each support distinct—that is, is there any overlapping between the supports? Have you included additional details for each major support? Which major support has the strongest details? Which has the weakest? What details can you add to strengthen your paragraph?

If you are revising an essay, circle or highlight the topic sentence of each body paragraph. Then look back at your thesis and answer the following: Does the topic sentence of each body paragraph clearly relate to the thesis? Is each topic sentence distinct? Which body paragraph is the strongest? Which is the weakest? What details can you add to strengthen your essay?

Use the answers to these questions to determine where you need to create additional supporting details or delete ineffective or insufficient support.

Locate Your Concluding Idea. If you are revising a paragraph, examine your concluding sentence. Then reread your topic sentence. If you are revising an essay, look closely at the restatement of the thesis in your concluding paragraph, and then reread your thesis in the introductory paragraph. Does your composition end where it begins? Will the reader come full circle at the end of your composition—that is, will the concluding idea help unify the composition for the reader? Are you satisfied with the effectiveness of the composition's conclusion? If not, try other approaches until you are confident that the reader will finish the last sentence with a clear sense of your composition's focus.

Outline Your Composition. Most students associate outlines with the planning stage of the writing process. Yet an outline can also be helpful in the revising stage. Using an outline will allow you to check the skeleton of the composition and determine whether the focus of the composition is clearly expressed and supported. Is the organization of your paragraph or essay a logical extension of your main idea? Will the organization of your paragraph or essay be easy for your reader to follow? (For information about outlining, consult Appendix A.)

Strategies for Coherence

The root of the term *coherence* is *cohere*, which means *to hold together*. Effective compositions feature sentences and paragraphs that "hold together" so that the ideas flow smoothly from one to another. The strategies offered below will help you revise your compositions for coherence.

Read Aloud from the Beginning of Your Composition through Your First Major Point. If you are revising a paragraph, you will probably only need a few sentences. Check the flow between your topic sentence and first major point.

Can you easily follow the movement between these two ideas? Will your reader be able to move smoothly from one idea to another?

If you are revising an essay, read your introduction and first body paragraph. Are there any sentences that are difficult to read or that break the flow of your writing? Is the movement between your opener and thesis statement in the introductory paragraph easy to follow? Is the movement between the thesis statement and the topic sentence of your first body paragraph smooth?

After You Have Made Any Needed Revisions, Read this Section Again and then Read the Second Major Point. Check the flow between your first and second major points. Is there a transitional expression present to help the reader make the connection between these two points? If not, try adding one. Read this section again. Is the transition smoother? You may have to try several transitional expressions before you find a good fit. Also check the movement from the major points to the supporting details. Are transitional expressions needed here as well?

If you are still not satisfied with the flow of your composition, try repeating key words from the topic sentence or thesis at critical points to improve coherence.

Read Your Composition Aloud from Beginning to End. Check the end of your composition. Is the transition between the last major point and the conclusion of your composition clear, or does the concluding idea seem "tacked on?"

Review the Order That You Use to Present Your Ideas. Do you use spatial, chronological, or emphatic order in your composition? Is the order of ideas a natural progression from the topic sentence or thesis statement? Are any of the details out of logical order? If you use emphatic order, does your strongest point appear last?

If you are writing an essay, what order of presentation do you use within each body paragraph? Is the order of presentation consistent from one paragraph to the next? If you are unsure whether your order of presentation is effective, try moving around different sections of your composition. Is your composition stronger or weaker than before?

Strategies for the Computer

Word processing programs offer many benefits for writers engaged in the revision process. Before the advent of computers, writers had no choice but to type or handwrite individual drafts—a time-consuming task. Today the ability to create and save numerous files on a single disk has so simplified the task of revision that many writers do the majority of their revision work on the computer.

All of the above revising strategies are applicable to computer-generated compositions. Instead of highlighting or circling main ideas, supporting details, and concluding ideas, the writer can place these sentences in a different font—**bold,** *italics,* or <u>underline</u>—or in another size font so they can be easily spotted. To make the composition easier to read aloud, the writer can print a copy and make handwritten additions or deletions that can later be entered into the text file. In addition, word processing programs offer special features to aid in revision, including

- Copy and paste
- Cut and paste
- Outlining
- Word count

Copy and Paste. You can find this feature in the editing menu of most word processing programs. (Word processing programs do not distinguish between editing and revising.) When you copy and paste, you select a portion of text from an open file and place it in a different location in the same document or in a different document. This feature allows you to revise your document by bringing in information from other computer-generated text without disturbing its original location.

Cut and Paste. This feature, similar to copy and paste, is also in the editing menu. When you cut and paste, you also select a portion of text from an open file and move it to another place in the same document or in a different document. However, when you cut and paste, you delete the portion of text from its original location.

Some novice computer users are unwilling to try copy and paste and cut and paste features because they fear "messing up" their compositions. Fortunately, word processing programs also offer an undo feature that will allow you to reverse your choice on your next stroke of the keyboard.

This ability to move sections of documents from one location to another is an invaluable asset to writers engaged in revising their compositions. If you are word processing your composition and discover you are unhappy with the order you use to present your ideas, you can move text to another location and, if you do not like the new arrangement, return to the previous order.

Outlining. Some word processing programs do not offer outlining features, and for those that do the capabilities vary greatly. In general, outlining features allow you to identify main portions of the text by numbering them and assigning headings and subheadings. Once you have outlined your composition, you can then arrange and rearrange different sections of your composition.

Outlining programs are particularly beneficial to "chunk" writers—authors who compose each paragraph (or section) of a document separately and then later arrange the sections in a logical order.

For additional information about your word processing software's features, consult your user's guide.

FOCUS ON EDITING STRATEGIES

The editing stage, like the revising stage, requires time and energy. If you try to edit your work too soon after you complete your revised draft, it will be difficult for you to read with an *objective eye*. If possible, get away from your writing for a while, and let your composition "cool." Then return in a few hours or even a few days to edit your work.

A high energy level is also a prerequisite for effective editing. If you are sleepy or preoccupied, you will be less likely to possess the concentration needed to edit your work. Also, if you have waited until the last minute to edit your work and are rushing through the process, you will probably overlook errors that could have been easily corrected.

General Editing Strategies

Mistakes in spelling, punctuation, and grammar generally result from

- Not knowing the correct form in Standard American English dialect
- Not concentrating and thus making careless mistakes

Unfortunately, these mistakes can distract your reader, who must slow down reading your composition to try to figure out what you were trying to say. The strategies below can help you edit your compositions so that your message has its best chance of reaching the reader.

Read Your Composition Aloud to Yourself or to Someone Else. The keys to this editing strategy are to read exactly what you have written, read with expression, and listen to yourself. Many writers read what they think is on the page instead of what is actually there. Read your composition slowly so that you can hear every word. If you are reading your composition to someone else, ask your audience to let you know if you begin reading too quickly.

Be sure to bring your voice to a full stop at every period. When you do so, you will hear your voice drop. This technique is an excellent way to check for run-ons, comma splices, and fragments.

Listen to the rhythm of your sentences. Are there any sentences over which your voice stumbles? If so, check to see if words have been omitted or if the sentence needs rewording.

Ask Someone to Read Your Paper to You. Ask your reader to read exactly what is written and not to fill in what is missing. If possible, choose someone who reads expressively so that you can listen to the rhythm of your writing. Pay close attention to sentences that the reader has trouble reading. These sentences may need additional words or punctuation to clarify the meaning.

Read Your Composition Line by Line. Try using a cover sheet to expose each line of your composition. This technique will force your "objective eye" to slow down and examine each word carefully. Otherwise, you may overlook spelling errors, punctuation errors, and word omissions.

Read Your Composition Backward Sentence by Sentence. While at first glance this strategy may seem silly, many student writers have found it helpful. Reading your composition backward one sentence at a time will interrupt the natural flow of your writing and force you to examine each sentence independently. This method works particularly well for students who sometimes write fragments.

Strategies for Spelling

Spelling errors are frustrating for writers and readers alike. Writers who wish to communicate their message clearly to readers know they must edit their work repeatedly for spelling errors. However, this process is time-consuming—especially for poor spellers. Psychologists are unsure why some people have more trouble spelling than others. What is agreed upon, however, is that spelling difficulties are not directly related to IQ. Many bright writers have trouble with spelling. Reasons for spelling difficulties can range from poor instruction in elementary school to specific learning disabilities. The following strategies will help good spellers and poor spellers alike eliminate misspelled words from their compositions:

Check Your Spelling by Using a Dictionary or a Hand-Held Spellchecker. An occasional spelling error is not a problem for many readers. However, frequent spelling errors are problematic, especially for educated readers, because they slow down the pace of the reading and distract from the message you are sending. Invest in a good collegiate dictionary—hardback for home and office and paperback for classroom use. Discipline yourself to carry your dictionary to class when you are writing an in-class composition. During the early stages of the writing process, taking the time to look up words in the dictionary can interrupt the thinking processes necessary for effective writing. Instead, as you are writing your experimental draft(s), circle words you think may be misspelled and then look them up as you are working on your later drafts.

Consider purchasing a hand-held spellchecker. If you are unsure how to spell a word, enter your best guess into the spellchecker. The spellchecker will then check the word against its dictionary (most dictionaries are at least 80,000 words) and suggest a possible spelling. This technique is good for those writers who have difficulty visualizing how to spell a word but can recognize the correct spelling when they see it.

Learn Basic Spelling Rules

Rule 1: *Use* ***-i*** *before* ***-e*** *except immediately following the letter* **c**. *Use* ***-ei*** *immediately following the letter* **c** *or in words where* ***-ei*** *sounds like* ***ay***.

believe	receive	neighbor
niece	conceive	weigh
relieve	deceive	eight

Exception: When the letter -c makes the -sh sound, the letter -c is followed by -ie.

sufficient	efficient	ancient

Other Exceptions: These words do not follow the rules above.

weird	their	foreign
height	neither	either
seize	society	

Rule 2: Drop the final -e when you add an ending that begins with a vowel. Keep the final -e when you add an ending that begins with a consonant.

ride + ing = riding	move + ing = moving
time + er = timer	manage + er = manager
hope + less = hopeless	move + ment = movement
time + less = timeless	manage + ment = management

Rule 3: When you add an ending to a word ending in -y, change the -y to -i if the letter before the -y is a consonant. Do not change the -y if a vowel appears before the -y.

dry + ed = dried	deny + ed = denied
rely + ed = relied	enjoy + ment = enjoyment
delay + ed = delayed	buy + er = buyer
cry + er = crier	relay + ed = relayed
angry + ly = angrily	

Exception: Always keep the final -y when you add -ing.

drying	denying	relying
enjoying	delaying	buying

Rule 4: When you form plurals, add -es to words ending in ss, x, z, ch, sh, or o. Always add -es when you form a plural by changing a final y to i.

kisses	tomatoes	countries
axes	potatoes	babies
buzzes	churches	flies

Rule 5: In one-syllable words that end in a single vowel between two consonants, double the final consonant when you add an ending.

stopped	stirring	crammed
rotted	stunning	stubbed

Rule 6: *In words of more than one syllable ending in a single vowel between two consonants and with a stress on the second syllable, double the final consonant when you add an ending.*

committed	occurring	expelled
transmitted	preferring	compelled

While each of these rules has some exceptions, mastering them will help you improve your spelling.

In the application letter below, circle misspelled words and write the correct spelling in the margin. Use the above spelling rules as your guide.

3522 Feildstone Lane
Hometown, SC 29999

Foriegn Imports, Inc.
2531 Business Avenue
Large City, NY 05231

Dear Mr. Jones:

I would like to apply for the sales manager position you advertised in last week's <u>Hometown News.</u> Recently I completed my degree in business management, and I beleive you will find both my work expereince and my educational background have prepared me well for this position.

Although I have been a full-time student for the last four years, I have never stoped working in sales—primaryly in retail department stores. I have siezed every opportunity to distinguish myself as an outstanding salesperson. Now that I have completed my degree, I am ready to move into sales managment. I am especially interested in car sales and am a long-time member of the Foreign Car Soceity.

I am commited to excelent customer service and would like the chance to interveiw for this position. I have enclosed my resume for your consideration.

Sincerly yours,
Melissa Smith

Check for Commonly Confused Words. Below are some words that writers often confuse. Confusing these words changes the meaning of the sentence and can confuse your reader.

Accept: a verb meaning *to receive*
Except: a preposition that means *excluding*
Will you **accept** this gift?
Everyone is going **except** her.

Advice: a noun
Advise: a verb

> Your **advice** was helpful.
>
> Can you **advise** me further?

Affect: a verb meaning *to influence*
Effect: a noun meaning *a result*

> Will your procrastination **affect** your grade?
>
> The **effects** of the drug are unknown.

Breath: a noun pronounced *breth* (short *e* vowel as in *death*)
Breathe: a verb pronounced *breeth* (long *e* sound, rhymes with *seethe*)

> Take a deep **breath** and then dive into the water.
>
> Singers must learn to **breathe** correctly.

Choose: verb meaning *to select* (rhymes with *fuse*)
Chose: past tense of *choose* (rhymes with *hose*)

> Karen will **choose** a new couch tomorrow.
>
> Karen **chose** a new couch last week.

Conscience: noun meaning *knowledge of good or bad acts*
Conscious: adjective meaning *aware and awake*

> He had a guilty **conscience** because of his misdeeds.
>
> The patient is not yet **conscious.**

Hear: verb meaning *to listen*
Here: adverb indicating a location

> Did you **hear** Denise say that her parents were **here** to pick her up?

Know: a verb (*to understand*)
No: opposite of *yes*

> I did not **know** there was **no** food in the house.

Knew: past tense of *know*
New: opposite of *old*

> I **knew** we would need a **new** car soon.

Lead: verb meaning *to guide* (rhymes with *seed*); noun meaning *a metal substance* (rhymes with *head*)
Led: past tense and past participle of *lead*

> I will follow if you **lead** the way.
>
> I need more **lead** for my mechanical pencil.
>
> The limousine **led** the funeral procession.

Lie: See Chapter 5.
Lay: See Chapter 5.

Loose: adjective meaning *untied* or *unwound* (rhymes with *moose*)
Lose: verb meaning *to misplace* or *to fail to win* (rhymes with *fuse*)

> The necklace was so **loose** that it nearly fell off her neck.
>
> Did you **lose** your necklace?

Passed: past participle and past tense of verb *to pass*
Past: noun referring to a time before the present; preposition that means *beyond*

The car **passed** by very quickly.

Did you go **past** our house last night?

So much has happened in my **past.**

Quiet: opposite of *noisy*

Quite: synonym for *very*

I was **quite** happy that my house was so **quiet.**

Raise: verb meaning *to lift* or *increase;* noun meaning *increase in salary*

Rise: verb meaning *to move without assistance*

Did you receive that **raise** you requested?

Every morning I get up before the sun **rises.**

Sit: verb; opposite of *to stand*

Set: verb meaning *to place*

Are you planning to **sit** on this couch all day?

Will you **set** those dishes on the table?

Than: word used in comparisons

Then: adverb that means *later*

She is a better runner **than** her brother.

I will see you **then.**

Their: third person plural possessive pronoun

There: adverb indicating location

They're: contraction for *they are*

Dan, Patricia, and Lee left **their** golf clubs at home.

There is the golf course.

They're not going to play well **there** without **their** golf clubs.

Through: a preposition

Threw: past tense of verb *to throw*

Over the river and **through** the woods is grandmother's house.

She **threw** the ball to home plate.

To: a preposition

Too: adverb meaning *also* or *more than enough*

Two: the number

Len is going **to** a reunion this weekend.

Two of his co-workers are going **too.**

Were: plural past tense of verb *to be*

Where: adverb indicating direction

Where were you last weekend?

Weather: a noun meaning *climactic conditions*

Whether: a subordinating conjunction used like *if*

The **weather** today is stunningly beautiful.

Do you know yet **whether** you can go with me?

Whose: possessive form of *who*

Who's: contraction for *who is*

Whose house is that?

Who's the new student in the class?

Your: second person possessive pronoun
You're: contraction for *you are*

You left **your** jacket at my house last night.
You're going to have to go to **your** friend's house without me.

EXERCISE 10.2

In the letter below, use the above list to check for confused words. Cross out any confused words and write the correction in the margin.

Foreign Imports, Inc.
2531 Business Avenue
Large City, NY 05231

3522 Fieldstone Lane
Hometown, SC 29999

Dear Ms. Smith:

I am pleased to except your application for sales manager at Foreign Imports. I am quiet impressed that you worked you're way threw school. However, I am also concerned weather your background in department store sales is sufficient preparation for the demands of this position.

My advice too you is to come in for an interview next Tuesday so that you can discuss your academic preparation in sales management. We are expanding our business, and I am sure their will be employment opportunities that you may chose to pursue. In this rapidly changing business environment, you never know what may lay ahead.

Cordially,
Jonathan Jones

Create Your Own Personal Spelling List. Keep a list of words you misspell in your compositions. Underline, circle, or capitalize the difficult part of each word.

reCEIve	aCCoMModate	oCCuRRed

Another helpful strategy is to underline, circle, or capitalize the small word inside the larger word.

inFINITE	misSPELLed	conSCIENCE
corRESPOND	foREIGN	GOVERNment

Strategies for Grammar and Punctuation

One of the major goals of this textbook has been to provide you with a review of grammar and punctuation rules. With knowledge comes understanding. However, you must still work diligently (as all writers do) to reduce the number of grammatical and punctuation errors in your compositions.

One effective strategy is keeping a checklist of the grammatical and punctuation errors that occur in your compositions. A simple method is to create a column for each of the following: *comma splices, run-ons, fragments, subject–verb agreement, verb tense, pronoun–precedent agreement, pronoun case, dangling modifiers, misplaced modifiers,* and *faulty parallelism.* For punctuation errors create a column for apostrophes, commas, and other (hyphens, dashes, etc.). Then for each paper record the number of errors you made in each of these categories.

Look for patterns of errors. Which types of mistakes do you make most frequently? Which types of errors do you rarely make? Use the answers to these questions to guide your editing. For example, if you have trouble with fragments, then read your essay through looking just for fragments. If you often fail to use apostrophes, then look especially for contractions and possessive nouns. In other words, try to tailor your editing to fit your pattern of errors.

Strategies for Diction

The term *diction* refers to *word choice.* Every writer's goal is to use the correct word for the desired meaning. However, many writers find themselves

- Using the same word too many times
- Using words that are too vague
- Writing sentences that contain deadwood (unnecessary words)

These diction problems can interfere with the reader's reception of the writer's message.

If you find yourself repeatedly using the same word, try using a thesaurus (a dictionary of synonyms and antonyms). Replace the word with its synonym, and then read your sentence aloud to see if the meaning of the sentence is clear. Keep in mind that while the thesaurus is an excellent way to find synonyms, you are responsible for making sure the synonym fits in the context of the sentence. If you are unsure of the exact meaning of a synonym, consult a dictionary.

Some words such as *thing, aspect, it,* and *this* are often so general that they are meaningless. When you use these words, make sure your reader knows exactly to what you are referring. Avoid using the words *it* and *thing* when you can use a specific noun instead. If you use the word *this,* make sure you follow it with a noun. If your references are unclear, your reader may have to reread your previous sentences to see what you are trying to communicate— an inconvenience for any reader.

Vague: I knew **it** would be the hardest **thing** I have ever done.

Clear: I knew working for my dad would be the hardest job I have ever done.

Vague: **This** is important for my future success.

Clear: This interview is important for my future success.

Go through your sentences and cut out the deadwood. Consider eliminating such phrases as *I believe, I think, in my opinion, personally I think, I feel, it seems to me that, it appears to me that, I guess that.* Since your name is on your composition, your reader knows that your ideas are being presented; therefore, the phrases listed above are probably needless fillers.

Deadwood	**Edited Sentence**
Personally I think I will never own a gun.	I will never own a gun.
It seems to me that convicted felons should not be released until they have served their full sentences.	Convicted felons should not be released until they have served their full sentences.

Prune unnecessary adverbs such as *very, really, definitely,* and *quite* from your sentences. Your sentences will be just as forceful without them.

Deadwood	**Edited Sentence**
In my opinion convicted felons should **definitely** serve at the **very** least eighty percent of their sentences.	Convicted felons should serve at least eighty percent of their sentences.

Remove any phrases from your sentences that are redundant—that is, which unnecessarily restate an idea that appears earlier in the sentence.

Deadwood	**Edited Sentence**
Immediately we knew **right away** we would miss the plane.	Immediately we knew we would miss the plane.
It is my **honor** and **privilege** to introduce Senator Smith.	It is my honor to introduce Senator Smith.

EXERCISE 10.3

Edit the following paragraph for vague words, repetition, and deadwood.

In my opinion the most important part of the job application process is the interview. The applicant should prepare for the interview well in advance of the scheduled date. It seems to me that it is very, very important that the applicant learn some things about the company before the interview. These things may include how long the company has been in existence, how many workers the company employs, and how much profit the company made in the previous year. Also the interviewee should anticipate the questions the interviewer will likely ask. This will also help reduce anxiety in the interview. For example, the interviewer will likely want to know why the applicant left the last job, what the applicant's strengths and weaknesses are, and what salary the applicant expects. Also the prospective employee should make a list of questions to ask at the end of the interview. It may include such questions as "When will I hear from you?", "What benefits does the company offer?" and "When does the job begin?" Thinking ahead will increase the chances of a successful interview.

Strategies for the Computer

Many writers draft their compositions solely on computers. Therefore, much of the editing takes place on the computer screen. All the strategies above also apply to writing with a computer even though some modifications are necessary on a computer screen. For instance, the writer can edit his or her paper for word omissions, repeated words, or spelling errors by moving the cursor through each word slowly and reading each sentence aloud. It is also possible to scroll through the document line by line and/or format the document in a different point size so you can easily read your composition. In addition to the strategies above, word processing software can offer the writer powerful editing tools including

- Spellchecker
- Thesaurus
- Grammar checker

Like any technology, these tools have clear benefits and limitations. Even with their limitations, however, many writers cannot imagine editing a document without them.

Spellchecker. Editing your compositions for spelling becomes a much easier process when you use a spellchecker. A spellchecker allows you to verify the spelling of many (but not all) of the words in your document. Most spellcheckers have between 80,000 and 100,000 common words in their dictionaries. The spellchecker selects a possible misspelled word and then asks the writer to verify whether the word is spelled correctly or needs correction. If the writer is unsure about how to spell a word, the spellchecker will present possibilities. If the word is spelled correctly, the writer can ask the program to ignore the suggested spelling once or throughout the document. If the word is misspelled, the writer can request that the program substitute the correct spelling once or at every occurrence.

Many spellcheckers offer the writer a chance to add words to the dictionary. Check your word processing program user's guide for options specific to your software. If this option is available, you may want to add specialized terms to the spellchecker's dictionary.

You may also have the option to exclude words from the spellchecker. For example, you can ask the spellchecker not to check any proper nouns. The spellchecker cannot recognize whether names are misspelled, but if you do not exclude proper nouns, many spellcheckers will select every word beginning with a capital letter.

Some word processing programs even have a feature that allows you to add typing errors or spelling errors you commonly make. These errors—*hte* for *the* or *beleive* for *believe*—will then be corrected automatically as you type.

No spellchecker is perfect, however. A spellchecker cannot recognize sound-alike words (see "Confused Words" section above), nor can it recognize omitted word endings such as *-s*, *-ed*, or *-ing* if the base word is spelled correctly. Because the spellchecker cannot understand the context in which the word appears, it cannot distinguish between *from* and *form* or between *an* and *and*. If the word used in the text matches a word that appears in its dictionary, the spellchecker will not recognize it as a misspelling.

EXERCISE 10.4

If you have access to a computer, enter the text of the letters in Exercises 10.1 and 10.2. Then run a spellchecker on each letter. Which words did the spellchecker fail to identify as misspellings?

Thesaurus. Many word processing programs feature a thesaurus, a specialized dictionary of synonyms and antonyms. Every writer has experienced the frustration of trying to find just the right word and being unable to come up with it. Another common frustration is repeating a word such as *nice*, *important*, or *pretty* so many times that the word becomes almost meaningless. Using a thesaurus can help relieve this frustration.

When you use a computer thesaurus, you select a word in your document. Then you can use the thesaurus to check this word against its dictionary and suggest synonyms and antonyms. If you are unsure of the meaning of a word, a thesaurus can often provide a definition. Once you have considered the thesaurus' suggestions, you can either replace the word or ignore the suggestion.

Unfortunately, no word processing program can read the context of your composition and recognize whether a word is used correctly. Therefore, you should consider each synonym carefully. If you have doubts whether a particular synonym will fit into the sentence, try reading the sentence aloud and listening. Does the synonym improve the sentence?

EXERCISE 10.5

Enter the text of Exercise 10.3 into your word processor. Place your cursor on words repeated unnecessarily. Then use the word processing program's thesaurus (if available) to locate a synonym. Replace the word with a synonym. Does this replacement improve the sentence? If so, leave the replacement in the paragraph. If not, return to the original wording.

Grammar Checker. Many word processing programs include grammar checkers. Like other computer tools such as the spellchecker and thesaurus, the grammar checker has both benefits and limitations.

One of the benefits is that many grammar checkers offer the writer a choice of styles. For example, for a business letter the writer can choose business style or for an academic essay a formal style. Other possibilities may include casual style or even a style customized by the writer.

Additionally, grammar checkers can help you locate common grammatical errors including fragments, comma splices, run-ons, subject–verb agreement errors, pronoun–antecedent agreement errors, and pronoun case errors. If you have been keeping a grammar checklist and know certain types of errors that frequently appear in your writing, you may be able to customize the grammar checker to look for these error patterns. Consult the user's guide to your word processing software for additional information.

Another benefit is the grammar checker's ability to determine readability. The grammar checker uses various formulas involving word length and sentence length to calculate a grade level. Then the writer can use the readability statistics to help determine whether the reader will be able to understand the written message.

Grammar checkers sometimes frustrate writers because they use grammatical terms that many writers do not understand. For instance, many grammar checkers will tell the writer that a sentence is written using a verb in the passive voice. However, the term *passive voice* is unfamiliar to many writers. All action verbs in English grammar have voice—either active or passive—depending on whether the subject of the sentence is doing the action expressed in the verb or receiving it. If the verb is in the *active voice*, the subject is doing the action expressed in the verb. If the verb is in the *passive voice*, the subjective is receiving the action expressed in the verb.

Ruth **decorated** her house. (Who decorated the house? *Ruth*, and *Ruth* is the subject of the sentence. Therefore, the verb *decorated* is in active voice.)

The house **was decorated** by Ruth. (Who decorated the house? *Ruth*, but *Ruth* is not the subject of the sentence. The subject is *house*. Therefore, the verb *was decorated* is in passive voice.)

Some other examples are

Kristen **performed** the solo at the end of the dance recital. (The verb *performed* is in active voice.)

The solo at the end of the dance recital **was performed** by Kristen. (The verb *performed* is in passive voice.)

Kevin **fixed** the computer. (The verb *fixed* is in active voice.)

The computer **was fixed** by Kevin. (The verb *was fixed* is in passive voice.)

Graham **completed** the landscaping work. (The verb *completed* is in active voice.)

The landscaping work **was completed** by Graham. (The verb *was completed* is in passive voice.)

Generally, sentences with active voice verbs are preferable to those with passive voice verbs because sentences with active voice verbs are shorter and more direct. Passive voice verbs consist of a main verb and one or more helping verbs, so the writer needs more words to complete the sentence. Another problem is that in some sentences with passive voice verbs the subject is not stated at all:

The house was decorated.

The solo was performed.

The computer was fixed.

The landscaping work was completed.

To change a sentence with a passive voice verb to one with an active voice verb

- Locate the verb and remove the helping word.
- Locate the performer of the action and place at the beginning of the sentence (drop the preposition *by* if present in the sentence).
- If nothing in the sentence is performing the action expressed in the verb, add a subject.
- Rewrite the sentence accordingly.

The house was decorated by Ruth. **(passive)**

Ruth decorated the house. **(active)**

The landscaping work was completed. **(passive)**

Graham completed the landscaping work. **(active)**

The grammar checker on your word processing software may use other unfamiliar terms as well. If you need further information, consult an English handbook of grammar and usage.

EXERCISE 10.6

Type the following paragraph onto your computer screen. Then use the grammar checker to locate passive voice verbs. Rewrite all sentences with passive voice verbs so that the verbs are in active voice.

During the interview the applicant must demonstrate self-confidence. The eyes must be focused on the interviewer at all times. Looking down at the floor or up at the ceiling can signal a lack of interest in the job. Attention must also be given to the prospective employee's dress. A conservative suit with a light-colored shirt and simple tie should be worn by male applicants. A solid-colored dress with appropriate accessories is a good choice for female applicants. A dark-colored skirt and light-colored blouse may also be worn by women. Clothing should be attractive but not flashy. Dressing well will boost the applicant's self-esteem. Finally, the interviewee's responses to the questions must favorably impress the interviewer. Questions should be answered by the applicant in a measured, calm voice. A good trick is to wait just a few seconds before responding—even when the answer is clear. The interviewer will be impressed by the applicant's ability to give a thoughtful response. Focusing attention on the interviewer, dressing appropriately, and answering questions thoughtfully are all signs of a confident applicant.

FOCUS ON CONFERENCES WITH TUTOR/TEACHER

Taking the time to talk with a tutor and/or teacher about your revised and edited drafts can help boost your grades and increase your confidence in your writing. Because these conferences are so important, you should maximize your conference time. Here are some suggestions.

♦ **Prepare for the conference.** Reread your draft(s) just before the conference. Write a list of questions to ask the tutor/teacher. If you prefer, write questions in the margins of your draft. Your goals are to reduce your anxiety about the conference, make a favorable impression, and increase your productivity.

♦ **Keep the focus of the conference on revising as well as editing.** A sure way to sabotage a conference is to walk into the tutoring center or teacher's office and demand, "I need someone to proofread my paper." Tutors and teachers do not like to think of themselves as proofreading services.

Instead, begin with an emphasis on revising. Use the peer review guide questions from this text as a starting point and then fill in with your own questions. You can also use the revision questions from this chapter.

Then move to editing considerations. Place a question mark or some other mark at the end of lines where you have questions about spelling, word choice, or grammatical correctness.

♦ **Allow plenty of time.** Another way to sabotage a conference is to announce, "This paper is due next period." First, the tutor or teacher may already be conferencing with someone, and you may have to wait or come back at another time. Second, good conferences take time, and additional conferences are often desirable. A better response would be, "This paper is not due for a day or two. Can I come back tomorrow and show you another draft?"

◆ **Take notes during the conference.** Make changes on your draft(s) during the conference or take notes on a separate sheet of paper. These notes will enable you to revise and edit your composition according to your tutor/teacher's suggestions.

◆ **Keep in touch.** Your tutor/teacher will want to keep track of your progress. If you make a good grade on your composition, share your success. If you do not do as well as you would like, let the tutor/teacher know you would like to continue to work toward higher grades.

As you continue to learn more about the writing process, the grammar of the English language, and the development of paragraphs and essays, your confidence in your ability to write well will grow. Your increased knowledge and confidence will serve you well in both the classroom and the workplace.

Writers as Spiders

In each chapter this section has offered on-line support for you as a writer. Many of the web addresses provided for you have been associated with writing centers at colleges and universities. If you would like to explore other on-line writing centers and check out their resources for revising and editing your compositions, see

http://departments.colgate.edu/diw/NWCAOWLS.html

If you would like to review many of the editing strategies presented in this book, visit

http://www.osu-okmulgee.edu/faculty/carsten/grammar.htm

In addition to colleges and universities, the federal government offers assistance to those writing not only in the classroom but also in the workplace. For example, a helpful site for business writers who wish to rid their compositions of deadwood and repetition is

http://www.pnl.gov/ag/usage/deadwood.html

Commonly confused words continue to present a challenge for many business writers because spellcheckers are of little help in this area. For more homonyms and other confused words, see

http://www.csun.edu/~hflrc001/confuse.html

You can find an exercise on homonyms at

http://www.journalism.indiana.edu/tutorial/tutorial.html

As you progress into other writing courses, remember to use the active voice of the verb whenever possible. If you would like more information about active versus passive voice, consult

http://kamhi.english.rhodes.edu/center/gram/passive.html

http://www.columbia.edu/acis/bartleby/strunk/strunk.html#13

As you continue to crawl through the World Wide Web for writing assistance, keep in mind that this web is constantly changing shape. Web pages come and go, but the Web will continue to be a vital resource for writers who wish to improve their skills.

APPENDIX A

Tips for ESL Students

WRITING STYLE

Researchers tell us that writing in a language other than our own involves more than just knowing the correct word or grammatical point. We must also have knowledge of the culture because ideas are bound to the culture. If the style of writing seems unusual, communication may not adequately take place even when the words and grammar are correct. Here are some ideas to help you become more successful as you compose paragraphs and essays for English-speaking readers.

1. **Be direct from the beginning.** In an essay, put the main point in the thesis statement at the end of the introductory paragraph. In a body paragraph, clearly state the main point in the topic sentence at the beginning of your paragraph.

2. **Go directly to the main points.** Present your ideas in a linear, logical fashion as you build paragraphs and essays.

3. **Avoid getting off topic.** Make sure every example and detail supports the topic sentence and thesis. Follow your outline carefully.

4. **Consider the difference between written and oral language.** You may hear native English speakers use fragments and other incorrect grammatical structures; however, when you write, you should use the Standard American English dialect, which is taught in your textbooks. Also, you may hear a word or an expression but not be able to produce it in writing because the English language has so many irregular pronunciations and spellings. Refer to your English course texts and dictionaries when you encounter these problems.

5. **Write your own ideas as you follow your instructor's guidelines.** Do not copy words or take your ideas from a published source unless you use the correct documentation procedure. This procedure is usually taught in college-level courses. The instructor wants you to share YOUR unique ideas, present your opinions, or challenge existing ideas. In a democracy, every individual has the right to express well-supported claims. The reader may not necessarily agree with your ideas, which is certainly an appropriate and acceptable response, but the reader will take your well-supported ideas seriously.

6. **Immerse yourself in the language as much as possible** to see significant improvement in your ability to read, write, and speak English fluently. Do more than the assigned written work in your classes. Reading and conversing will help you master the rules and structures because repetition plays a key role in learning. Finally, remember that it is natural to make mistakes. When you use your mistakes to improve, you will learn, grow, and progress more rapidly.

GRAMMAR AND LANGUAGE

A word may be used in different ways in a sentence, and a word's part of speech depends on its usage. For example, the word **play** can be used as a noun in "We went to see the <u>play</u> at the Tampa Bay Performing Arts Center," and as a verb in "The football team will <u>play</u> its first game on Saturday." Here are some tips to help you become more accurate in your use of the English language.

1. **Choose the correct noun form.** Nouns are words used to name a group or class of people, places, or things. Some nouns can be counted, but others cannot be counted because they represent mass quantities or abstractions. For example, <u>you can count the number of pens</u> on your desk, but <u>you cannot count the amount of knowledge</u> in your head.

   - **Count Nouns** can be singular or plural (note different plural endings):

     | **Singular** | one book | one church | one story | one woman |
     | **Plural** | two books | three churches | four stories | five women |

   - **Count Nouns** following **one of** are written in the plural form:

     <u>One of</u> the **poems** was written by Robert Frost.

   - **Noncount nouns** are singular (a list of some noncount nouns follows the example):

Example	**Knowledge** <u>opens</u> many doors.
Abstract Ideas	understanding, love, hate, intelligence, advice, knowledge, information, faithfulness, honor, peace, laundry, time, etc.
Activities	tennis, bowling, homework, writing, etc.
Liquids	oil, blood, milk, water, coffee, etc.
Gases	oxygen, steam, etc.
Diseases	cancer, pneumonia, flu, etc.
School subjects	mathematics, history, etc.
Food	bread, rice, lettuce, etc.
Natural elements	rain, snow, wind, weather, thunder, etc.

- Some nouns may be **countable or noncountable** depending on usage:

  Time flies so quickly.   In **times** like this, we must demand the truth.

2. **Use modifiers to qualify and describe ideas.** Modifiers include determiners (a, an, the), pronouns, adjectives, and adverbs. You can improve your writing style by using a variety of modifiers.

  - Precede **singular Count Nouns** with

    a, an, the, this, that, other, another

    one, any, every, each, neither, either, some of the

  - Precede a non specific noun with **a** or **an** and precede a specific noun with **the**

    We went on <u>a vacation</u> to <u>the Rocky Mountains</u>.
    On <u>a clear day</u>, we could see snow on <u>the mountains</u>.

  - Do not use **the** before gerunds in most cases. Gerunds are nouns formed by combining a verb +ing.

    Swimming keeps the muscles toned, and **eating** nutritious food keeps the mind focused.

  - Use **other** to mean "different," and use **another** to mean "additional."

    The **other** hospital was too far away.   **Another** doctor was added to the case.

  - Precede **plural Count Nouns** with

    the, these, those, some, many, a lot of, few, a few, quite a few

  - Do not use **the** before **Noncount Nouns:**

    <u>Love</u> is a strong emotion.   <u>Coffee</u> is my favorite morning drink.

  - Precede **Noncount Nouns** with one of the following:

    much, any, some, a little, lots of, a lot of, this, that

  - Use **any** to indicate a negative element, and use **some** to indicate certainty. Use either **any** or **some** for an uncertain idea:

    She <u>didn't</u> want **any** octopus, but she <u>did</u> eat **some** lobster.

    The others at the party <u>weren't sure</u> if they wanted **any** seafood at all.

  - Place **adjectives** near the nouns or pronouns to which they refer.

    The **rich** <u>woman</u> stepped into the **elegant** <u>limousine</u>.
    The <u>children</u>, **tired and happy**, ran into the house.

- Do not change the form of the **adjective** if the noun or pronoun is plural.

  The students sat around the **long tables** in the library.

- Put a **long list of descriptive adjectives** in the following order:

  judgment, physical characteristics, condition, composition, and origin or trade name.

  The **beautiful, tall, old, oak** tree stood near the lake.
  The **efficient, new, metal, Japanese** clock works well.

- Place **adverbs** which modify verbs, adjectives, or other adverbs in the appropriate position in the sentence. Sometimes, you can place adverbs in different positions in the sentence without changing the meaning.

  Quietly, Mother <u>opened</u> the door to the baby's room.
  Mother **quietly** <u>opened</u> the door to the baby's room.

  Other times, you must put adverbs in a particular position for the meaning to be clear or to place emphasis on a particular idea.

  John felt **especially** <u>happy</u> yesterday. (The emphasis is placed on "happy.")
  John felt happy **especially** <u>yesterday</u>. (The emphasis is placed on "yesterday.")

3. **Use gerunds carefully.** Gerunds are nouns formed by using verb + ing.

   - Usually, you will use the **gerund** form as the subject of the clause or as the object of some verbs and prepositions.

     Use gerunds as subjects:
     Shopping is Cathy's favorite thing to do.
     Working late helps Cathy earn more money to spend in the stores.

     Use gerunds as objects:
     Jim avoided **hitting** the car that moved into his lane.
     He talked about **buying** a new truck with better brakes.

   Learn the difference between the gerund and the progressive verb form, which also uses the -ing ending. The following examples use progressive verbs:

   Alicia was **working** on her paper until late into the night.
   She was **trying** to get ahead in her history class.

Avoid fragments with gerunds:

> **ERROR:**   **Playing** tennis in college.
> **CORRECT:**   **Playing** tenis in college was my dream.

4. **Use correct verb forms and place all verbs in the correct order.**

- **Basic form** of the verb (hope, be, work, life, etc.)—used after an <u>auxiliary verb</u> and in the <u>infinitive verb</u> phrase

   The new 3-D whale movie finally <u>did</u> **arrive** at Ross Aquarium. (<u>Did</u> is an auxillary verb.)
   We didn't want <u>to</u> **be** late. (<u>To be</u> is an infinitive verb phrase.)

- **Auxiliary** verbs (be, do, and have are the most common)—used with a <u>main verb</u> to add more meaning to the idea, to express a negative thought, or to ask a question.

   Eventually, they **did** <u>open</u> the doors.
   Unfortunately, three exhibits **did** <u>not contain</u> any sea life.
   We asked the tour guide, "What exhibit **has** the aquarium <u>planned</u> to add next year?"

- **To be:** Never use the basic form of a verb after any form of the verb **be**.

> **ERROR:**   We **were** watch the angel fish in the aquarium.
> **CORRECT:**   We **were** <u>watching</u> the angel fish in the aquarium.

- **Modal** verbs (present tense = will, can, shall, may, must; past tense = would, could, should, might)—used to express a condition or possibility. Remember to keep all modal verbs in the same tense.

   The aquarium **might** add a special room where visitors **could** touch starfish and crabs.

- **Linking** verbs (be, seem, appear, become, look, sound, smell, and feel are some common linking verbs)—used to convey a condition of being, becoming or feeling and link the subject to the complement which follows the verb.

   The diver who fed the large fish from inside the tank **seemed** confident.
   I'd **feel** scared getting in the tank with so many large fish.

- **Simple present** and the **progressive** verb tenses:

   Use the **simple present tense** to tell what happens regularly, what happens in the present, or what is considered true. Also, you can use some present tense verbs to tell about the future.

   I **speak** Greek at home with my parents. (This happens regularly.)
   When I have an English test, I **study** with my sister, not my parents. (This happens in the present.)

My sister, Irene, always **gets** A's and B's on her college essays. (This is true.)

Irene **plans** to get a job as a translater. (This tells about the future.)

Use the **progressive tense** to indicate the action continues or occurs habitually.

I **am working** at the Athena Restaurant to pay for my tuition. (The job will continue.)

Greek customers **are** always **asking** me to speak to them in Greek. (The request occurs habitually.)

5. **Determine word order by the type of sentence you write.**

- **Declarative statements** present a fact and contain at least one **subject** and a <u>verb</u>, usually in that order; sometimes they may contain more than one subject and verb.

  The museum **display** <u>showed</u> the desert animals in their natural habitats.

  The **snakes, rabbits,** and **birds** <u>looked</u> alive.

  Although the **animals** <u>do</u> not <u>require</u> a lot of water, **they** <u>do need</u> some shade from the sun.

- **Inverted sentences** put the **subject** after the <u>verb</u>. For example, sentences beginning with **There** or **Here** will follow this pattern.

  There <u>were</u> five **students** waiting in line.

- **Questions** are usually inverted, and sometimes the complete <u>verb</u> is separated by the **subject!**

  <u>Were</u> the **students** in the right registration line?

  What time <u>were</u> **they** <u>supposed</u> to register?

- **Questions beginning with** the noun question words, **who** and **what,** are followed by the <u>verb</u>.

  "**Who** <u>wants</u> to register now?" Dr. Morrison, the counselor, asked them.

  "**What** <u>happened</u> to your registration cards?" she asked.

6. **Remember to include these necessary sentence elements.**

- We use **pronouns** so much in English! Make sure you know exactly what the pronoun replaces to avoid confusion. You must use the correct pronoun to indicate gender and number.

  The **mountains** near the town of San German, Puerto Rico, are beautiful. **They** are covered with many tropical plants.

My **parents** bought a house near the mountains. **They** liked the house just the way **they** found it.

My **mother** said the house was perfect because it allowed **her** to live away from town.

- Choose and use prepositions **in, on,** and **at** carefully when referring to time and place:

Time:

in a period of time—**in** a few days, **in** an hour
in a particular month or year—**in** June, **in** 1998
in a period of time during the day—**in** the morning
on a specific day—**on** Monday, **on** Sept. 24, **on** Veterans' Day
on time
at a definite time—**at** 9:00, **at** lunch time

Place:

inside a specific place—**in** the desk drawer, **in** his pocket, **in** the room
at a specific place—**at** the park, **at** my mother's home
on top of something—**on** the desk, **on** the mountain, **on** my street

- Always include the **infinitive** marker **to** before the base form of a verb.

I'd like **to** return to San German **to** see my aunt and uncle.

7. **Avoid these problems with verbs and pronouns.**

- **Negatives:** Put the 's' for third person singular only on the **auxiliary verb**.

ERROR: Andrea **doesn't** has a hobby
CORRECT: Andrea **doesn't** have a hobby.

- **Past tense:** Change only the form of the **auxiliary verb** to mark past tense.

ERROR: My friend, Thien, **didn't** had a hobby until he discovered car races.
CORRECT: My friend, Thien, **didn't** have a hobby until he discovered car races.

- **Prounouns:** When you use a **pronoun,** do not also use the noun it replaces.

ERROR: Erika's hobby is horseback riding. Erika **she** goes to the barn every day.
CORRECT: Erika's hobby is horseback riding. **She** goes to the barn every day.

Writers as Spiders

Here are some helpful Web sites. Also consider using search engines to find information because Web sites may disappear.

ESL Resources for Students

http://owl.english.purdue/esl/ESl-student.html

On-Line English Grammar

http://www.edunet.com/english/grammar/toc.html

Grammar Quizzes

http://www.aitech.ac.jp/~iteslj/quizzes/grammar.html

Portland Community College Links for Students

http://thor.pcc.edu/~ap-sec/links.htm

English Pages

http://www.pratique.fr/~green/english.html

English Grammar for ESL Students

http://www.gl.umbc.edu/~kpokoy1/grammar1.htm

Selected Links for ESL Students

http://www.aitech.ac.jp/~iteslj/ESL.html

ESL Grammar Notes #1: Count and Noncount Nouns

http://www.fairnet.org/agencies/lca/grammar1.html

ESL Grammar Notes #2: Articles

http://www.fairnet.org/agencies/lca/grammar2.html

ESL Grammar Notes #3: Verb Tenses

http://www.fairnet.org/agencies/lca/grammar3.html

APPENDIX B

Outlining

Outlining is a tool to help you shape your paragraph or essay. An outline

- Presents the main idea, major supports, and minor points of your composition
- Previews your composition for your reader

Some writers outline before they begin to draft their compositions. These writers use outlines to help them in the planning stage of the writing process. Once they have finished the composition, they then revise the outline. Other writers do not outline until they have finished their revised drafts. These writers use outlining to check whether the main ideas of their compositions have sufficient support and whether the supporting ideas are logically arranged.

Two types of outlines are commonly used by writers: informal and formal. An *informal outline* identifies the main idea as well as the major and minor points of your composition but does not use conventional outline form. For example, a cluster such as the one that appears in Chapter 2 can serve as an informal outline. So can a list of your composition's major and minor supports. A *formal outlining* uses standard outline form consisting of headings and subheadings to identify main ideas, major points, and supporting details. This appendix focuses on the formal outline. You can use a formal outline for either a topic sentence paragraph or an essay.

Formal outlines appear in one of two formats: topic or sentence. In a *topic outline* all parts of the outline consist of short phrases (groups of words without a subject and a verb). The topic outline is the most common type of formal outline. Topic outlines are especially useful for lengthy writing assignments such as research papers or even books. In a *sentence outline*, on the other hand, every part of the outline consists of a complete sentence. The sentences that appear on the sentence outline (with the exception of the topic sentence) do not have to be worded exactly as they appear in the composition, but they do have to express the same thought. Sentence outlines are helpful for assignments such as speeches or in-class essays.

It is important that writers not confuse the reader by mixing topic and sentence outline form. One of the editing tasks of the writer is to check to be sure that if a sentence outline is used, no phrases appear on the outline, and that if a topic outline is used, no sentences appear on the outline.

Formal outlines, whether topic or sentence, follow certain conventions.

- A Roman numeral (*I, II, III*, etc.) identifies the topic sentence of a paragraph (or in a lengthy essay a major division of the paper).
- Capital letters beginning with *A* identify major points.
- Numbers beginning with *1* identify minor points.
- Lower case letters beginning with *a* identify supporting details for minor points.
- Each level of the outline is indented under the preceding level.
- Punctuation and capitalization are standardized (see examples below).
- All levels of the outline should be grammatically parallel when possible.
- All parts of the outline represent divisions of the preceding idea. Therefore, every *A* is followed by a *B*, every *1* by a 2, and every *a* by a *b*.

Formal Outline for Paragraphs

The conventions of a formal outline do not lend themselves to all types of paragraphs. For instance, narrative paragraphs that are arranged using chronological order and observation paragraphs that use spatial order are generally not outlined. However, formal outlines are helpful for development-by-example paragraphs and comparison/contrast paragraphs. You do not need to outline every idea in your paragraph, but you should include your major and minor supports.

Here is the formal outline pattern for paragraphs.

I. Topic (or topic sentence) of paragraph
   A. Major support #1
      1. Minor support for #1
      2. Additional minor support for #1
   B. Major support #2
      1. Minor support for #2
      2. Additional minor support for #2

Other major supports (C., D., etc.) can be added as well as additional minor supports (3., 4., etc.). Note also that the concluding sentence is not outlined.

Sample

Topic Outline for Comparison/Contrast Paragraph—Point-by-Point

Here is a formal topic outline for the sample comparison/contrast paragraph (point-by-point pattern) that appears at the end of Chapter 6.

I. Myakka River State Park versus Hillsborough River State Park
   A. Size
      1. Myakka
      2. Hillsborough
   B. Trail
      1. Myakka
      2. Hillsborough
   C. Terrain
      1. Myakka
      2. Hillsborough
   D. Rivers
      1. Myakka
      2. Hillsborough

Sample

Topic Outline for Comparison/Contrast Paragraph—Block

Below is the formal topic outline for the sample comparison/contrast paragraph (block) at the end of Chapter 6.

I. Tent campers versus motor home campers
   A. Tent campers
      1. Comforts
      2. Expense
      3. Amount of work
   B. Motor home campers
      1. Comforts
      2. Expense
      3. Amount of work

Sample

Sentence Outline for Development-by-Example Paragraph

Following is a sentence outline for Kathryn Figueroa's development-by-example paragraph at the end of Chapter 3.

I. Developing math skills in college will help prepare me for a career as a registered nurse.
   A. I have to calculate almost every day.
      1. I must figure out dosages.
      2. I must reach the correct answer.
   B. I must measure liquids.
      1. I must make conversions.
      2. I must calculate the rate of flow for continuous flows.

Notice how the sentences on this outline (except for the topic sentence) are worded differently from the way they appear in the paragraph in Chapter 3. Note also how the sentences representing major and minor points are expressed in parallel form (for more information about parallelism, see Chapter 9).

FORMAL OUTLINE FOR ESSAYS

Formal outlines of essays differ from those of paragraphs. Because the body of the essay is longer than the body of a paragraph, the outline for an essay will be more extensive and may require additional levels.

Furthermore, the thesis statement appears at the top of the essay outline as a guide for both the writer and the reader. Introductory and concluding paragraphs are generally not outlined.

The pattern for formal essay outlines is

Thesis

I. Topic (or topic sentence) of first body paragraph
   A. Major support #1
      1. Minor support for #1
      2. Additional minor support for #1
   B. Major support #2
      1. Minor support for #2
      2. Additional minor support for #2
II. Topic (or topic sentence) of second body paragraph
   A. Major support #1
      1. Minor support for #1
      2. Additional minor support for #1
   B. Major support #2
      1. Minor support for #2
      2. Additional minor support for #2 etc.

If you need to outline more extensively, you can add levels where needed (as long as you have at least two points at each level), as follows:

I.
    A.
        1.
            a.
            b.
                (1)
                (2)
                    (a)
                    (b)
        2. *etc.*

Sample

Topic Outline for Contrast Essay

Here is a topic outline for a contrast essay, "Corporate Funeral Homes versus Family-Owned Funeral Homes" by Deborah Klingensmith. This essay appears in Chapter 7.

Corporate Funeral Homes versus Family-Owned Funeral Homes

Thesis: Although corporate funeral homes and family-owned funeral homes both provide services for the community, they operate their businesses differently.

I. Corporate funeral homes
    A. Staffs
        1. Large
        2. Standard wages
    B. Community involvement
        1. Limited
        2. Outside buying
    C. Business practices
        1. Reception of families
        2. Payment arrangements
II. Family-owned funeral homes
    A. Staffs
        1. Small
        2. High wages
    B. Community involvement
        1. Extensive
        2. Local buying
    C. Business practices
        1. Reception of families
        2. Financial arrangements

Sample

Sentence Outline for Development-by-Example Essay

When Kathryn Figueroa extended her development-by-example paragraph to form an essay, she developed the following sentence outline:

College Skills for Future Success

Thesis: I plan to learn academic skills in college that will enable me to be a registered nurse and further my career.

   I. Developing math skills in college will help prepare me for a career as a registered nurse.
      A. I have to calculate almost every day.
         1. I must figure out dosages.
         2. I must reach the correct answer.
      B. I must measure liquids.
         1. I must make conversions.
         2. I must calculate the rate of flow for continuous flows.
            a. I must calculate the rate for intravenous infusions.
            b. I must calculate the rate for artificial feedings.
  II. A nurse must not only possess excellent math skills but also strong communication skills.
      A. I must speak with other staff members.
         1. I must speak professionally.
         2. I must speak articulately.
      B. I must document patient records.
         1. I must include every action.
         2. I must write concisely.
 III. Being a nurse requires comprehensive knowledge of anatomy and physiology.
      A. I must learn the functions and locations of body organs.
         1. Organs are interdependent.
         2. I will learn what causes organs to malfunction.
      B. I will learn to recognize symptoms of diseases.
         1. Recognizing symptoms can mean saving a life.
         2. Nurses often must relay patient information to the doctor.

Outlines—whether informal or formal, topic or sentence—are tools to help you plan and shape your compositions. Learning to outline will help you bring your ideas into focus and strengthen your composition skills.

APPENDIX C

Manuscript Form

When you are ready to submit your finished draft to your reader, you should prepare your work so that it creates a positive, lasting impression. You should make sure that you have fulfilled any special requests your reader may have made. For example, your reader may ask that you submit your finished work in a folder, turn in all your drafts, staple your drafts together, or that you not write on the backs of the manuscript pages. Taking special care to meet your reader's requirements will help assure that the message of your paragraph or essay is well-received.

Many college instructors ask that students prepare manuscripts using the Modern Language Association (MLA) format. The MLA format is one of several major format styles used to prepare manuscripts in college classrooms. You will learn more about the MLA format when you learn to write research papers. This appendix limits its focus to

- Preparation of a title page
- Page numbering
- Spacing
- Margins
- Titles

PREPARATION OF THE TITLE PAGE

Some manuscripts using MLA format include a title page that is separate from the rest of the text. A sample format for a separate title page is shown in Figure C.1.

MLA format provides an alternative to a separate title page. This alternative uses a heading which appears in the upper left hand corner of the first page of text. The heading is immediately followed by the title of the paper and the beginning of the text (see Figure C.2).

PAGE NUMBERING

If you use a separate title page, begin numbering your document on the first page of text. The page number 1 will appear in the upper righthand corner and will be followed by the title repeated from the title page and the beginning of the text, as shown in Figure C.3.

Title of Paper

Student's Name
Course Title
Instructor's Name
Date

Figure C.1   Sample format for title page—separate page

Student's Full Name   Student Last Name   1

Instructor's Name

Course Title

Date in Day Month Year Style

                              Title of Paper

Beginning of text . . . .
. . . .

Figure C.2   Sample format for alternative to separate title page

If you do not use a separate title page, the number 1 will appear on the same page as your heading, title, and text (see sample page above).

Whether you use a separate title page or not, on each subsequent page your last name followed by the page number will appear, as shown in Figure C.4.

SPACING

If you are word processing your manuscript, double space the entire manuscript. If you are handwriting your manuscript, check with your reader about spacing. Many readers prefer that handwritten manuscripts be double spaced to make them easy to read and edit.

MARGINS

Whether your manuscript is word processed or handwritten, your left and right margins should be defined. For word processed manuscripts, follow these general guidelines unless your reader has other preferences:

- Set your left margin at 1 to 1.5 inches.
- Set your right margin at 1 inch.

                                       Student Last Name   1
                              Title of Paper
Beginning of text . . . .
. . . .

Figure C.3   Page numbering when using a separate title page

Campbell 2

Text . . . .
. . . .

Figure C.4 Subsequent page numbering

- Set your top margin at 1 inch.
- Set your bottom margin at 1 inch.

TITLES

A title is a phrase (usually of three to five words) that appears at the beginning of your composition. Think of your title in the same way you think of a title of a book on a library shelf. Will the title of your composition pique your reader's interest? Does the title reflect the focus of your composition?

Your title does not have to be catchy to be effective. If you have trouble composing a title for a paragraph, find your topic sentence and write down the key words. Then write a title that includes these words. If you are writing a title for an essay, consider the most important words in your thesis statement.

In general, follow these guidelines when writing your title:

- Do not place your title in quotation marks (unless, of course, your title is quoting someone else's words).
- Do not underline your title.
- Do not follow your title with a period.
- Capitalize the first and last words.
- Capitalize all other words except conjunctions (*for, and, nor, but, or, yet, so*), articles (*a, an, the*) and prepositions under four letters in length.

Following the guidelines above will help you present a composition pleasing to the eye. Students who prepare their finished drafts carefully are well on their way to achieving success.

APPENDIX D

Glossary of Key Grammatical Terms

The definitions of key grammatical terms used in this textbook appear below. For further information about each of these terms, consult the pages listed in the index.

Action verb   Word or group of words expressing an action performed by the subject

Active voice verb   Verb of a sentence in which the subject performs the expressed action

Adjective   Word modifying (describing) a noun or pronoun by answering *what kind of, which one,* or *how many*

Adverb   Word modifying a verb, adjective, or another adverb by answering *where, when,* or *how*

Antecedent   Noun for which the pronoun is a substitute

Appositive   Noun renaming or identifying the noun immediately preceding it

Clause   Group of grammatically related words with a subject and a verb

Comma splice   Two independent clauses connected by a comma alone (no coordinating conjunction present)

Comparative form of adjective   Adjective form comparing two persons, ideas, or things and generally formed by the use of the *-er* ending or the word *more*

Comparative form of adverb   Adverb form comparing two persons, ideas, or things and generally formed by the use of the word *more* or *less*

Complete subject   Noun or pronoun forming the subject (including any descriptive words surrounding it)

Compound adjective   Adjective consisting of more than one word

Compound subject   Subject consisting of more than one noun and/or pronoun

Conjunction adverb   Adverb joining two independent clauses

Coordinate adjective   Two or more adjectives that can be reversed without changing the meaning of the sentence

296

Coordinating conjunction   Word used (with a comma) to join two related independent clauses. Remember *FANBOYS* (*for, and, nor, but, or, yet, so*).

Coordination   Process of joining two or more related independent clauses

Dangling modifier   Phrase modifier that appears at the beginning of a sentence but does not modify (describe) the subject of the sentence

Dependent clause   Group of words with a subject and a verb but without grammatical independence (does not form a complete thought)

Essential clause   Clause beginning with *who* or *which* and necessary for identification of the noun preceding the clause

Fragment   Any group of words without grammatical independence (does not form a complete sentence)

Gender   Denotes whether a singular pronoun is male, female, or neuter

Helping verb   Verb that accompanies (helps) the main action verb of the sentence

Imperative sentence   Expresses a command

Indefinite pronoun   Pronoun that does not refer to a specific person, place, or thing: *anyone, someone, no one, everyone, anybody, somebody, nobody, everybody, each, either, neither, some, all, none, both*

Independent clause   Group of words with a subject and verb and grammatical independence (forms a complete thought)

Infinitive phrase   Group of words beginning with the word *to* and followed by a verb and sometimes a noun or pronoun (object of the infinitive)

Inverted sentence   Sentence in which the subject does not come before the verb

Irregular verb   Verb that does not form its past tense by adding *-ed* ending

Linking verb   Verb that does not express action but joins the subject to the words that follow the verb and that describe or rename the subject

Misplaced modifier   Modifier that is separated in the sentence from the word it modifies

Modifier   Word, phrase, or clause that provides additional information about another word or group of words in the sentence

Nonessential clause   Clause beginning with *who* or *which* and providing additional (but not necessary) information about the noun preceding the clause

Noun   Word identifying a person, place, or thing

Number   Denotes whether noun, pronoun, or verb is singular or plural

Objective case pronoun   Pronoun that is used following an action verb or as an object of the preposition: *me, you, him, her, it, us, you, them*

Passive voice verb   Verb of a sentence in which the subject receives the expressed action

Past participle   Verb form used with a helping verb

Past tense   Verb expressing action or state of being that has already taken place

Person   Way of classifying nouns and pronouns: *first person, second person, third person*

Personal pronoun   Pronoun referring to a specific person, place, or thing and classified as *first person, second person,* or *third person*

Phrase   Group of grammatically related words without a subject and a verb

Possessive case pronoun   Pronoun that shows possession: *my, mine, your, yours, his, her, hers, its, our, ours, their, theirs*

Prepositional phrase   Group of words beginning with a preposition and ending with a noun (the object of the preposition)

Present tense   Verb expressing action or state of being that is taking place in the present

Pronoun   Word that substitutes for a noun

Pronoun–antecedent agreement   Grammatical principle that states that a pronoun must agree with its antecedent in number, person, and gender

Relative pronoun   *Who, whoever, whom, whomever, whose, which, whichever, that*

Run-on   Two independent clauses with no punctuation to join them

Sentence combining   Use of coordination and/or subordination to join sentences

Shift in person   Unnecessary movement from the use of one type of personal pronoun (e.g., first person) to another type of personal pronoun (e.g., second person)

Simple subject   Main noun or pronoun that forms the subject

Subject   Noun or pronoun that tells who or what is performing the action expressed in the verb or who or what is being discussed

Subject–verb agreement   Grammatical principle that states that a verb must agree with its subject in number and in person

Subjective case pronoun   Pronoun that can be used as the subject of a sentence, following a linking verb, or in most comparisons with *than* or *as: I, you, he, she, it, we, they*

Subordinate clause   Same as dependent clause

Subordinating conjunction   Word or word group that introduces a dependent (subordinate) clause

Subordination   Process of joining one or more dependent (subordinate) clauses to an independent clause

Superlative form of adjective   Adjective generally formed by use of *-est* ending or word *most* and used to compare three or more persons, places, or things

Superlative form of adverb   Adverb generally formed by use of the word *most* or *least* and used to compare three or more persons, places or things

Tense shift   Unnecessary movement from one verb tense to another

Answers to Selected Odd-Numbered Exercises

Exercise 1.1

P	1.	A lawyer's brief in support of a client's innocence
I	2.	An airline's list of airfare rates to China
I	3.	A scientific article on the effects of pollution on the ozone layer
P	4.	A political candidate's speech on the day before elections
X	5.	A teenager's diary
P	6.	A job application letter
P	7.	A charity's appeal for additional funds to feed the homeless
P	8.	A newspaper editorial in support of a new sports stadium
I	9.	A technical manual for installing an ice maker in a refrigerator
E	10.	A column about relatives who are really space aliens

Exercise 1.3

G	1.	A movie review in a daily newspaper
S	2.	A review of an art exhibit in a magazine for art historians
S	3.	A cookbook for lovers of Louisiana Cajun cooking
G	4.	An instruction manual for a portable television
G	5.	A textbook for freshman composition students
G	6.	A cookbook for beginning cooks
S	7.	A technical manual for repairing videocassette recorders

__S__	**8.**	A review of a new classical music CD for a magazine for classical music lovers
__G__	**9.**	A review of a new CD for a local newspaper
__G__	**10.**	A guide to a foreign city for first-time visitors

Exercise 2.5

__X__	**1.**	Students who attend college while employed face many challenges.
__OK__	**2.**	Young people often face the pressure to consume alcoholic beverages at an early age.
__X__	**3.**	There are many problems facing adolescents today.
__OK__	**4.**	Working college students must budget study time carefully.
__OK__	**5.**	A good parent maintains an active interest in his or her child's homework.
__OK__	**6.**	An effective teacher uses class time wisely.
__X__	**7.**	Exercising regularly is beneficial in many ways.
__X__	**8.**	Good parents are hard to find.
__X__	**9.**	There are many characteristics of an effective teacher.
__OK__	**10.**	One benefit of regular exercise is weight control.

Exercise 2.7

The answers to these questions will, of course, vary. Here are some possible responses.

1. Fans of Chinese food can enjoy moderately priced meals at Sum Ho Chinese Restaurant.
2. Home computers can help users manage their finances.
3. Even some elementary school children carry weapons to school.
4. Exposure to secondary smoke can cause respiratory problems in infants.
5. The number of juveniles arrested for violent crimes is on the rise.

Exercise 2.9

One characteristic of a good teacher is excellent preparation. To begin with, a good teacher prepares ahead of time for the next day. For instance, if her class is supposed to have a reading assignment, she also reads the material in case there are any questions. Also a well-prepared instructor devises an outline of what she will teach the next day. In addition, a good teacher always give sufficient notes and provides a review prior to a test. For example, she gives her class ample time to study notes, ask questions, and consult for extra help. Furthermore, she budgets her time well in order to cover the required curriculum. For instance, she does not get behind on her assignments and does not cram work in all at once. When budgeting her class time, she always follows up on specific dates when information is to be covered. Finally, a well-prepared teacher keeps each student informed of his or her progress throughout the course. If the student is going great work, the teacher will comment to the student and give him or her confidence to continue. On the other hand, if a student is not doing well in the course, the teacher detects the problem and takes whatever means are necessary to help the student and see that he or she is taking the right steps toward improvement. An excellent teacher prepares herself daily to meet her students' educational needs.

Exercise 2.11

1. One proposal (to reduce the number) (of firearms) (in America) is gun-swap programs.

2. These gun-swap programs offer various incentives (in exchange) (for guns).

3. (For example), (in New York City) citizens were offered a gift certificate (for toys) (in exchange) (for turning) (in a firearm) (at a police station).

4. (During a 14-day period) (in December 1993), approximately 1200 firearms were brought (to police stations) (in the city).

5. (In Los Angeles) guns could be swapped (for tickets) (to concerts and sporting events).

6. Approximately 400 firearms were exchanged (in Los Angeles' gun-swap program).

7. Other cities are thinking (about a gun-swap program).

8. Various civil rights organizations and church groups have supported these programs and encouraged local sponsors.

9. Can gun-swap programs really make a difference (in firearms reduction)?

10. What incentives will be needed (for these programs) (to continue)?

11. Communities must either try innovative ways (of firearm reduction) or accept the number (of firearms) (in America's streets and homes).

Exercise 2.13 (See 2.11 on page 301 and 2.12 below)

Exercise 2.12

1. Another (proposal) (to reduce the number) (of guns) (in the United States) is an increase (in gun dealers' licensing fees).

2. These are more gun (dealers) (in the United States) than McDonald's restaurants, (according to one study).

3. Every (one) (of the gun dealers) must pay a licensing fee (to the federal government).

4. Gun (dealers) currently purchase a three-year license (for $200 or $66 a year.)

5. This (fee) had previously been just $10 a year.

6. Most business (owners) (in this country) pay higher licensing fees.

7. This (increase) (in the licensing fee) might discourage some people (from becoming gun dealers).

8. A recent (suggestion) is raising that fee (to a minimum of $600.00).

9. (You) Think (about this question).

10. Would raising this (fee) affect the number (of handguns) (in circulation)?

11. (You) Imagine the estimated 200 million guns currently (in America's streets and homes).

12. American (citizens) and government (officials) should carefully consider this proposal.

Exercise 2.15

  IC   1. Some criminal justice experts are not enthusiastic about gun-swaps.

DC/IC   2. (Because) there are so many guns on America's streets, gun-swap programs will not result in a significant firearms reduction.

  IC   3. Many of the guns have not been used for years.

  IC   4. Some guns do not function properly

  IC   5. Some gun owners may even use the money from the gun-swap to purchase a new gun.

IC/DC   6. Police personnel must be used to process the guns (which) are swapped in exchange for money or certificates.

IC	7.	<u>Is</u> this <u>use</u> of manpower effective in crime reduction?
IC	8.	Other <u>means</u> of gun control <u>would be</u> more effective.
DC/IC	9.	(If) gun <u>owners</u> <u>were required</u> to renew their license every four years, police <u>officials</u> <u>could monitor</u> the number of legal gun owners.
IC	10.	Criminal justice <u>experts</u> <u>should work</u> with communities to find effective ways to reduce the number of guns in our streets and homes.

Exercise 3.1

1. Insufficient
2. Sufficient
3. Sufficient
4 Insufficient
5. Insufficient

Exercise 3.5

A true friend is trustworthy. If I share a secret with her about a coworker. I do not have to worry about her repeating my secret. Last year I experienced a problem with my supervisor. When I mentioned this problem to one of my "friends". She went straight to my supervisor's office and repeated what I had said. This betrayal of loyalty is not characteristic of true friendship. When I have a problem communicating with my children. I sometimes express my frustration to a friend. A true friend will set aside what she is doing. Because she knows it is important for me to have an outlet for my frustration. I know a true friend will not be disloyal and talk about me behind my back. If she does. I will no longer be able to trust her. Because true friends are hard to find. A friend who is trustworthy is a treasure. Who is worthy of my trust in return.

Exercise 3.7

If I win the lottery. I want to visit several sites in Florence, Italy. Including the Florence Cathedral. I want to stand in the middle of the cathedral and gaze at Brunelleschi's dome. I also want to walk in the passageway between the inner dome and the outer dome and admire Brunelleschi's architectural feats. Such as the use of herringbone brickwork to support the weight of the dome. Then I want to see Ghiberti's doors on the Florence Baptistry and admire the figures cast in gilded bronze. For example, Abraham, Isaac, Ghiberti himself, and Ghiberti's son. Touring the Uffizi Museum, I can gaze admiringly on the great works of Botticelli. Such as *Primavera* (*Allegory of Spring*) and *The Birth of Venus* (which I call *Venus on the Half Shell*). Finally, I would love to place flowers on my uncle's grave. He was shot down over Italy two weeks before the end of World War II. I want to see the place where he has rested all these years. When my winning numbers come in. I will be packed and ready to catch a plane to Florence.

Exercise 3.9

The waterfalls in the North Georgia mountains offer an abundance of delights for summer hikers. For instance, Minnehaha Falls, located near Rabun Beach Recreation Area in Rabun County, is just a short, moderately easy hike from Bear Gap Road. Although finding the unpaved Bear Gap Road and the trailhead to the waterfalls can be an adventure. Once there, the falls are enticing stairsteps of rock and water. A log at the foot of the falls is easily accessible for hikers. Who may have sore feet and a meditative spirit. Anna Ruby Falls in Unicoi State Park is a double waterfall. An unusual sight in these Georgia Hills. The falls, named after the daughter of a farmer who discovered them, are located at the end of a paved, one-quarter mile hike from a parking lot managed by the U.S. Forest Service. In the summer hikers can enjoy the cool walk along Smith Creek. Listening to the creek tumble over logs and large boulders. For those who are clever enough to bring along a picnic lunch. There are several rocks in the stream suitable for a picnic spread. Although these waterfalls in the North Georgia mountains are enjoyable any time of year. A summer hiker will especially appreciate the cool water on a hot day.

Exercise 3.11

Much of Rembrandt's life was full of sadness even though he enjoyed a brief, happy marriage to Saskia van Uylenburgh. The years between 1635 and 1642 brought him much suffering. During this seven-year period, (*comma optional*) his mother, sister-in-law, and three infant children died. This period ended with the death of Saskia just a few weeks before she turned 30. The years after his wife's death were very difficult, for Rembrandt loved his wife dearly. She left him with his beloved only child named Titus. Later Rembrandt fell in love with his housekeeper named Hendrickje

Stoffels. This gentle, loving woman bore him a daughter, and she outlived both Rembrandt and her mother. Hendrickje, however, died at the age of 37. Titus also died before his father, and his death deeply saddened the aging artist. Rembrandt died on October 4, 1669, at the age of 63.

Exercise 3.13

It's easy to contrast Rembrandt's career with that of his contemporary, Jan Vermeer. One of the major differences between these two artists' work is the subjects of their paintings. Rembrandt's subjects were often religious such as his painting of Jesus' parable of the prodigal son. This painting, entitled *The Return of the Prodigal Son,* shows the son's return to his father's household. The son is kneeling as his father's arms encompass him. The expression on his father's face is compassionate; he's celebrating his long-lost son's return. Vermeer, on the other hand, painted very few paintings with religious subjects. He was more interested in commonplace subjects, particularly scenes of everyday Dutch life. One of Vermeer's most famous painting is *A Lady Weighing Gold.* In this painting a lady stands at a wooden table with a pair of scales in her right hand. She's weighing her gold, and the scales aren't perfectly in balance. On the table are the lady's pearls and a couple of the lady's gold necklaces. The look on the woman's face is serene as she gazes at her scales.

Exercise 3.15

Peter Paul Rubens was the greatest Flemish painter of the seventeenth century. Rubens was born June 28, 1577, in Westphalia, Germany. Rubens' father had moved to Germany after being exiled from Flanders. However, after his father's death in 1587, his mother's desire to move back to Flanders led her to relocate the family in Antwerp. In addition to painting, Rubens' lifelong interests included diplomacy and travel. In 1600, he went to Italy to serve in a diplomatic post and study Italian art. Rubens like to paint in a highly dramatic, colorful style. For example, in his painting, *Descent from the Cross,* Mary's figure is dressed in a bright red cloak. The other figure's clothing is not colorful at all. The painting's background is dark, but Jesus' figure is brightly illuminated as he is removed from the cross. Through the dramatic contrasts between light and dark, the viewer's attention is drawn to the central figures of Jesus and his mother, and the viewer can sense the painting's pathos.

Furthermore, Rubens' figures are often robust and passionately bold. In 1630, four years after his first wife's death, Rubens married a sixteen-year-old girl, Helena. To celebrate his love for her, he painted *The Garden of Love.* The painting's dimensions are large—6'6" by 9'3½"—another characteristic of his paintings. On the canvas' left side are two figures. One is a self-portrait of Rubens in a large, black Flemish hat holding his wife's hand and back gently as if they are dancing. Pushing them into the garden is a small, rounded cupid. In the center of the painting are many female figures awaiting their lovers in the garden. Above them are various cupids with arrows pointing toward the painting's center. In the painting's background is the porch of the house. Art historians believe this was the outside of Rubens' home, which still stands today. The viewer's impression is that all of the figures appear to be enjoying the garden's delights. The artist's purpose is clear—he desires a happy marriage in the new house he has bought for his bride.

Exercise 4.1

<u> X </u> **1.** I will never forget all the good times I had on my trip last summer.

<u> OK </u> **2.** I can still remember the first moments of my first day in first grade.

<u> OK </u> **3.** On August 25, 1983, in a casino in Las Vegas, I learned a valuable lesson.

<u> OK </u> **4.** One afternoon last summer my family and I took an unforgettable rafting trip on North Carolina's Nantahala River.

<u> X </u> **5.** During my senior year in high school I made many decisions which would affect the rest of my life.

Exercise 4.5

<u> N </u> **1.** One autumn night my brother, my sister, and I waited impatiently for my father to come home from work.

<u> CO </u> **2.** Our hopes were high; we wanted to go to the state fair.

<u> CO </u> **3.** We did not want to beg, for whining would only make him angry.

<u> N </u> **4.** We decided, instead, to put on sad faces and wait for him to notice.

<u> CO </u> **5.** The plan worked, and soon my father noticed our unhappiness.

<u> CO </u> **6.** Then he told us to go get in the car; he had a surprise for us.

<u> N </u> **7.** We ran outside and saw "State Fair or Bust" written on the car windows.

<u> CO </u> **8.** My father has been dead for almost 20 years, yet every Father's Day I remember his kindness on that autumn night.

Exercise 4.7

It was a hot night in New York City. My husband and I decided to sit out on the fire escape by my sister's apartment. We had been chatting awhile when we noticed a disagreement erupt between two homeless men on the street below. They were arguing quite loudly. / Soon after they began to scuffle. A few minutes later their girlfriends got involved. The women were screaming and punching each other. By this time a crowd of people had gathered below. / At the same time an eighteen-wheel produce truck pulled up to the stoplight on the corner. Suddenly, both women pulled each other to the ground. The light turned green. / The wheels of the truck slowly started to move. Both women heard the truck. / Only one could get up. My husband and I started screaming as did the rest of the crowd. / It was too late. The truck had rolled over the woman in the street.

Exercise 4.9

One of my most exciting experiences occurred two years ago when five of my friends and I went whitewater rafting on the Nantahala River in North Carolina. Our rafting trip began with safety instructions. / Our instructor told us to keep our feet securely tucked under the seat at all times. Then we were told that if we fell out of the raft into the swiftly moving current, we should not try to walk to shore even though the water would only be a few feet deep. / Instead we were to do a "whitewater swim." A "whitewater swim" involves floating feet first down the river using the lifejacket to keep afloat. One of my friends had been whitewater rafting many times. / He decided to be our raft guide. The guide sits in the back of the raft. / His responsibility is to steer the raft around rocks and other obstacles in the river. We soon departed down the river. / We were confident that we would have a successful trip. The water was beautiful on that summer day. / The sun glistened playfully on its surface. At first we responded well to the challenges that the river offered us. / Then we began to relax and quickly forgot the safety instructions. Suddenly, a small ripple in the water became our guide's undoing. The drop in the river at first appeared shallow. / It was, in fact, much deeper than we thought. The back of the raft came down in this "hole" in the river. / It landed on a rock submerged just a few inches below the water. The raft acted like a trampoline, bouncing our guide several feet in the air and into the water. Trying to be a hero, our guide attempted to walk to the edge of the river. Fortunately, he slipped on a rock, fell into the water, and began a "whitewater swim." The rest of us took the raft to the bank. / Realizing he was not hurt, we laughed as he climbed back into the raft. The next time we go rafting, we will listen to the safety instructions—and not our "experienced" guide.

Exercise 4.11

It seemed like we waited for hours for the highway patrol and ambulance to arrive on the scene. As the paramedics took us inside the ambulance, I realized my knees and legs were hurting. The paramedics determined my nose had been broken. / The dash of the car had cut and scratched my legs. Mike was told he would be okay but would probably be sore for a few days. The highway patrol arrived and filled out a report. I was not ticketed for the accident. / The conditions were hazardous. Then I had to notify my parents. The officer telephoned my mother and explained the situation. Because of his expertise, my mother stayed calm. / She soon arrived to comfort me. Now the first thing I do every time I get into the car is buckle my seatbelt. The accident happened almost three years ago. / The memory of the collision, however, is still vivid. The officer at the scene of the incident said, "If you had not had the seatbelt on, you probably would not have survived the crash." Because of the speed I was traveling, I would have been thrown through the windshield upon contact with Mike's vehicle. Accidents occur without warning. / There is not enough time to fasten the seatbelt when the driver realizes he or she is about to crash. I learned that wrecks can occur on even the most untraveled roads and when they are least expected. My advice is "buckle up."

Kerri Carlisle

Exercise 4.13

Last summer my husband, Dan, and my daughters, Jenny and Leah, took a day trip to the Smoky Mountains. Just inside the national park was our first stop, Fontana Lake. The green-colored lake looked so inviting on that hot day that my husband decided to go for a swim and proceeded to take off his shirt. "Watch out," we cried. "That water sure looks cold." "Don't worry," he replied. "I'll be all right." We sat on the bank in the shade and continued to yell at him. I screamed, "You don't know how deep that water is. You're going to break your neck." He replied, "You're just jealous." Then we saw him jump into the water. "Yikes!" he screamed. We looked to see him scrambling back to the shore like a clown shot from a cannon. "What's wrong?" we cried. When he reached the shoreline, he grabbed his shirt and ran through the poison ivy to the car. When we crawled into the car with him, we felt the heat blasting through the vents. "Where's the air conditioning?" we cried. "I'll never complain about being hot again," Dan whined. Then we all laughed until we cried.

Exercise 5.1

__OK__   1.   My two-year-old daughter, Frances, is beautiful when she sleeps.

__X__   2.   The students in Ms. Campbell's English class are all interesting.

__OK__   3.   My favorite photograph is a picture of me taken when I was a carefree toddler.

__X__   4.   This photograph of twenty-five family members at last year's family reunion is a personal favorite.

__OK__   5.   The gold pocket watch lying on the table intrigues me.

__X__   6.   All the guests at my sister's wedding enjoyed themselves at the reception.

__OK__   7.   The young boy playing in the sand looks intently at his sand castle.

__X__   8.   The mountains look lovely in the distance.

__OK__   9.   The waterfall is lovely in the early morning light.

__X__   10.   The students, waiting for class to begin, are gathering outside the classroom door.

Exercise 5.3

The twenty-one-inch nutcracker stands guard on the fireplace's mantel. At the top sits a sable-colored, Cossack-style helmet made of fake fur. Below the helmet protrudes his gray hair. His face is colorful. His dark black eyebrows are striking. Below are his black eyes, petite nose, black mustache, and red mouth ready to crack a nut at any opportunity. To the left, his bent arm holds a pole topped by a red flag. To the right his arm rests by his side. His military-style jacket is green. To the right and left of his jacket are five white buttons. His red pants match the red of the flag and the jacket's cuffs. At the bottom his black boots stand on a red base. The nutcracker's figure is imposing.

Exercise 5.7

Adjacent to the desk area is her single bed with a light oak spindle headboard resting against the wall. Geometrical designs in hot neon colors **decorate** her white background bedspread. At the top of the bed near the headboard **are** a seven-inch, hot pink troll doll and a white, lace-trimmed heart pillow. Her five-drawer chest beside her bed is stuffed with jeans, T-shirts, socks—all hanging out of the drawers. A black drawing table with an adjustable light, black stool, and a two-drawer night-stand **make** up the rest of the room. Neither the top of her drawing table nor the surface of the nightstand **is** clear. On the top of the nightstand is the cage for her pet cockatiel, Tweeters. The contents of Tweeters' cage **litter** the nightstand's surface as well as the dull, brown carpet. There **are** school awards and posters of a famous cat hanging on the off-white wall. My daughter's room is never very clean, but it is definitely colorful.

Exercise 5.9

The red sports car is intriguing as it sits in the car lot. Its sleek exterior design and its aerodynamic style **attract** my attention. Each of its exterior features **is** graceful including its wide tires with shiny aluminum wheels and sculpted, curved lines. The tinted windows as well as the glistening paint **add** to the sporty effect. In the interior **are** many attractive features including roominess in both the front and the back. A six-footer would have no trouble comfortably driving this car, and three screaming kids could easily fit in the back seat. The leather-covered seats and precision dashboard add to the beauty of the interior. The specs on this car **point** to its potential power on the road. A 210-horsepower, 24-valve, V-6 engine offers power while front-passenger air bags and anti-lock brakes **provide** safety. Unfortunately, on the window **are** the prices for all the special options this car offers its lucky owner. This sleek beauty along with all its attractions is a treat for the eye but not for the wallet.

Exercise 5.11

In my son's aquarium one particular fish, known as Bluey, **provides** a fascinating show of beauty and awe-inspiring violence. He **is** a betta splendons, commonly known as a Siamese fighting fish. His color **is** a vivid blue with imperceptible, iridescent gold flecks. The blue **fades** to a deep purple in the valley at the base of his tail. His scales **are** so tiny that he **appears** cloaked in a soft, velvety robe. Bluey's body **is** less than an inch-and-a-half long; his tail **is** another inch-and-a-half of veil-like fins. These fins **hang,** when he **is** still, like the wet hair of a mermaid. This tail **is** the most remarkable trait of a betta. Like a crepe paper streamer, it **floats** behind him as an afterthought. As he **rises** toward the top of the tank, the light **illuminates** his tail, and it **changes** to a deep, blood red. It **is** not as long as it once was, having been nipped away by a challenging subordinate. Bluey's head **is** shaped like the prow of a graceful sailing ship of old. His eyes **appear** to be small, dark buttons attached to either side of his head. His tidy mouth **is** turned up in indignation—a princely pout. The milky-white area **is** separated by the start of his gills, which spread apart into a V-shape and **disappear** into black on the lower side of his head. Immediately behind each gill **is** a small, fan-shaped fin, which **appears** to be the fish's main source of propulsion. As he **swims,** the fins **move** back and forth with a twisting motion to the top and bottom and **appear** translucent, except for the slight bit of blue that **trims** the edges. Just behind and below these fins **are** two long strands of midnight-blue fins that resemble a mustache. This refined, elegant fish **rules** the tank.

Debra Bates

Exercise 5.15

Both girls had long, brown hair. One was wearing a solid, forest-green shirt that only covered about two-thirds of her upper body. She had a matching scrunchy holding her hair in a ponytail along with matching colored socks and nail polish. I doubt that her neon-orange pager was in her color scheme when she spent two hours staring in the closet trying to figure out what would look best on her five-feet, eight-inch, one-hundred-and-thirty-five-pound body. The other girl wore white tennis shoes with loose blue jeans. She had on a huge, multi-colored shirt that looked as if she had just been in a paint fight with someone and apparently lost. She had huge, lime-green loops hanging from her ears that looked like trial issues of the hula hoop. My overall impression of her was that she looked as if her friend had decided to go out and stopped by to see if she wanted to go. She probably took five minutes to pick up the shirt and jeans off the floor, put them on, look in the mirror, and say, "What do you think?" to her friend.

Andy Warren

Exercise 6.1

1. Unfocused
2. Focused
3. Unfocused
4. Focused
5. Unfocused

Exercise 6.3

The novel, *One for the Money,* is **better** than the novel, *Two for the Show.* First, the characters in *One for the Money* are **more realistic.** Mary Penny is like many women who have suffered from poverty. She is **more cautious** than Joe Vegas, the main character of *Two for the Show,* about investing in get-rich-quick schemes. She is **more likely** to hold on to her money and **less likely** to play the slot machines. Second, the plot moves **more quickly** in *One for the Money.* The author creates **greater** suspense by using foreshadowing. Overall, the plot is **less predictable** than the plot of *Two for the Show.* Third, *One for the Money*'s ending is **better.** It is **more interesting** and **more satisfying.** *Two for the Show*'s ending is pointless and aggravating. In sum, *One for the Money* is a **better** buy than *Two for the Show*.

Exercise 6.5

The camping facilities at Lake Jenoway and Lake Lee are quite different. Lake Jenoway scattered throughout the camping area has bathrooms and shower facilities whereas Lake Lee has no shower facilities and few restrooms. Lake Jenoway's camping area also features water and electricity hookups. However, all camping sites at Lake Lee are remote. Campers do not have access to electricity using tents. They must carry their water jugs to the water fountain which are empty. Lake Jenoway offers many family contests. Campers at Lake Lee can view the moon and stars who are bored, but no planned activities are provided. Families always crowd Lake Jenoway with small children, so the camping area is often noisy. On the other hand, the only noise in Lake Lee's camping area is the chirping of millions of crickets. Before deciding to camp at Lake Jenoway or Lake Lee, campers should carefully consider their needs.

Exercise 7.7

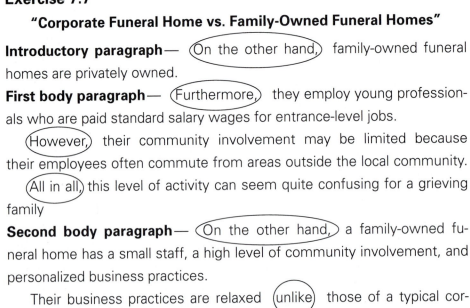

"Corporate Funeral Home vs. Family-Owned Funeral Homes"

Introductory paragraph— On the other hand, family-owned funeral homes are privately owned.

First body paragraph— Furthermore, they employ young professionals who are paid standard salary wages for entrance-level jobs.

However, their community involvement may be limited because their employees often commute from areas outside the local community.

All in all, this level of activity can seem quite confusing for a grieving family

Second body paragraph— On the other hand, a family-owned funeral home has a small staff, a high level of community involvement, and personalized business practices.

Their business practices are relaxed unlike those of a typical corporate funeral home.

"Two State Parks"

First body paragraph—Both parks, located along rivers, have excellent canoe launch facilities and also offer canoe rentals on site.

In addition, food and drink concessions are available at both parks.

Second body paragraph— (In fact,) it is Florida's largest state park.

(In contrast,) Hillsborough, which covers 3000 acres, can boast of its distinction as the oldest state park.

Hillsborough River, (however,) lies on very flat, low marshlands.

The featured rivers of each park (also) differ.

(On the other hand,) the Hillsborough River offers several actual white water rapids—indeed a rarity in Florida.

(Despite their differences,) both of these parks offer rewards for those who appreciate a glimpse of Florida's natural wonders.

Concluding paragraph—Myakka River and Hillsborough River State Parks (both) offer their visitors reasonable fees, excellent recreational facilities, and an abundance of wildlife, (yet) their size and terrain vary.

Exercise 7.9

Not every college student knows what (he) **wants** to pursue as a major. Many students can remember that growing up (they) wanted to be teachers or doctors or police officers. However, a person's childhood fantasies don't always become (**his or her**) choices later. A boy who once dreamed of fighting fires when (he) was younger may decide that the life of adventure is not for (him) after all. Or a girl who wanted to be a doctor may decide that **she is** not willing to spend so much time in training. As an adult, (**he or she**) may decide to pursue a job in the business field. Often freshmen and sophomores will delay making (their) career choices. However, a student with enough hours to graduate may still be unsure what (**he or she**) **wants** to do once (**he or she**) **gets** that diploma.

Often a student makes a career choice as a freshman and discovers that when (**he or she**) **is** a sophomore or junior (**he or she**) **wants** to change (**his or her**) major. Either the strong influence of a teacher or excitement over subject matter may have (its) influence on a student's change of heart. Very often either a group of students or an individual student will want to pattern (**himself or herself**) after an important person in (**his or her**) life. Each student must decide for (**himself or herself**) on what grounds (**he or she**) will make (**his or her**) choices. Deciding on a major is not easy, but college students should not put off this decision for too long.

Exercise 7.11

One type of student who decides to attend college is the recent high school graduate. **High school graduates** often **go** to college because of **their** parents' and friends' expectations. If **they are** in the classroom for **their** parents and friends and not for **themselves, they** will probably lack an interest in **their** course work. **They** will often be bored in class and will not listen to the teacher's instructions or complete **their** homework on time. In addition, **they** may not have a clear career goal and will be undecided about **their** major because **they are** not motivated to make a career choice. **These students** often **end** up with a weak grade point average and may even withdraw from college. This lack of motivation is fortunately not typical of every eighteen-year-old first-year college student. **New high school graduates** often **have** a specific career goal. Therefore, **they** will take interest in **their** course work, ask questions, in class, listen carefully to the instructor, and complete **their** homework in a timely manner. **They** will declare a major as soon as possible. Because **they have** a clear goal, **they** will do well in school.

Another type of student attending college in the returning student. Sometimes **returning students enter** the college classroom because of a divorce. **They** may have depended on **their** spouse's income, but now **find they need** employment. Because **they need** a vocational skill, **they decide** to return to college. Also **they** may want the intellectual stimulation of a college classroom. **They** may want to pursue an interest in a particular subject. Another reason **students return** to the classroom is **they want** to change **their** career. Therefore, **they need** additional job training. **Returning students are** usually highly motivated. **They are** enthusiastic about **their** course work, **take** careful notes, and **are** punctual in completing **their** assignments. As a result, **they** will do well academically.

Exercise 8.5

A woman **who** is experiencing domestic violence should seek refuge in a shelter for battered women. **She** and her children should leave their residence as soon as possible after the abuse occurs. At the shelter **she** and her children will be safe and can receive counseling. In counseling she will realize that it is not **she** but her abuser who is the perpetrator of the violence. Also she will find that other women are experiencing the same type of abuse as **she.** The counseling will likely benefit her children as much as **her.** Entering a shelter is difficult, however. She must leave all but a few possessions behind at her home. The children **whom** she may be traveling with may experience anxiety. She may resist counseling because she feels her problems can be worked out between **her** and the man in her life with no outside help. Furthermore, her community may not have a shelter for her children and **her.** Despite **its** drawbacks, a shelter can offer battered women a lifeline. Every abused woman should consider taking this important step.

Exercise 9.3

1. **F**
2. **F**
3. **O**
4. **O**
5. **F**
6. **O**
7. **T**
8. **T**

Exercise 9.5

List five repeated phrases or clauses.

1. I have a dream today.
2. Free at last.
3. Let freedom ring.
4. One day
5. With this faith

List five examples of parallel structures.

1. . . . the sons of former slaves and the sons of former slave owners. . .
2. . . . every valley shall be exalted, every hill and mountain shall be made low. . . and the glory of the Lord shall be revealed.
3. With this faith we will be able to hew out of the mountain of despair a stone of hope. With this faith we will be able to transform the jangling discords of our nation into a beautiful symphony of brotherhood.
4. Let freedom ring from the prodigious hilltops of New Hampshire. Let freedom ring from the mighty mountains of New York. Let freedom ring from the heightening Alleghenies of Pennsylvania!
5. . . . all of God's children—black men and white men, Jews and Gentiles, Protestants and Catholics—will be able to join hands and sing in the words. . .

Exercise 10.1

3522 **Fieldstone** Lane
Hometown, SC 29999

Foreign Imports, Inc.
2531 Business Avenue
Large City, NY 05231

Dear Mr. Jones:

I would like to apply for the sales manager position you advertised in last week's <u>Hometown News</u>. Recently I completed my degree in business management, and I **believe** you will find both my work **experience** and my educational background have prepared me well for this position.

Although I have been a full-time student for the last four years, I have never **stopped** working in sales—**primarily** in retail department stores. I have **seized** every opportunity to distinguish myself as an outstanding salesperson. Now that I have completed my degree, I am ready to move into sales **management.** I am especially interested in car sales and am a long-time member of the Foreign Car **Society.**

I am **committed** to **excellent** customer service and would like the chance to **interview** for this position. I have enclosed my resume for your consideration.

Sincerely yours,

Melissa Smith

Exercise 10.3

~~In my opinion~~ The most important part of the job application process is the interview. The applicant should prepare for the interview well in advance of the scheduled date. ~~It seems to me that~~ It is ~~very, very~~ important that the applicant learn some ~~things~~ facts about the company before the interview. These ~~things~~ facts may include how long the company has been in existence, how many workers the company employs, and how much profit the company made in the previous year. Also the interviewee should anticipate the questions the interviewer will likely ask. This anticipation will also help reduce anxiety in the interview. For example, the interviewer will ~~likely~~ probably want to know why the applicant left the last job, what the applicant's strengths and weaknesses are, and what salary the applicant expects. Also the prospective employee should make a list of questions to ask at the end of the interview. It may include such questions as "When will I hear from you?", "What benefits does the company offer?", and "When does the job begin?" Thinking ahead will increase the chances of a successful interview.

Index

325